THE PAKISTANI
MASTERS

THE PAKISTANI MASTERS

BILL RICQUIER

With Foreword by Wasim Akram

TEMPUS

For Anita and Guy
with love

Frontispiece: Family conference: Mushtaq, Hanif and a youthful Sadiq Mohammad pictured during the Pakistan tour of England, 1967.

First published 2006

Tempus Publishing Limited
The Mill, Brimscombe Port,
Stroud, Gloucestershire, GL5 2QG
www.tempus-publishing.com

British Library Cataloguing in Publication Data.
A catalogue record for this book is available from the British Library.

ISBN 0 7524 3928 6

Typesetting and origination by Tempus Publishing Limited
Printed in Great Britain

CONTENTS

ACKNOWLEDGEMENTS

As always there are plenty of people to thank. Holly Bennion and Rob Sharman at Tempus, for helping things go smoothly; Wasim Akram, for agreeing to write the foreword and making a number of helpful suggestions; the amazing Wati Kassim for all her hard work; Anita for her continued encouragement; Rob Higham and Malcolm Merry for their friendship and insights; Neil and Ben Jenkinson for their various errands of mercy; Peng Ow for all her help; and Christopher Chew, John Child, John McKenzie, Andre Monza, David Pierce and Shashi Tharoor.

Bill Ricquier
Singapore
April 2006

FOREWORD

I am very pleased to write the foreword to this book on Pakistani cricketers. I believe that over the years Pakistan has provided the world with some of the most exciting cricketers around and Bill Ricquier has done a good job in choosing and writing about many of the best of them.

The players chosen include Abdul Hafeez Karder, who was the first captain of Pakistan, and go right up to the modern day with current stars such as Shahid Afridi.

While I was working in Singapore in early 2006, Bill and I had a chance to discuss some of these terrific players together.

I have no doubt the book will be very interesting for all fans of Pakistan cricket and should do very well.

Wasim Akram
Lahore
April 2006

INTRODUCTION

The relationship between England and Pakistan as cricketing nations has always been 'interesting'.

Things started to go wrong almost as soon as Pakistan achieved Test status. Their first tour of England in 1954 was a success on all fronts. Accorded the popularity that the English always give the underdog, they astonished the cricketing world by winning the last Test, the great medium-pacer Fazal Mahmood proving too good for an admittedly below-strength batting line-up. In 1955/56 the MCC sent an 'A' side to Pakistan and, on this tour, an incident occurred that in some ways set a pattern for the future. The 'A' side was a young team not perhaps prepared to cope with the rigours of touring in Pakistan. The absence of diversion after stumps were drawn proved a severe trial and a prank was played one evening, the not-very-subtle denouement involving the drenching with water of a senior Pakistan umpire, Idris Begh. It gave rise to a not-inconsiderable 'diplomatic incident' and it somehow encapsulated a 'clash of cultures'.

Once the initial shock-waves from the Idris Begh affair had receded, relations stabilised. This was helped to some extent by Pakistan's poor record in England: they were not regarded remotely as a cricketing threat, although they were very hard to beat at home. They lost a five-Test series very heavily in 1962 (when off-spinner Haseeb Ahsan returned home early with, allegedly, a suspect action, never to play Test cricket again) and a three-Test series equally heavily in 1967. In the 1970s the genial Intikhab Alam brought two sides to England full of popular and talented cricketers such as Majid Khan, Mushtaq Mohammad and Asif Iqbal. The English crowds found their combination of playing attractive cricket and not actually beating the home team irresistible.

But by the early 1980s Pakistan, for the first time since A.H. Kardar in the 1950s, had a captain who was able to co-ordinate his players' mercurial talents. This was the Oxford-educated Imran Khan. In 1982 he led his country to what almost became their first series win in England. The Pakistanis were convinced that a major factor in their losing the final Test was an erroneous umpiring decision by David Constant.

When England's injury-hit party toured Pakistan in 1983/84 the hosts won handsomely. Ian Botham, leaving early for home injured, observed that Pakistan was the sort of place you sent your mother-in-law to, a remark that was dissected by cultural commentators from both countries for years afterwards.

By 1987 Pakistan were a leading cricket nation. They toured England, (managed by – well well! – Haseeb Ahsan) and won a five-Test series 1-0, the tour being packed with 'incidents' gleefully handled by the ebullient Pakistani manager. That winter the sides met again in Pakistan. Although the two teams did not, like the Australian and English teams of 1921, make the journey on the same boat, it rapidly became clear that this was too much of a good thing. The English, not for the first or last time, adopted a siege mentality. There were some, to put it mildly, highly questionable umpiring decisions and, alas, one of the abiding memories of cricket in the 1980s is the picture of the England captain Mike Gatting and umpire Shakoor Rana engaged in a shouting match on the second evening of the Second Test at Faisalabad. The match and the tour itself were in jeopardy. The long-term effects of the incident were considerable. Gatting, who many felt was the best English captain of his generation, was sacked the following year. And Imran Khan – not involved in the series as a player – stepped up the campaign he had been waging for years for 'neutral' Test match umpires.

It was thus with some trepidation that England awaited the Pakistan tourists under their maverick captain Javed Miandad in 1992. The Pakistanis, fresh from a World Cup triumph in which they defeated England in the final, won an increasingly fraught series 2-1. England's win at Headingley was helped by a decision on a run out by umpire Ken Palmer in favour of Graham Gooch that was so manifestly wrong that photographs of it adorned buses in Pakistan's cities for weeks. The tour culminated with allegations of ball-tampering in a one-day international when the ball was replaced during the England innings. The officials, whether the English TCCB or the ICC match referee Deryck Murray, refused to say why and the ball has remained locked in a safe at Lord's. Allan Lamb, who was batting at the time, had his say in a Sunday tabloid and English cricket's domestic showpiece final was marked by the unusual spectacle of Lamb being served with a libel writ as he walked out to bat by his former teammate and erstwhile Pakistan opening bowler Sarfraz Nawaz. Ball-tampering allegations also formed a prominent part of another libel case brought by Ian Botham and Lamb against Imran, the latter asserting that ball-tampering was a regular feature of the English game.

That case formed a surreal backdrop to the beginning of Pakistan's next series in England, in 1996. By then relations on the field were much better. This was in large measure due to the two captains. The Pakistan captain Wasim Akram was a county teammate and friend of his English counterpart Mike Atherton. Pakistan were again too good for England, winning the series 2-0.

The two countries did not meet again in Test cricket until 2000/01. Pakistan had been through a series of match-fixing inquiries; indeed there were muttered complaints about the wisdom of England's warriors having to do battle with these allegedly dodgy characters. So there was some consternation when, soon after the England team arrived in Pakistan, allegations were made that their senior player, Alec Stewart, had accepted money from a bookmaker. Stewart vehemently, and no doubt justifiably, denied the allegations. On the field, England enjoyed their most successful tour of Pakistan. It was certainly better than their most recent tour, in 2005, when they must have thought of themselves as world champions after beating Australia for the first time for almost twenty years.

Plus ça change... when Pakistan were beating England in the late 1980s and early 1990s there were two things that really irritated the English: the Pakistanis' ability to swing the old ball; and their habit of continually using substitute fielders. By 2005, both were part of an Ashes masterplan. When Sarfraz Nawaz or Wasim Akram swung the old ball, it was time for a special inquiry; when Simon Jones did it, it was, according to the voice of authority – Mark Nicholas on Channel Four – the result of months of hard work.

The Pakistani Masters does not purport to be a history of these events or of Pakistani cricket generally. But it is difficult to ignore them in writing profiles of the brilliant players who have represented Pakistan over the last fifty years. In selecting the players, I have not adopted the restriction followed in *The Indian Masters* and chosen only players who have played domestic cricket in England. That would have meant missing out such leading figures as Abdul Qadir, Hanif Mohammad and Inzamam-ul-Haq. Again, though, there are difficult choices. I have had to leave out, among others, those splendid left-handed openers Saeed Anwar and Aamir Sohail, the underrated all-rounder Nasim-ul-Ghani and two men who played a great deal of county cricket, Khalid 'Billy' Ibadulla, and Younis Ahmed.

A perfect XI? How about: Hanif Mohammad, Majid Khan, Zaheer Abbas, Javed Miandad, Inzamam-ul-Haq, Imran Khan, Wasim Akram, Wasim Bari, Abdul Qadir, Waqar Younis, Fazal Mahmood. If the wicket is expected to turn, Mushtaq Mohammad would replace Fazal Mahmood and bat at number six. In one-day cricket, Shahid Afridi would replace Hanif Mohammad.

Note on the Statistics

The statistics are up to date as of 15 May 2006. Thus, the Test match statistics include the Sri Lanka *v.* Pakistan series in March/April 2006. The one-day international statistics include the series between India and Pakistan in Abu Dhabi in April 2006. Figures for Tests and one-day internationals do not include games for the ICC World XI or the Asia XI. A.H. Kardar's Test figures include Tests played for India. Figures for players involved in the English domestic season of 2006 are up to date to the round of Cheltenham & Gloucester Trophy fixtures that concluded on 14 May 2006.

A.H. KARDAR

If Hanif Mohammad was Pakistan's W.G. Grace – and many would say such an accolade is not far-fetched – Abdul Hafeez Kardar was its Lord Harris. A useful cricketer but not an outstanding one, a forthright character with a devotion to cricket and doing what was best for it in his own country and beyond, an administrator of unimpeachable integrity and indomitable authority, Kardar did much to shape Pakistan's cricket during its first twenty-five years of Test status. Ramachandra Guha called him 'perhaps the greatest cricketer-ideologue born outside the West'.

It would be wrong to underestimate his prowess as a player. He was a very handy all-rounder, an idiosyncratic left-handed middle-order batsman and a medium-pace left-arm bowler who could turn to spin if the conditions were suitable.

Abdul Hafeez Kardar was born and raised in Lahore and played for the Muslims in the Pentangular tournament. In 1945/46 he made 37 and 86 not out against the Australian Services XI at Eden Gardens, Calcutta. He did enough generally to be picked for the team that toured England in 1946 under the Nawab of Pataudi. He only had moderate success on the tour, scoring 348 runs at 17.45 and doing little in the three Tests he played in, although he showed what he was capable of in making 43 with some crisp drives and cuts in the First Test and an obdurate 35 in the second. He then went up to Oxford to read Philosophy, Politics and Economics at University College and obtained blues in 1947, 1948 and 1949. It was a good period for Oxford, who were led in the first year by the great New Zealander Martin Donnelly. Kardar proved himself an extremely capable all-rounder. He also played for Warwickshire from 1948 to 1950, receiving his county cap in 1949. He scored 1,312 runs for them in all at 22.87 and took 112 wickets at 28.42. He scored a hundred against Middlesex at Lord's in 1948. Geoffrey Howard, then secretary of Lancashire, remembered him being sent off the field at Old Trafford by Warwickshire's captain Tom Dollery for not trying hard enough. His main achievement at Warwickshire was to marry the chairman's daughter. Then he went back home.

This is not the place to review the events surrounding Partition, the process whereby Pakistan – East and West – emerged as an independent Islamic country separated

— traumatically — from a simultaneously independent India. Suffice it to say that, as Scyld Berry put it, at the time of independence, Pakistan did not even have headed notepaper. As far as cricket was concerned Kardar simply took it and moulded it more or less as he pleased. His first task was to ensure that Pakistan obtained Test status. There was no doubt that this would depend on how they performed in the two unofficial Tests played against the MCC after England's series in India in 1951/52. Kardar led the Pakistan side and they won the second match. Test match status followed.

Kardar captained Pakistan in their first 23 Tests. By force of personality as much as anything else he ensured that Pakistan attained respectability as a Test-playing country more swiftly and with more assurance than any new entrant since the original members, England and Australia. Pakistan became exceptionally difficult to beat at home. This was always a mantra of Kardar's: they were not beaten at Karachi until 2000/01. In those 23 Tests, Pakistan beat each of the other Test playing countries at least once (of course, they did not play South Africa) and, after their first series in India, lost only one series, Kardar's last, in the West Indies in 1957/58.

Of critical importance, for obvious reasons, was Pakistan's first Test series in India in 1952/53. It was, as India-Pakistan series are today, a gesture of goodwill in difficult times: the two neighbours had already fought their first inconclusive war over Kashmir in 1947/48. But relations had calmed down and there was enormous interest in the cricket in both countries. The First Test, at the Ferozeshah Kotla stadium in Delhi was attended by India's president and watched by capacity crowds of 25,000. India won by an innings but the new boys fought back at once and gained their historic first Test victory at Lucknow, a city famous for its predominantly Muslim heritage. Pakistan won by an innings and 13 runs. India won the next game, at the Brabourne Stadium in Bombay, by 10 wickets and the other two games were drawn. Kardar top-scored with 79 in the rain-interrupted match at Madras. Everyone seemed satisfied with the series result and the tour, generally, had been a great success. For Kardar it had been something like a pilgrimage, certainly when it took the team to places of historic interest to Muslims, like Lucknow and Hyderabad. As Guha put it, in Kardar's view Muslim rule in the princely states had brought civilization to backward India.

The next assignment was very different but just as important: a tour of England in 1954. Kardar himself had considerable cricketing experience there and lots of old friends (not to mention drinking companions: no doubt this was not mentioned at team meetings). It would scarcely be an exaggeration to describe the tour as a triumph. Pakistan shared the four Test series 1-1: even Australia had not won a Test on their first visit to England. Pakistan's famous victory at The Oval owed something perhaps to some strange decisions by England's selectors — the Pakistanis themselves would not have claimed to be as good a side as England — but all agreed that Pakistan's players had acquitted themselves exceptionally well in deeply alien conditions. Kardar himself had a reasonable tour, making almost 800 runs at 28. He made 139 with 24 fours in a losing cause against Yorkshire. His best effort in the Tests came at The Oval where, in a low-scoring match, he made 36 out of 133 in Pakistan's first innings. But it was his calm and authoritative leadership that constituted his greatest contribution.

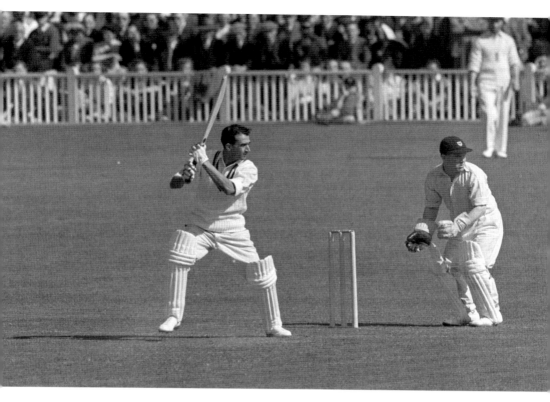

A.H. Kardar batting for the Pakistan tourists against Worcestershire in the opening match of the 1954 tour. Hugo Yarnold is the wicketkeeper.

In January 1955 India began a three-month tour of Pakistan. All five Tests were drawn, setting a pattern that came to be difficult to alter. The series generated phenomenal interest, particularly in Lahore — recently a multi-cultural city populated by many Hindus and Sikhs as well as Muslims — and Karachi, where the Fifth Test was played at the newly constructed National Stadium. But the cricket rarely matched expectations, as Pakistan's captain was the first to admit. 'The crowds,' he wrote, 'were the real heroes of the tour, displaying remarkable patience watching dull, lifeless cricket.' Almost the only entertaining piece of batting in the series came in Pakistan's second innings at Karachi when the opener Alimuddin (103) and Kardar (93) put on 155 for the fifth wicket in even time.

The first part of the 1955/56 season was taken up with a tour by New Zealand, who played three Tests, of which Pakistan won two. For the first time, Pakistan's dominant bowlers were spinners — Zulfiqar Ahmed, Shuja-ud-din (whose book on Pakistan cricket is a monumental labour of love) and Kardar himself: he took 10 wickets in the series. Up until then the most successful bowlers had been the pacemen Fazal Mahmood and Khan Mohammad.

There followed the visit of an MCC 'A' team led by Kardar's old Oxford teammate, the future Test and County Cricket Board secretary Donald Carr. There were four unofficial 'Tests'. The first, at Lahore, was a dull draw, dominated by an immensely slow century from Hanif Mohammad. The second, at Dacca, and the third at Peshawar were won by Pakistan. Kardar made 78 at Dacca and took 11 for 65 at Peshawar. The fourth game at Karachi, which Kardar missed through injury, was won by MCC 'A'. During the Peshawar game the incident occurred that provided the only reason why the tour is remembered, namely the 'ragging' of a Pakistani umpire, Idris Begh, by members of the MCC 'A' side. Begh had been of considerable assistance to Kardar when he took his 11 wickets, particularly in the first innings when four of Kardar's – or Begh's – victims were leg before. There was a big fuss about the incident for a little while, but it blew over, as these things do. Stephen Chalke, in his splendid book about Geoffrey Howard, the MCC 'A' manager, has a lovely story about it:

'At close of play [in Karachi] Governor-General Iskander Mirza summoned Geoffrey Howard and Hafeez Kardar to talk, and he listened carefully to what the two parties had to say [about Begh]... He paused to reflect. "I have to say that I form the view that Idris Begh, as an umpire, is a cheat." "But he's the best we've got," Hafeez protested. "The best umpire? Or the best cheat?"'

In Pakistan's historic first Test against Australia at Karachi in October 1956, which Pakistan won by 9 wickets, Kardar made the game's highest score, 69.

Kardar retired at the end of the Caribbean tour in March 1958 and was appointed chairman of selectors. There was a feeling that his retirement might be a bluff and that he was waiting to be asked to return when it was clear there was no effective successor but, if that were so, the ploy failed. An embarrassing net prior to the tour of India in 1960/61 put paid to any idea of a comeback. His involvement in politics in the Punjab limited Kardar's participation in cricket in the 1960s, generally a dispiriting time for Pakistan. But he served periodically as chairman of selectors. He was heavily involved in the unhappy ending of Hanif Mohammad's Test career. The Little Master's form had declined perceptibly after his century against England at Lord's in 1967. He played in the First Test against New Zealand in 1969/70. At the end of the match, Kardar sent the press to the home dressing room: Hanif had an announcement to make about his future. But there was no announcement; Hanif retired before the Second Test.

Kardar became president of the Board of Control for Cricket in Pakistan in 1972. The reorganisation of domestic cricket in Pakistan, so that teams were sponsored by leading companies such as Habib Bank and Pakistan International Airlines, was essentially his idea. It helped provide financial support for players and administrators (in the 1970s Haseeb Ahsan was PIA's sales manager in London). Opinions differed as to how successful it was. Javed Miandad was a great supporter of the general principle, although Imran Khan thought the system failed to cure the ills of the domestic game. Kardar himself thought that further restructuring would be necessary.

At the international level, he was genuinely radical and innovative. Many of his ideas became general currency in time. He was one of the first administrators to question the necessity of a veto in the hands of England and Australia regarding decisions of the International Cricket Council. He successfully advocated a limitation of bouncers in the inaugural World Cup. In the 1970s, he wanted to see Test cricket spread to Sri Lanka and other Asian countries and he was an early supporter of the principle of neutral umpires. Ray Robinson once wrote that it must have been a source of great encouragement to the Pakistan team to have their president watching them regularly when they were playing away from home. Robinson was as shrewd as they come. Was there a hint of irony? When Pakistan recorded their famous Test victory over Australia at Sydney in January 1977, respected Pakistani journalist Qamar Ahmed wrote that, 'Pakistan owes its success much to the absence of the pavilion captainship of BCCP president A.H. Kardar whose presence in every Test played abroad resulted in terrible disaster for the team and the team members.'

Kardar resigned at the end of the West Indian tour in 1977. He continued to live an active public life, his final appointment being as Pakistan's ambassador to Switzerland.

ABDUL HAFEEZ KARDAR
Left-hand bat, slow left-arm
Born: 17 January 1925, Lahore, India
Died: 21 April 1996
Major Teams: India, Pakistan, Muslims, Northern India, Oxford University, Warwickshire
Also Known as: Abdul Hafeez

TESTS
(1946-1957/58)

	M	I	NO	Runs	HS	Ave	50	Ct
Batting & Fielding	26	42	3	927	93	23.76	5	16

Bowling	Balls	R	W	Ave	BBI	SR	Econ
	2712	954	21	45.42	3/35	129.14	2.11

FIRST-CLASS
(Career: 1943/44-1955/56)

	M	I	NO	Runs	HS	Ave	100	Ct
Batting & Fielding	174	262	33	6,832	173	29.83	8	110

	R	W	Ave	BBI	5	10
Bowling	8,448	344	24.55	7/25	19	4

ABDUL QADIR

'Mummy, I want to be a leg-spinner when I grow up.'

How often, one wonders, is that plaintive cry heard? Not very, is almost certainly the answer. Even in those households where cricket is a dominant theme when the little ones are dandled on the knee, it will be the likes of (and I promise you that this is the one and only time in this book that that egregious phrase is used, and I maintain that it is not superfluous here) Brett Lee, Shoaib Akhtar, Andrew Flintoff and Sachin Tendulkar whose images stoke the fires of childish and parental ambition. You have to be a bit older to want to be a leg-spinner; old enough to know that there is, alas, a rough that goes with the smooth, that every cloud has a nasty dark bit just behind that nice fluffy corner, and that, like it or not, God is a batsman. As Ian Peebles, a considerable leg-spinner himself and one of the most enjoyable of cricket writers, said, a leg-spinner has to prepare himself for the hideous days when everything goes wrong and the glorious moments when everything goes right.

The mechanics of 'back of the hand' bowling – the leg-break or the slow left-armer's equivalent, the chinaman – leave much scope for error. Finger spin has its own techniques and demands but the actual spin is imparted by a flick of the finger; the turn of a leg-break requires a combination of movements in shoulder, wrist and fingers that if not co-ordinated correctly can send the ball sailing over the batsman's head or dribbling towards him – or not, as the case may be – along the ground. The ball comes out of the side of the hand and turns to the off – to the right-handed batsman – or at least that is usually the plan. Some hundred years ago or so the Middlesex and England amateur Bernard Bosanquet – father of the colourful television newscaster Reginald – discovered with the aid of a tennis ball that if he turned his wrist further, so that the ball came out of the back of the hand, it would turn from off to leg rather than from leg to off – (rather like Flanders and Swann's honeysuckle and bindweed). This became variously known as the 'bosie', the googly, the wrong'un, or – in the subcontinent, more formally and engagingly, the 'wrong one'. The masters usually but not always try to make the googly difficult for the batsman to distinguish from the leg-break; that, indeed, is usually the point of it. That is good if you can do it, but not the only way to prosper. Shane Warne, the Australian maestro, has a wrong 'un most Test batsmen could spot on a foggy evening in Manchester after the pubs have closed but it has not stopped him taking 600 Test wickets. Leg-spinners have all sorts of additional variations – flippers, which go straight and apparently at increased speed, top spinners and sliders. Ultimately there is only so much you can do with a cricket ball but, as Warne has triumphantly demonstrated over many years, a keen cricketing brain and an indomitable competitive spirit and self-confidence, when allied to supreme natural gifts, can get you almost anywhere. But the physical strains and stresses incurred in order to produce these variations can have serious consequences of various types; Warne's shoulder and fingers have been ravaged by years of hard work, while Peebles, striving to produce the perfect googly, lost his leg-break altogether.

Leg-spinners are often intriguing personalities. The Australian Arthur Mailey – Australia, with its hard, bouncy wickets, is a natural setting for leg-spin – was a great early exponent operating before and after the First World War. Cartoonist, raconteur and landscape painter, he too was a great writer on the game. The leg-spinner's leg-spinner, he was a whimsical character and a prodigious spinner of the ball. He took many Test wickets but his favourite analysis came in Victoria's record score of 1,107 against New South Wales in 1926/27: Mailey took 4 for 362. 'A chap in the outer kept dropping his catches,' Mailey said. 'I was just finding my length when the innings finished.'

Leg-spinners are generally of two types rather like waves – rollers and breakers. Mailey was a breaker, giving the ball an almighty tweak. One of his successors in the Australian side, Bill O' Reilly, was more of a roller, bowling at pretty well medium pace, like Anil Kumble or the post-war England bowler Doug Wright. He turned his googly more, and loathed batsmen with a passion. Don Bradman, with whom he had an uneasy relationship, thought he was the best. His great contemporary, Clarrie Grimmett was different – slower, more controlled, with immensely subtle variations of flight and pace and, according to Peebles, a googly that was 'more an instrument of propaganda than deception'. They were sometimes joined in the Australian eleven by Leslie 'Chuck' Fleetwood-Smith, the first purveyor of the chinaman to attain regular success at Test level; a terrific spinner of the ball, a match-winner on his day, but inconsistent and sometimes lacking discipline, on and off the field. At The Oval in 1938, when England made 903 for 7, he took 1 for 298; even Mailey must have thought that was a bit much.

After the Second World War, Australia started exporting wrist-spinners to England. Bruce Dooland, Colin McCool and the left-armers Jack Walsh and George Tribe seemed at least as good as the Test rivals they left behind, Doug Ring and Jack Hill. But Ring and Hill had an understudy with them on the Ashes tour of 1953 who looked a good bet as a batsman and fielder too, an impression he confirmed when he toured again in 1956. When he returned to England as Australia's captain in 1961, Richie Benaud was the most influential cricketer in the world. Many would argue he has yet to surrender that position.

By the time he gave up playing Benaud was the leading wicket-taker in Test cricket, as Grimmett had been before him. That says something about the potency of the top-class wrist-spinner. Tich Freeman, the Kent leg-spinner of the 1920s and

1930s tormented county batsmen for years but struggled at the highest level. In recent times, Ian Salisbury has had a similar experience, enjoying considerable success with Sussex and then Surrey but seldom troubling Test batsmen. Wrist-spin and Englishness have rarely gone well together. In Yorkshire, wrist-spinners were always looked upon with great suspicion. Johnny Wardle, who won a Test series in South Africa with his chinamen and googlies, was never allowed to bowl them north of the Watford Gap; he had to stick to the orthodox stuff.

Now, of course, leg-spin has suddenly become fashionable. England won the Ashes in 2005 but the leading bowler in the series was the incomparable Warne. The greatness of Warne has been at least in part to have combined some of the disparate and apparently incongruous attributes of Grimmett, O'Reilly and Fleetwood-Smith; astonishing accuracy and control, prodigious turn, subtle variations, the aggressive intent of a fast bowler and a cricketing brain surely rarely equalled. He is a genius and a larrikin.

Few people now dispute that Warne is the greatest leg-spinner of all time. Many indeed assert that he is the greatest bowler of all time. The Englishman S.F. Barnes, a difficult bowler to classify, is perhaps his strongest challenger in both categories but comparisons between sportsmen from such widely differing eras are rather pointless. What can be said without any doubt is that Warne is the best leg-spinner since the imam's son from the backstreets of Lahore, Abdul Qadir, and that Qadir was the best since Benaud.

Since Warne's emergence – in a way thanks to it – unorthodox spin has made a remarkable comeback. Australia themselves have a second leg-spinner, Stuart MacGill, who would be a first choice in most Test sides. One of the remarkable things about Qadir was that he was, literally, unique in his time. The 1980s was a period dominated by pace. This was most clearly demonstrated in the West Indies but it was true everywhere to some extent. Even in India, where there had been one of the great post-war leg-spinners in Subhash Gupta and a veritable galaxy of spinners after him, the leading bowler by a distance in the 1980s was Kapil Dev. Generally, spinners were used primarily to give the pacemen a rest and block an end, men like John Emburey, John Bracewell, Roger Harper, Greg Matthews. As a match-winning, attacking leg-spinner, Qadir was an anachronism, and a delight.

As today's watchers, whether at the ground or perhaps to an even greater extent on television, can testify, cricket has no more enthralling spectacle to offer than an attacking leg-spinner with plenty of variety. This is why Warne is so compelling. Qadir was similar, in a different class to any of his contemporaries. When he toured places like England, where some county batsmen had perhaps never played a bowler of his type, he could be devastating.

For instance, there was genuine excitement when Qadir went to England with Imran Khan's team in 1982 and tied county batsmen in all sorts of knots. Even Robin Marlar (an old curmudgeon even when young) described him as 'a joy'. The normally down-to-earth Jack Bannister waxed as rhapsodically as a Lake poet about Qadir's bowling in an article written after the Lord's Test of that year. It was understandable. In England, to a far greater extent than in Australia, a good leg-spinner really was a rare treat. Qadir was almost like a freak show exhibit in an upmarket Victorian fairground.

Abdul Qadir, 1978.

Like Warne, Qadir was wonderful to watch, with a marvellous action rippling and writhing with aggressive intent. He would toss the hard-spun ball from hand to hand fast, licking his fingers like a man shuffling cards. His left arm was raised, as if in greeting to the batsman, in the manner of a diffident traffic policeman or a reluctantly remonstrative schoolmaster admonishing a tiresome class, before he began his approach to the wicket with a few walking paces, his arms going back and forth as if he was winding himself up mechanically as much as psychologically. Then came a bouncy four-pace run to the crease before he delivered the ball with a distinctive arm action, fast and loose, and quickly and powerfully followed through. His pace was similar to Warne's; just right, not too fast, not too slow. He had all the tricks. He spun his leg-break hard, and his googlies – yes, he had two – were difficult to spot. Like Warne in his younger days, he had a marvellous flipper – he shattered Graham Gooch's stumps with one in the Lahore Test in 1987/88. He had two – at least – top spinners. People delighted in his subtlety, his artistry. Like all artists, he needed a patron and in Imran Khan he had both a loyal and a powerful one. Indeed, Scyld Berry, playing Peter Brough to Phil Edmonds' Archie Andrews in the England player's book on great bowlers, said that Imran sometimes overbowled Qadir. Imran always wanted Qadir in his side, and he usually got his way. One occasion when he did not was in the third and deciding Test against India at Bangalore in 1986/87. Javed Miandad urged Imran to pick Iqbal Qasim instead of Qadir; Imran reluctlantly agreed, and Iqbal Qasim in effect won the match.

Then there was the artistic temperament. Qadir was notoriously moody. He looked moody. You can see it in his face, his eyes. Physically he hardly changed (apart from the beard). Muscular, slightly podgy, hair all over the shop, five-and-a-half-feet tall, he is one of those people whose appearance will hardly alter between the ages of eighteen and sixty. Warne, writing in 2001, said he thought Qadir could still have been playing Test cricket then. But his moods did swing. Occasionally, away from his native land, he suffered the cruel and unusual punishment of having an appeal for leg before turned down. This could trigger a decidedly feisty reaction. The depths were plumbed during the tense final day of the Bridgetown Test in 1987/88 when Pakistan were desperately trying to maintain their 1-0 lead and become the first team since Ian Chappell's Australians in 1972/73 to beat the West Indies in a home series. Qadir was a key figure in this endeavour but he became distracted when a couple of close appeals were turned down. Things deteriorated markedly when he became the target of abuse from a spectator. Qadir was not the first cricketer to have been victimized in this way but he was the first to react by clambering over the fence into the crowd, singling out the perpetrator and thumping him in the face – twice. Only diplomatic intervention prevented him from being prosecuted. He was left out of the team that toured India in 1983/84 for disciplinary reasons. Javed Miandad sent him home from a tour of New Zealand in 1984/85, also for disciplinary reasons: Qadir launched an attack on the selectors. More than once there were personal distractions that delayed his arrival on a tour or interrupted its smooth progression.

How good was Qadir? He was the second Pakistani after Imran to take 200 Test wickets. Benaud was highly impressed, as was Ian Botham, who called him the best leg-spinner he ever faced: 'only' could have done just as well. Warne, who met Qadir at his home in 1994, said he was one of the true greats. His novelty and the sheer fascination of watching him inevitably make up part of the equation when calculating how to assess his quality. In England, his reputation rested to a considerable extent on his achievements on the 1982 tour. He caused havoc in the county games. Pakistan secured three innings victories before the start of the one-day series, against Sussex, Glamorgan and Worcestershire, and in these games he took 7 for 44 and 6 for 78, 5 for 31 and 4 for 20 and 4 for 30 and 4 for 75 respectively. There was a glitch at Southampton when promising middle-order batsman Mark Nicholas scored an unbeaten century in a Hampshire victory: Qadir took 0 for 114. Did England miss a trick here? He took 6 for 77 against Leicestershire in another innings victory before the start of the Test series. Although he did little in the First Test (3 wickets in 69 overs), he played a big part in Pakistan's historic victory in the Second Test at Lord's. In England's first innings, he bowled a long and aggressive spell on the third afternoon, earning a reprimand from Pakistan's favourite umpire, David Constant, after dancing a jig – on a length – in the course of one of many appeals for leg before. He caused profound, almost embarrassing, problems for Derek Pringle and Ian Greig. Qadir took 4 for 39 in 24 overs. In England's second innings, as Chris Tavare and Botham in particular fought hard to stave off defeat, Qadir took 2 for 94 in 37 overs, finishing the innings by dismissing last man Robin Jackman with the new ball. There was just enough time left for Pakistan to secure their win.

When he next toured England in 1987, there was an unusually wet summer, even by English standards. He arrived late because his wife was unwell and by early August he probably wished he had not bothered to come. But at The Oval, with Pakistan making a massive total, he took 7 for 96 in England's first innings and then, when they followed on, 3 for 115. England saved the game easily. That was by some distance Qadir's best innings and match analysis in a Test outside Pakistan. That is the question mark regarding Qadir's stature as a great bowler. He was unquestionably a great bowler in Pakistan. There, he took 168 Test wickets at 26.08. Elsewhere, he took 68 wickets at 47.58. The difference – one really should say the contrast – is startling. On his first visit to England in 1978, he made no impression at all, taking 6 wickets – on the whole tour, not in the Tests – at 66.00. Australia also rarely saw the best of him. He had a hard time of it there in 1983/84, taking 12 wickets in the five Tests at an average of 61. He had the Maileyesque figures of 5 for 160 in the Boxing Day Test at Melbourne. He took the last 4 wickets while 16 runs were added but earlier Graham Yallop had made 268. Australia had quite a few left-handers in their top order – Wayne Phillips, Kepler Wessels, Allan Border and Rod Marsh as well as Yallop – and this sometimes seemed to be a problem for Qadir. He had fared much better in Pakistan fifteen months earlier when Australia had lost all three Tests in the series and Qadir had taken 22 wickets at 25.54. He was the outstanding player in the series and the Australians found his variety and control too much to deal with. At Faisalabad in the Second Test he took 11 wickets – 4 for 76 and 7 for 142. Graeme Wood – another left-hander – defended stolidly in the first innings and Greg Ritchie made a fine unbeaten century in the second but nobody else had much of a clue.

Abdul Qadir bowling for the Rest of the World against the MCC in the Bicentennial match at Lord's in 1987. Even the umpire looks perplexed.

West Indian batsmen had occasional hiccups against spin bowlers – even quite modest spin bowlers – and Qadir had his share of success against them in the two drawn series in 1986/87 (at home) and 1987/88 (away). In the First Test at Faisalabad in 1986/87 the West Indies, having bowled Pakistan out for 328 in their second innings, needed 240 to win in four sessions. But their batsmen were utterly confounded by Qadir. He came on as soon as the openers were out, with the score on 16 for 2. He dismissed Larry Gomes and Richie Richardson in three balls and then Viv Richards for a duck. He took 5 for 13 in 7 overs and West Indies finished the fourth day on 43 for 9. When he caught and bowled Malcolm Marshall the next morning they were 53 all out: Qadir took 6 for 16. He finished the series with 18 wickets at 20 apiece.

In the Caribbean eighteen months later he again bowled well but inconsistently. He was still suffering slightly from a kidney ailment diagnosed during the series against England late in 1987 and he missed the opening games of the tour. He did not take a lot of wickets in the historic win in the First Test at Georgetown but the wickets he took were important. He troubled all the upper order in the first innings, and his dismissal of Gus Logie with a flipper was the break that enabled Imran to burst through with a spell of 4 for 29 in 9 overs. Pakistan secured a lead of 143 but were handicapped when West Indies resumed their second innings after the rest day by Imran's temporary absence due to an injured foot. Qadir again made a vital breakthrough, bowling Phil Simmons with a top-spinner in the third over of the day. He also dismissed Richie Richardson and Carl Hooper before Imran returned to finish the job. In the Second Test at Port-of-Spain he bowled wonderfully well. In the first innings he took 4 for 83, including the threatening Richards caught at slip for 49 off 45 balls. In the second innings, he took 4 for 148. Marshall was his 200th Test wicket. At the thrilling climax of the game, he came in at number eleven to play out a tense final over from Richards to secure a draw.

It was the home series against England in 1987/88 that saw Qadir at his most fiendish. He had always been partial to England batsmen on Pakistan's pitches. He had made his debut against England in 1977/78, taking 6 for 44 in his second Test at Hyderabad. Bowling into the rough he troubled all the batsmen; only Geoff Boycott (run out for 79) showed the technical nous to deal with him.

In 1983/84, the England players arrived in Pakistan after a controversial and disappointing tour of New Zealand. They were badly hit by injuries which deprived them of their captain Bob Willis and their leading player Ian Botham. Having asked for a truncated tour they got their wish, and found themselves facing Qadir in the First Test at Karachi almost as soon as they got off their – much delayed – flight from Auckland. Pakistan won the match by 3 wickets but it was not really as close as the result suggests. The Pakistan batsmen panicked in their pursuit of a modest target of 65, slow left-armer Nick Cook taking 11 wickets in the match. The key figures though were Qadir, who bowled brilliantly to take 5 for 74 and 3 for 59, and David Gower who made 58 and 57; no other England batsman made more than 28 in either innings. The Second Test, at Faisalabad, was a high-scoring draw; Gower, now England's acting captain, made 152 and Qadir took a solitary wicket. The Third Test, at Lahore, was also drawn. England struggled in their first innings, making 241. Gower failed for once, and Qadir took 5 for 84. Pakistan responded with 343. England's second innings was built around Gower's six-and-three-quarter-hour innings of 173 not out. Qadir took a further 5 wickets for 110, Pakistan were set 243 to win and would probably have got them but for a nervous middle-order stutter and some blatant time-wasting.

It is difficult to think of a more sustained spell of success by a batsman against Qadir at home than this performance of Gower's. It demonstrated again Qadir's vulnerability against left-handers, a criticism occasionally levelled against Warne too. When Warne first toured England in 1993, and announced himself with his first ball in an Ashes Test, it sometimes seemed that Gower was the only English-qualified batsman between the ages of twenty-one and forty who was not going to be considered for selection. None of the new faces selected prospered, except Graham Thorpe, and he had been dropped within a year.

The 1987/88 series was probably the most controversial Test series since the Bodyline tour of 1932/33. After the series in England in 1987, which Pakistan won 1-0, Qadir had a good World Cup in the subcontinent – as Scyld Berry noted, and as became true of Warne, Qadir on his day was a captain's dream. He could be both a shock bowler and a stock bowler. He had often been a successful one-day bowler with two match awards in the previous World Cup in England. Then came England's visit. The seeds of the trouble in 1987/88 had been sown long before, but the immediate *causus belli* was the attitude of the English cricket authorities, at the start of the 1987 tour, to the Pakistanis' request to withdraw umpires David Constant and Ken Palmer from the Test match panel for the duration of the tour. The request was rather disdainfully refused. The Pakistan tour manager, Haseeb Ahsan, muttered darkly that Pakistani umpires would officiate on England's tour: this was a reference to the fact that neutral umpires – from India – had stood in two of the Tests against the West Indies in 1986/87. The presence of Pakistani umpires was not in itself a problem; various Pakistani officials performed with distinction in the World Cup. The real difficulty was the appointment of two umpires – Shakeel Khan and Shakoor Rana – who had not been thought suitable for the World Cup. Shakeel Khan was very inexperienced; Shakoor Rana had more than once been the object of criticism from touring sides: the New Zealanders had almost walked off in protest after Javed Miandad was given not out leg before in a Test at Karachi in 1984/85. Ironically – perhaps uniquely – television replays suggested Rana's decision was right.

Qadir captained Pakistan in the one-day series that preceded the Tests. England won all three games. A good indication of the relationship between the teams came in the second game at Karachi. The result was clear well before the end – Pakistan were not going to reach the target of 270. The finale was not of purely academic interest, however. Off the last ball of the match, Pakistan's opener, Rameez Raja, turned a ball off his legs and ran one and turned for a second. Running back to the striker's end he intercepted the ball as it was thrown towards the wicket and batted it away. England appealed and Rameez was given out obstructed the field – for 99.

Shakeel Khan stood in the First Test at Lahore, which Pakistan won by an innings. There were seven leg befores in England's two innings, compared to one in Pakistan's innings (although the dismissal that gave rise to most on-field protestation was Shakeel's adjudication that Qadir had been stumped). England were convinced that five of those lbws – all to Qadir – were not out – plus two absolute shockers successfully claimed by the wicketkeeper, Ashraf Ali, off Iqbal Qasim in the second innings and David Capel's dismissal to a catch at slip. Even the *Nation* newspaper said that the umpiring was 'deplorable'. England, though, made it difficult for themselves to claim they occupied the moral high ground by displaying unprecedented levels of dissent. First there was the captain, Mike Gatting, waiting, posed on one knee after being given out for a duck in the first innings stretching well forward to sweep. It culminated with Chris Broad having to be persuaded by his opening partner, Graham Gooch, to leave the field, after being adjudged to have been caught behind off a ball that he seemed to have missed by some distance. Rana officiated in the Second Test, at Faisalabad, where the inevitable flashpoint occurred just before close of play on the second day, when he and Gatting engaged in an extraordinary – shocking, really – shouting match about a fielder being moved behind the batsman's back. A day's play was lost while 'crisis talks' were held. That Test and the third, at Karachi, were drawn.

The umpiring controversy dominated the series. It thus obscured and deflected attention from a quite extraordinary display of leg-spin and googly bowling from Abdul Qadir. In the first innings of the Lahore Test, he took 9 for 56, still statistically the seventh-best analysis in Test history and the best against England. Qadir himself said the first 15 overs he bowled in that innings constituted his best bowling in Tests. In his third over – the fifteenth of the match – he fooled Gooch with a flipper. Tim Robinson and Gatting were both out to leg-breaks and England were 50 for 4 at lunch. That soon became 94 for 8 but Neil Foster and Bruce French took the total to 175. Pakistan made 392 and then Qadir was at England again. He took 4 more wickets in the second innings before retiring with what was thought to be a side strain. It was subsequently diagnosed as kidney stones. He took 7 wickets in the blighted game at Faisalabad and 5 in each innings – off 104 overs – at Karachi. In the course of his 5 for 88 in the first innings, he had a spell of 3 for 6 in 6 overs – and still found time to have an argument with a spectator. In all he took 30 wickets in the three Tests, at 14.37. Iqbal Qasim took 10. Nobody else on either side took more than seven. In the Karachi match, he also made his highest Test score, 61, hitting 4 sixes and 6 fours.

The series against England and the West Indies in 1987/88 were the climax of Qadir's career. He was unable to reproduce quite the same quality after that. In 1988/89 Australia had their equivalent of the Gatting tour, arriving in Pakistan almost expecting to be defeated however they played. Pakistan won the first game at Karachi by an innings and the other two Tests were drawn. In the First Test, Qadir took 5 wickets in the match, but the damage was mainly done by Iqbal Qasim. In the acrimonious tour of New Zealand that came a few months later he took 6 for 160 in the drawn Test at Auckland. He struggled against India in 1989/90, taking 6 wickets in four Tests. In an exhibition match at Peshawar that was originally scheduled to be the first one-day international, he was hit for 27 in an over, including 3 sixes. The batsman was the sixteen-year-old Sachin Tendulkar. When Pakistan toured Australia a few months later, their leading leg-spinner was Mushtaq Ahmed.

Qadir remains a legendary figure. People visit him in the way they would visit a seer, or a survivor from some distant and historic age. He is revered too: Danish Kaneria worships the loops he weaved. Warne, and Kumble too, went to see him, to pay homage and seek counsel. Rahul Bhattacharya visited him at his home in Lahore in 2003 as Berry had done in 1987. Bhattacharya's book *Pundits from Pakistan* is the best tour book since Berry's *Cricket Odyssey* and ranks with the best, by Jack Fingleton and Alan Ross. Bhattacharya asked the question, 'Why leg-spin?' From twelve or fourteen years of age, Qadir had wanted to be a leg-spinner. Leg-spinners made things happen. It was simple really. "I could bowl the same ball in ten different ways... I've seen people bowling in one style, and that's it. But not me. I wanted to do miracles, you see.'"

ABDUL QADIR KHAN
Right-hand bat, leg-break & googly
Born: 15 September 1955, Lahore
Major Teams: Pakistan, Punjab, Lahore, Habib Bank

TESTS
(1977/78-1990/91)

	M	I	NO	Runs	HS	Ave	50	Ct
Batting & Fielding	67	77	11	1029	61	15.59	3	15

	Balls	R	W	Ave	BBI	5	10	SR	Econ
Bowling	17,126	7,742	236	32.8	9/56	15	5	72.56	2.71

ONE-DAY INTERNATIONALS

	M	I	NO	Runs	HS	Ave	SR	Ct
Batting & Fielding	104	68	26	641	41★	15.26	75.50	21

	Balls	R	W	Ave	BBI	5	SR	Econ
Bowling	5100	3454	132	26.16	5/44	2	36.63	4.06

FIRST-CLASS
(Career: 1975/76-1995/96)

	M	I	NO	Runs	HS	Ave	100	50	Ct
Batting & Fielding	209	247	43	3,740	112	18.33	2	8	83

	Balls	R	W	Ave	BBI	5	10	SR	Econ
Bowling	49,036	22,314	960	23.24	9/49	75	21	51.07	2.73

LIST A RECORD

	M	I	NO	Runs	HS	Ave	Ct
Batting & Fielding	147	91	29	869	41★	14.01	29

	Balls	R	W	Ave	BBI	5	SR	Econ
Bowling	7,014	4,606	202	23.09	5/31	3	34.72	3.99

ASIF IQBAL

For spectators in England in the late 1960s and the 1970s there were few more enjoyable sights than a big innings from Asif Iqbal. There was something uninhibited about his batting. When he joined Kent in 1968 he seemed to personify the perceived advantages of the 'instant' registration of overseas players. Of medium height, fit and athletic with a lean and hungry look, but often with a smile on his face, his approach to the game seemed Caribbean in its enthusiasm. There were two innings in particular which symbolised this freedom of spirit: Asif's century for Pakistan against England at The Oval in 1967, and his 89 for Kent against Lancashire in the Gillette Cup final of 1971. The first of these innings was more startling, not only because Asif was largely unknown in England and was ostensibly playing as a bowler, but also because of the context of the game and the series.

It could not be said that his success in 1967 was totally unexpected. Like all his contemporaries in the Pakistan side, by definition, Asif was born in pre-partition India but, unusually, he actually played first-class cricket in India. The nephew of Ghulam Ahmed, the Indian off-spinner, he played for Hyderabad in the Ranji Trophy in 1960/61. Later that year he migrated to Karachi. On his Test debut at Karachi against Australia in October 1964, he opened the bowling with fellow debutant Majid Jahangir Khan. Batting at number ten in the first innings he scored 41, and he made 36 in the second. He was the leading wicket-taker on the tour to Australia and New Zealand in 1964/65, taking 18 wickets at 13.77 in the three Tests against New Zealand. In the opening first-class game of the tour against Queensland, he and Intikhab Alam put on 116 in rapid time for the sixth wicket in the tourists' second innings. The New Zealand segment of the tour also revealed his batting potential. In the First Test at Wellington, New Zealand set Pakistan 259 to win and at one point they were 19 for 5. Asif, at number eight, made a match-saving 52 not out. Nonetheless, his primary role in Pakistan's side appeared to be as opening bowler – he had learned much about swing bowling in English conditions while on tour with the Pakistan Eaglets in 1963.

In 1967, in the First Test at Lord's, he opened the bowling, dismissing Colin Milburn early on. England made 369. Pakistan were 99 for 6 when Intikhab joined captain Hanif Mohammad in a stand of 40; then Asif put on 130 with Hanif. Asif made 76. Pakistan reached 354 and the game was drawn. England won the Second Test at Nottingham by 10 wickets. The Oval Test seemed to be going the same way when Pakistan, facing a deficit of 224, staggered to 65 for 8, the fast-medium swing of Ken Higgs having accounted for five of the top six. That was the score when Intikhab joined the number nine, Asif. They put on 190 in 175 minutes for the ninth wicket, the record stand for that wicket in Tests until it was overtaken by Mark Boucher and Pat Symcox at Johannesburg in 1997/98, against Pakistan. Asif's 146 was the highest score made by a Test number nine until Ian Smith's 173 for New Zealand against India in 1989/90. England needed 34 to win. Asif dismissed Colin Cowdrey and Brian Close before they got them.

The records were splendid but they were in a sense beside the point. Asif seemed to be playing a different sort of game from anybody else involved in the series. Ken Barrington was England's leading run-scorer. He spent more than five hours making 148 at Lord's and almost seven hours making 106 – with 6 fours – at Trent Bridge. Pakistan were not immune. When Close set them 257 to win in three and a half hours at Lord's Javed Burki and Khalid Ibadulla scored 8 runs in 40 minutes and 23 in the first hour. That was the way it was in 1967.

But not for Asif. Of course, you could say he had nothing to lose, but again that was not really the point. He was upset by suggestions that a beer match would be put on to compensate spectators for an early finish and was determined that England should bat again. There was nothing abandoned about his stroke making; he played his natural game, driving sumptuously and running quickly and eagerly between the wickets, always urging his partner on. In this great innings at The Oval, Asif made 50 out of 56 runs scored and reached his century in just over two and a quarter hours: the happy event was greeted by a tumultuous and rather alarming pitch invasion. In all he batted for just over three hours, hitting 2 sixes and 21 fours. All the bowlers suffered, Higgs being hit for 5 fours after Asif had reached his century.

Kent snapped him up and he proved an immediate success. He headed the batting averages in 1968. In 1970, the county won the championship for the first time since 1913. Among the batsmen – who included three England players in Colin Cowdrey, Brian Luckhurst and Mike Denness – it was difficult to ignore Asif, again not just because of the runs he made but because of the way he made them. He played a series of scintillating innings, often in the hunt for bonus points in the first innings that, in a tight campaign, could make all the difference. He was a match-winner at Cheltenham with a brilliant hundred on a crumbling wicket against Gloucestershire spinners John Mortimore and David Allen. The Gillette Cup innings came in the following year, 1971. Asif spent the first half of the summer with the Pakistan tourists, scoring a century in the Edgbaston Test. He headed Kent's first-class batting averages and was in prime form for the climax of the domestic season, the Gillette Cup final against one-day specialists Lancashire. People of a certain age – particularly if they live in Dorset – will probably say that this was the perfect one-day cricket match. A glorious late summer's day and a packed house

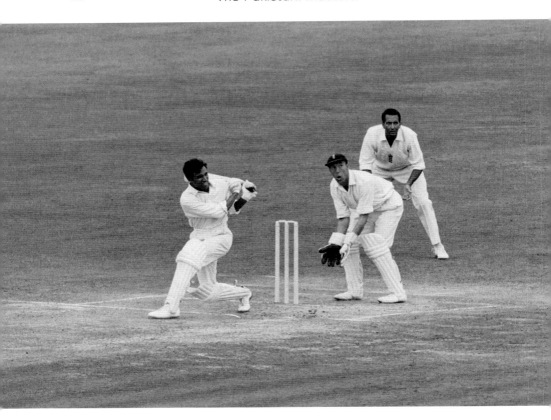

Asif Iqbal batting during the first Test against England in 1967; John Murray and Basil d'Oliveira look on.

at the game's noblest ground. Lancashire, whose captain Jack Bond won the toss, struggled for much of their innings. But their leading batsmen, Clive Lloyd, who got off the mark by hitting Asif for six, made 66, and local heroes David Hughes and Jack Simmons scrambled and slogged at the death. A target of 224 seemed competitive but gettable.

Kent had problems in their turn, particularly against Peter Lever and Ken Shuttleworth; they were 9 for 2, then 68 for 4. Asif and Alan Knott put on 37, and then Knott was run out. Asif took matters into his own hands with a thrilling array of strokes. He had taken the score to 197 for 6 when, having hardly lifted a ball off the ground all day, he hit a powerful drive off Simmons into what appeared to be a gap on the off-side. But the thirty-nine-year-old Bond, fielding in the covers, leaped to his right and took an amazing catch. It was unquestionably one of the abiding cricket images of the 1970s and it put an end to one of the great one-day innings of the decade: 89 out of 141 in two and a quarter hours. Lancashire won by 24 runs. Asif won the Gold Award for that innings and he was similarly rewarded in the Benson & Hedges Cup final against Worcestershire in 1973 when he made 59 and took 4 for 43. He continued to perform well for Kent, captaining the county to a joint championship with Middlesex in 1977 and leading them again in 1981 and 1982. His first spell in charge came to an end because of his involvement with World Series Cricket, but he carried on playing for the county and had one of his best seasons for them in 1978 when they won the championship outright. He played a series of brilliant innings, including a dazzling 171 in just over three hours in an innings victory over Gloucestershire at Folkestone.

Throughout the 1970s Asif was a key figure in Pakistan's middle order, usually batting at five or six. His style, which remained predominantly as aggressive and entertaining as it was in 1967, meant that he was unlikely to be the most consistent batsman in the side, and he had his ups and downs. But he played some marvellous innings, often when they were most needed. He was seen at his best on Pakistan's tour of Australia in 1976/77. This was a compelling series played by two sides that, somewhat to the surprise of the home supporters, if not players, turned out to be evenly matched: Australia had comfortably beaten Intikhab's team, comprising many of the same players, in 1972/73. Pakistan's batsmen had one stroke of great good fortune in 1976/77 in that the fast bowler Jeff Thomson was injured in the field during the first innings of the First Test at Adelaide and missed the rest of the series. Pakistan were up against it in that game, conceding a first innings lead of 182, but they fought back with style and determination in the second. Zaheer Abbas made 101 and Asif batted with resolution and fluency to score a magnificent 152 not out in four and a half hours. He put on 87 for the last wicket with Iqbal Qasim, who contributed 4 of them. The match was drawn. Australia overwhelmed the visitors in the Second Test at Melbourne, Dennis Lillee taking 10 wickets, but Pakistan achieved an historic victory at Sydney to secure a drawn series. The principal architect of that victory was Imran Khan, with 12 wickets, but Pakistan could not have won without Asif's brilliant century in the first innings. Australia had made only 211. Pakistan began confidently but kept losing wickets and the game was in the balance when Asif came in at 114 for 4. He added 94 with debutant Haroon Rashid and 116 with Javed Miandad to give Pakistan a substantial lead.

The Australian tour was followed by an equally intriguing series in the Caribbean, won 2-1 by the hosts. Pakistan were confronted by a fearsome pace attack of Andy Roberts and, in their debut series, Colin Croft and Joel Garner. Asif was not the only batsman to struggle. Pace had occasionally troubled him before: 'Butch' White of Hampshire gave him a rough time at Southampton back in 1968. Now he suffered more than most: 36 and 0 at Bridgetown; 0 and 12 at Port-of-Spain; 15 and 35 at Georgetown and 11 and 10 in the second game at Port-of-Spain. In the decisive Fifth Test at Kingston, he scored 5 in the first innings but finally came good in the second, Pakistan needed 442 to win when they began their second innings on the fourth morning but by lunch they had lost 3 wickets and when Asif came in the score was 51 for 4. He was dropped on 9 but the reprieve seemed to jolt him into form and he launched a dramatic assault. Croft and Garner both went for 4 an over.

When he was stumped off the leg-spinner David Holford on the fifth morning Asif had scored 135 with a six and 20 fours. Pakistan were all out for 301.

Asif was one of five Pakistanis signed by Kerry Packer's World Series Cricket, so his Test career was interrupted for a while; indeed, he initially announced his retirement from Test cricket. But, with the other Packer players, he returned for the all-important series against India in 1978/79. He made an attractive if slightly point-less century in the First Test at Faisalabad – the thirteenth successive draw between the two countries. But the other two Tests were different. Asif showed the value of his one-day experience in the two victories, each by 8 wickets, at Lahore and Karachi. At Lahore, Pakistan needed 126 in just over 100 minutes; Asif was 21 not out at the end. At Karachi it was much tighter: 164 in 100 minutes. Mushtaq shrewdly promoted Asif to open. Faced with defensive field placings Asif put on 97 in 9 overs with Javed Miandad for the second wicket before he was out for 44: Pakistan won with 7 balls to spare. That was an historic and celebrated triumph for Pakistan. Things were very different in the return series in 1979/80, when Pakistan made their first visit to India since 1960/61. Asif was the captain. He had been Mushtaq's vice cap-tain for some years and had led the side in the World Cup campaigns of 1975 and 1979. Back in 1966/67 he had led Pakistan in a series against an England Under-25 team captained by Mike Brearley and there had been a feeling then that he might have been Hanif's natural successor. But he had had to wait. Adding to the piquancy of his appointment for what was bound to be a hugely significant series was the fact that, on that previous tour, he had actually played against the Pakistanis for South Zone at his birthplace, Hyderabad, taking 4 for 52.

It was not a happy return. Pakistan lost the series 2-0. There were all sorts of reasons. One of their best bowlers, Sarfraz Nawaz, was left at home. Imran Khan was injured for some of the time. Too many of their batsmen, Asif included, under-performed. Discipline was said to be lacking. It has since been alleged that it was an open secret that Asif was in touch with gambling syndicates. Imran told the Qayyum inquiry into match-fixing that the first time he heard about match-fixing was on that tour. Asif was later to run cricket in Sharjah; a venue that, rightly or wrongly, came to be regarded with a degree of scepticism. Be all of that as it may, Asif announced his resignation as captain before the final Test at Calcutta. Imran said that Asif, always a lean and slight figure, lost a lot of weight in India because of the pressure.

It was a sad end to what had been a genuinely glittering international career. Still, that final Test in Calcutta had its consolations. It was his 59th Test; no Pakistani had played so many. And when he was out – run out – for 15 in the final innings – the last nail in the coffin of an always-improbable run-chase – he received a standing ovation from the crowd of 50,000 at Eden Gardens – every one of them Indian. Now that's not a bad send-off.

Syed ASIF IQBAL Razni
Right-hand bat, right-arm medium-pace
Born: 6 June 1943, Hyderabad, India
Major Teams: Pakistan, Hyderabad, Karachi, National Bank of Pakistan, Pakistan
International Airlines, Kent

TESTS
(1964/65–1979/80)

	M	I	NO	Runs	HS	Ave	100	50	Ct
Batting & Fielding	58	99	7	3,575	175	38.85	11	12	36

	Balls	R	W	Ave	BBI	5	10	SR	Econ
Bowling	3,864	1,502	53	28.33	5/48	2	0	72.90	2.3

ONE-DAY INTERNATIONALS

	M	I	NO	Runs	HS	Ave	SR	100	50
Batting & Fielding	10	8	2	330	62	55.00	70.81	0	5

	Balls	R	W	Ave	BBI	5	SR	Econ
Bowling	592	378	16	23.62	4/56	0	37.00	3.83

FIRST-CLASS
(Career: 1959/60–1982)

	M	I	NO	Runs	HS	Ave	100	50	Ct
Batting & Fielding	440	701	75	23,329	196	37.26	45	–	303

	Balls	R	W	Ave	BBI	5	10
Bowling	8,776	291	30.15	6/45	5	0	–

LIST A

	M	I	NO	Runs	HS	Ave	100	50	Ct
Batting & Fielding	259	244	30	5,989	106	27.98	3	33	101

	Balls	R	W	Ave	BBI	5	SR	Econ
Bowling	5,017	3,272	126	25.96	5/42	1	39.81	3.91

DANISH KANERIA

Danish Kaneria is that rarity, a Hindu playing cricket for Pakistan. He is the second: his cousin, Anil Dalpat, who kept wicket in 9 Tests in the 1980s was the first. He is also the latest in the line of an impressive succession of leg-spinners that started with the great Abdul Qadir.

In the general look of his action Kaneria is a true descendant of Qadir and Mushtaq Ahmed, but in one respect he is very different, Kaneria is over six feet tall and this makes him in some ways a very different sort of bowler. Qadir had been his boyhood idol and when he was in his early teens, Kaneria, like Qadir, was short, and – unlike Qadir – plump. Because he was so short he found bowling hard work, and developed a very high arm action. Then, all of a sudden, he shot up. He went to St Patrick's in Karachi, Javed Miandad's old school, and started bowling beautifully flighted leg-spin. As he grew taller and – slowly – fitter he found that his height was a real advantage. He was no longer having to toss the ball up. He had natural flight and the height from which he was bowling enabled him to bowl faster and generate exceptional bounce. This ability to gain bounce has turned out to be one of his strengths as a bowler. But there are others. He is extremely accurate for a bowler of his type, and rarely gets collared. At the same time, he has an aggressive, passionate temperament and is desperate to succeed. He will bowl for hours. And, finally, he has an extremely well-disguised googly.

He had played in a couple of first-class matches before playing in a game for Pakistan National Shipping Corporation against Habib Bank in 1998/99. Former Pakistan captain Saleem Malik was playing for Habib Bank and he noticed Kaneria. The bank signed him up and before long he was making his Pakistan Under-19 debut, against South Africa. He was one of the stars of the Under-19 World Cup in 2000, taking 5 for 17 against Australia, led by Michael Clarke.

When Nasser Hussain's England team toured Pakistan in 2000/01, there was talk of a new spinning sensation. That turned out to be rather exaggerated. On debut at Faisalabad, he took 2 wickets – good ones too, Marcus Trescothick and Alec Stewart – in England's first innings, for 89 runs in 34 overs. In the final Test at Karachi, he bowled 47 overs taking 2 for 80 in England's first innings, during which Michael

Atherton made a century in over nine and a half hours. Atherton's tactics were much criticised at the time but they were vindicated in the best possible way. England won by 6 wickets, Graham Thorpe and Hussain taking them to victory in sepulchral darkness as Pakistan's captain. Moin Khan, desperately tried to slow things down. He did not trust Kaneria with more than three overs.

He found Test cricket rather more to his liking against Bangladesh in 2001/02. In the first game of the Asian Test Championship at Multan – that city's first Test – he took 6 for 42 and 6 for 52. Four Pakistanis, including local hero Inzamam-ul-Haq, made centuries as Pakistan made 546 for 3 and won by an innings and 264 runs. When Pakistan

Danish Kaneria practicing in the nets, Colombo, 2006.

toured Bangladesh in January 2002, Kaneria helped himself to 7 for 77 in the First Test at Dhaka. In May that year Pakistan had another massive win, against New Zealand at Lahore, following a triple century by Inzamam. New Zealand had to follow on 570 behind and, after getting to 186 for 3, were bowled out for 246. Kaneria took 5 for 110.

Commendable though all this was, in a way, none of it proved very much: Kaneria needed to produce something in less favourable circumstances and/or against stronger opposition. At last, in October 2003, he did it. South Africa were making a short, rather hastily scheduled tour of Pakistan, whom they had recently thrashed at home. Mushtaq Ahmed had been recalled after his brilliant season for Sussex in the English County Championship and both spinners played. In the First Test at Lahore, South Africa won the toss and batted, making 320. Pakistan responded with 401. Herschelle Gibbs and Gary Kirsten were building a lead in South Africa's second innings when Kirsten tried to hook a Kaneria googly and edged a catch. That was 159 for 2 and they lost another 3 wickets for 4 runs in 13 balls. Kaneria bowled 28.3 consecutive overs and took 5 for 46. Pakistan won by 8 wickets. The Second Test at Faisalabad was drawn, and Pakistan had their first series win over South Africa.

When India made their historic tour of Pakistan in March 2004 Saqlain Mushtaq was initially preferred to Kaneria, but he fell well short of expectations in the First Test at Multan and the leg-spinner was recalled. He played his part in Pakistan's win in the Second Test at Lahore, demolishing the tail in the second innings with 3 for 14. He was one of the few Pakistanis to emerge with much credit from the disappointing tour of Australia in 2004/05, taking 15 wickets – only Glenn McGrath with 18, took more. He took 5 for 125 in 39.5 overs at Melbourne and 7 for 188 in 49.3 overs at Sydney, when Australia made 568. Shane Warne praised Kaneria's bowling in the series. Kaneria had at least learned something from the master: he was fined his match fee at Sydney for using obscene language after dismissing Clarke.

Success in Australia boosted his confidence and a number of impressive performances followed. He troubled all the Indian batsmen in the series there in March 2005, taking 5 wickets in an innings in the draw at Mohali and (in the first innings) in Pakistan's win at Bangalore. At Kingston, two months later he removed the heart of the West Indies batting – Ramnaresh Sarwan, Brian Lara and Shivnarine Chanderpaul – for 8, 0 and 0 respectively: West Indies folded for 141 (Kaneria 5 for 46) and Pakistan squared the series. Then, against England, he was a constant threat. Although England had triumphed over Australia at home in 2005, the most successful bowler in the series was Warne. Kaneria too made searching enquiries of the batsmen's techniques. He started the slump that led to the visitors' unexpected defeat in the First Test at Multan in November 2005. Andrew Strauss and Ian Bell seemed to have everything under control on the last morning but Kaneria, who finished with 4 for 62, dismissed them both and added the vital wicket of Andrew Flintoff, who was trying to hit his way out of trouble. England were all out for 172 and lost by 22 runs. Kaneria went wicket-less in the draw at Faisalabad. Then, in the Third Test at Lahore, he and Shoaib Akhtar were once again the match winners. England needed to bat through the final day, this time to avert an innings defeat. Again, before lunch, things appeared to be going smoothly, with Bell and Paul Collingwood batting sensibly and soundly. After lunch, Kaneria switched his attack to over the wicket and struck almost immediately as Collingwood edged a leg-break to Hasan Raza at slip. Soon afterwards, Raza held a much more difficult chance to dismiss Kevin Pietersen. Flintoff was bowled first ball by a perfectly flighted and pitched googly and Kaneria seemed unlucky not to have a hat-trick when umpire Darryl Hair declined to give Geraint Jones out leg before. Meanwhile, Shoaib was wreaking havoc at the other end. From 205 for 2 just after lunch, England collapsed to 248 all out, losing 8 wickets in 69 balls. Kaneria took 4 for 52. He had an outstanding season for Essex in 2004, taking more wickets (63) than anyone else in the Second Division of the County Championship. But they did not win many matches.

Danish Kaneria is an outstanding bowler but an ordinary fielder and a somewhat less than ordinary batsman. In a way that is a good thing. He is likely to be ignored for one-day internationals and can concentrate on breaking Test match records.

DANISH KANERIA
Right-hand bat, leg-break
Born: 16 December 1980, Karachi
Major Teams: Pakistan, Karachi, Habib Bank, Pakistan National Shipping Corporation, Essex

TESTS
(2000/01-2006)

	M	I	NO	Runs	HS	Ave	Ct
Batting & Fielding	36	48	24	126	15	5.25	11

	Balls	R	W	Ave	BBI	5	10	SR	Econ
Bowling	7,697	4,914	156	31.50	7/77	11	2	62.16	3.04

ONE-DAY INTERNATIONALS

	M	I	NO	Runs	HS	Ave	SR	Ct
Batting & Fielding	15	8	6	6	3★	3.00	33.33	2

	Balls	R	W	Ave	BBI	SR	Econ
Bowling	728	555	12	46.25	3/31	60.66	4.57

FIRST-CLASS
(Career: 1998/99-2006)

	M	I	NO	Runs	HS	Ave	Ct
Batting & Fielding	93	113	58	462	47	8.40	32

	Balls	R	W	Ave	BBI	5	10	SR	Econ
Bowling	24,535	11,662	445	26.20	7/39	33	5	55.13	2.9

LIST A

	M	I	NO	Runs	HS	Ave	Ct
Batting & Fielding	91	44	22	130	16	5.90	18

	Balls	R	W	Ave	BBI	5	10	SR	Econ
Bowling	4,683	3,180	138	23.04	5/21	3	0	33.93	4.07

FAZAL MAHMOOD

In her early years as a Test nation, Pakistan had few genuine stars. There was the captain, A.H. Kardar, whose personality dominated cricket in the country for many years. There was the Little Master, Hanif Mohammad, who from his teenage years often had to carry the team's batting. There was the redoubtable wicketkeeper-batsman Imtiaz Ahmed, scorer of Pakistan's first Test double century. But when it came to that most elusive achievement, winning Test matches, one name stood out above all others: the great medium-fast bowler Fazal Mahmood.

For cricket lovers in the West Fazal's legendary status is based on his performance in one match: the fourth and final Test between England and Pakistan at The Oval in August 1954. From the start of the tour Fazal had been a force to be reckoned with, taking 4 for 54 and 7 for 48 in an 8-wicket victory over Worcestershire in the opening match. After lunch on the third day, when the county, following on, had reached 156 for 1, his figures were 7 for 19 in 12 overs. He finished the tour with 77 wickets at 17.53. The First Test, at Lord's, was so badly affected by the weather that play did not start until the afternoon of the fourth day. Pakistan, put into bat, proceeded with extreme caution, scoring 50 for 3 in over two and a half hours. Next day, they were all out for 87. England scored much more quickly, but to little greater effect. When Len Hutton declared with the score on 117 for 9, Fazal and Khan Mohammad had bowled throughout the innings, the first pair of bowlers to do so in a Test match since Arthur Gilligan and Maurice Tate against South Africa at Edgbaston in 1924. Khan took 5 for 61 and Fazal 4 for 54. England achieved a huge innings victory at Trent Bridge and the Manchester Test, in which Fazal took 4 wickets, seemed to be heading in the same direction when the weather again intervened.

At The Oval rain again delayed the start, this time until mid-afternoon on the first day, Kardar won the toss and chose to bat. They slipped to 51 for 7 soon after tea. Kardar instigated a recovery of sorts and they reached 133. Further heavy rain freshened up the wicket before England's reply could get under way, and Fazal and Mahmood Hussain exploited the helpful conditions superbly. Fazal dismissed Hutton, Peter May, Denis Compton and Tom Graveney to reduce England to 92 for 6. Their final score was 130, Fazal's figures were 6 for 53. Again, he bowled throughout the innings.

With the pitch drying the English spinners took control and at one stage on the fourth morning Pakistan were 82 for 8. Wazir Mohammad and Zulfiqar Ahmed added 58 and England's target was 168. Hutton fell early to Fazal but England batted positively, May making a polished 53. Wickets fell regularly though – England seemed in a hurry to get the game over – and on the final morning, they still needed 43 to win with 4 wickets left. Pakistan took the last wicket at 12.30 p.m. and won by 24 runs. Fazal took 6 for 46, his victims including May, Compton and Godfrey Evans as well as Hutton.

There was probably only one bowler in the world at the time who could have exploited the conditions at The Oval better than Fazal and that was England's Alec Bedser, whose home ground it was. But Bedser was not playing. He and Trevor Bailey had been 'rested' for the game and there has sometimes been a tendency to see Pakistan's victory as having been achieved against a second-string attack. As one of the replacements was Frank Tyson, who helped win back the Ashes six months later when Bedser had been dropped, that seems a bit much. The comparison with Bedser, though, is a valid one, Fazal was often called 'the Pakistani Bedser'. C.L.R. James, who reported the Worcestershire game for *The Guardian*, described Fazal as a bowler of the Bedser type. But they were only similar up to a point. They were both big, strong men who bowled at just above medium pace. Both adhered with tireless precision to the old-fashioned virtues of line and length. Both had the ability to make the ball appear to hurry off the pitch. There, however, the similarity ended. Bedser was, not surprisingly, a classic English bowler, relying for the most part on seam and swing, and occasionally cutting the ball. Fazal, on the other hand, had started bowling quickish leg-breaks; then he changed his action and developed a leg-cutter more or less as a stock ball. He bowled the off-cutter too and had enough variations to be a handful on all surfaces. On the mat, though, he was a master. Most of Pakistan's home Test matches up to and including the Karachi Test against Australia in December 1959 were played on coir or jute matting stretched tightly over concrete.

The Oval was Pakistan's second Test win in their ninth match. The first had been against India on a jute matting pitch at Lucknow in 1952/53. Pakistan won by an innings. The match was a triumph for Fazal, who took 5 for 52 and 7 for 42. It was only by an accident of politics and chronology that he was not playing for India. Born in Lahore, the son of an economics professor who coached him enthusiastically, he played for North Zone before the Second World War and narrowly missed selection for the 1946 tour of England. He did get picked for the 1947/48 tour of Australia but had to drop out because Partition intervened.

On jute matting at Karachi in October 1956, he orchestrated Australia's demise by 9 wickets in the first meeting between the countries. The first day, it seems remarkable to relate now, produced 95 runs. Australia were all out for 80 and Pakistan made 15 for no wicket. Fazal and Khan bowled throughout Australia's innings, Fazal taking 6 for 34 in 27 overs. In the second innings, he took 7 for 80 in 48 overs, finishing the innings with 3 wickets in 4 balls. In a way this makes his achievements in England, in such different conditions, all the more commendable. And The Oval was no fluke. He was treated with wary respect in the Caribbean in the 1957/58 series, the main feature of which was massive scoring by both sides but particularly the West Indians. Their totals

Fazal Mahmood.

included 579 for 9, 790 for 3, and 410. Fazal bowled 320 overs and took 20 wickets at a cost of 764 runs. In the victory at Port-of-Spain he took 6 for 83. For the return series at home, he had succeeded Kardar as captain. Winning the toss and asking the visitors to bat on the mat at Karachi in the First Test, he had Conrad Hunte caught by Imtiaz in the first over. Fazal took 4 wickets in the first innings and 3 (including his hundredth Test victim, Gary Sobers) in the second; Pakistan won by 10 wickets. The Second Test was a low-scoring one at Dacca, which Pakistan won by 41 runs. It was another personal triumph for Fazal who took 6 for 34 and 6 for 66. West Indies won the final match by an innings. He had a 5-wicket haul against Australia at Karachi in 1959/60, in the last Test match played on matting.

He led Pakistan to India in 1960/61, in a series that was often very dull even by the standards of India-Pakistan contests at that time. Winning was never an ambition of either side. Not losing was all that mattered. Fazal took 5 for 26 in a rain-affected match at Calcutta – in 26 overs. At the gala dinner to celebrate – if that is the word – the end of the series, Fazal made a speech criticising the umpiring. In the First Test, Fazal had dismissed the Indian captain Nari Contractor and the umpire called 'no ball' when the batsman was halfway back to the pavilion; the official attributed the delayed call to some obstructive chewing gum. The two countries next played one another in 1978.

Fazal was sidelined after that series. Imtiaz Ahmed took over the captaincy for the home series against England in 1961/62 and Fazal only appeared in one Test. He was called up as a replacement during the dismal tour of England in 1962. There was never going to be a repeat of 1954.

Fazal Mahmood worked for many years as a police inspector in his native city of Lahore; as Scyld Berry said, he was never a man to be taken lightly. He was still working, as a director of a textile company, when he died in May 2005.

FAZAL MAHMOOD
Right hand bat, right arm fast medium-pace
Born: 18 February 1927, Lahore, India
Died: 30 May 2005
Major Teams: Pakistan, Lahore, Northern India, Punjab

TESTS
(1952/53–1962)

	M	I	NO	Runs	HS	Ave	50	Ct
Batting & Fielding	34	50	6	620	60	14.09	1	11

	Balls	R	W	Ave	BBI	5	10	SR	Econ
Bowling	9,834	3,434	139	24.70	7/42	13	4	70.70	2.09

FIRST-CLASS
(Career: 1943/44–1958/59)

	M	I	NO	Runs	HS	Ave	100	50	Ct
Batting & Fielding	112	147	33	2,662	100*	23.35	1	13	39

	Balls	R	W	Ave	BBI	5	10	SR	Econ
Bowling	25,932	8,837	466	18.96	9/43	38	8	55.60	2.04

HANIF MOHAMMAD

The most famous member of cricket's first family, Hanif Mohammad attained legendary status in his native land when he failed to overtake Len Hutton's record Test score of 364, at Bridgetown in January 1958. He is the third of five cricketing brothers born in Junagadh in the Kathiawar Peninsula, not far from the birthplace of Ranji; the family fled to Karachi in the tumult of Partition. Encouraged by a sports-loving mother, they became prolific run-scorers as schoolboys. All save the second brother, Raees, played for Pakistan. Hanif's son Shoaib duly became a highly proficient Test match batsman. But Hanif has left the most enduring mark on the game.

He was famously dubbed 'The Little Master'. As Ian Wooldridge said in his profile of Hanif as one of *Wisden's* Five Cricketers of the Year in 1968, both parts of the soubriquet fitted him well. He was – is – decidedly small, five foot three. That makes him noticeably shorter – all these things are relative – than Sunil Gavaskar – Hanif's real heir as Asia's most naturally gifted batsman – and Sachin Tendulkar, both of whom have been little masters in their turn. He is about the same height as Gundappa Viswanath and, among more modern players, Aravinda de Silva. When you saw de Silva do anything with a bat other than hit a ball – carry it out to the middle, for instance, or lean on it at the non-striker's end – it always seemed impossibly big. You do not get that feeling with Tendulkar, although he uses a very heavy bat. When that most perceptive, sympathetic and eloquent of cricket writers Ray Robinson first watched and recognised the quality of Hanif back in 1954, he observed that you could hardly see the little figure behind the great big pads.

The mastery was not dominance in the modern way of great batsmen such as Tendulkar or Vivian Richards. It was technical soundness, especially in back-foot defensive play, combined with quite phenomenal powers of concentration and endurance from a remarkably early age. His genuinely heroic feats – of which there were quite a few – also have to be seen in the context of Pakistan's status as a Test-playing nation. Hanif was there right from the start: he played in Pakistan's first Test, against India at Delhi in October 1952 (his elder brother Wazir joined him in the third). He was there when they achieved their first victories, against India in the Second

Test of that series at Lucknow, against England at The Oval in August 1954, against New Zealand at Karachi and Lahore in October 1955, against Australia at Karachi in October 1956 and against the West Indies – a consolation victory in a lost series – at Port-of-Spain in February 1958 (Wazir got a big hundred). It was often a struggle. They started amazingly well with those wins at Lucknow and The Oval. If one thinks of New Zealand and more recently Zimbabwe and particularly Bangladesh, Pakistan's early performances seem remarkable. And they quickly developed a reputation for being very difficult to beat at home. Hanif, if not exactly on his own then clearly the outstanding batsman in the side, was a crucial component of that reputation.

Like Tendulkar, Hanif had to learn from a very early age how to cope with fame and adulation. Like Tendulkar again, but perhaps rather surprisingly, much of that adulation came from India. Cricket did not really have mass appeal in Pakistan in the years immediately following independence. That was only achieved after Hanif's heroics in the Caribbean. But Pakistan's first Test tour, to India in 1952/53, provoked tremendous interest in the home country. Much of that interest was focused on the boyish-looking little wicketkeeper-batsman, already famous for his run-scoring. Playing for the tourists against North Zone at Amritsar, Hanif became the youngest player to score two centuries in a match (he was still – as far as we know – only seventeen). Both the President of India, Rajendra Prasad, – once a bitter opponent of the very idea of Pakistan – and Prime Ministrer Nehru met the tourists in Delhi and singled out Hanif for praise and wonder. His teammates nicknamed him 'Dilip' after a famous Indian movie star.

England's cricketers had come across Hanif earlier, before Pakistan achieved Test status. Indeed Pakistan's performances against the MCC tourists on their tour of the

Hanif Mohammad.

subcontinent in 1951/52 undoubtedly played a part in Pakistan's promotion. Pakistan won the two-match unofficial 'Test' series 1-0. Hanif, sixteen years old, opened the batting and kept wicket in both matches, batting with tremendous composure and a remarkably well-organised technique; Tom Graveney, who played brilliantly throughout the tour, was hugely impressed by his maturity.

An MCC 'A' side toured Pakistan in 1955/56 and again they saw a great deal of Hanif's batting. Those pads that Ray Robinson had noticed were certainly playing a part in his defensive technique. Hanif was quite unembarrassed about this aspect of his game. When he was a schoolboy, making his way in what then passed for domestic cricket (the game against the MCC at Lahore was his first-class debut), his coach, the Afghan-born former Indian wicketkeeper Abdul Aziz (father of the gifted Indian all-rounder Salim Durrani), used to plead with the umpires not to give him out leg before. The message seemed to get through. Umpiring was certainly a feature of the 1951/52 tour. It was still more of a feature of the 1955/56 tour. Even that most generous and objective of observers, Geoffrey Howard, who was manager of both touring sides, thought that the umpires overdid it when it came to Hanif, certainly on the 'A' tour. In 1987/88, at the height of the Faisalabad umpiring controversy, Graveney remarked that 'they've been cheating us for thirty-five years.'

For the record, Hanif played more Tests away from home (31, including 12 in England), than in Pakistan (24). His record in Pakistan was very good – 1,613 runs at 46.08 – but not so much better than his record away from home where he averaged over 42. He was out leg before ten times in Test cricket; once in that first series in India; three times in England in 1954; once in England in 1962; and five times in Pakistan – once against New Zealand in 1955/56 (he was out hit wicket in the first innings of the same game); twice, astonishingly in the Dacca Test against England in 1968/69 when he was batting at number seven, rather sadly; and in his last Test innings, against New Zealand, at Karachi in 1969/70. This proves nothing very much, although it could be said to lend support to Imran Khan's long-held belief that English umpires – along with all others – had an in-built home bias.

Hanif scored seven of his twelve Test centuries at home, many of them long, defensive innings in which elaborate ramparts were being put up to defend the citadel, often against India; the two countries soon became locked in a seemingly interminable series of enervating draws. The tone was set at Bahawalpur – the only Test played there – in January 1955. A result never looked likely. Pakistan in their only innings scored 312 in 164 overs, Hanif opening and making 142, his first Test century. Against the West Indies at Karachi in February 1959, he enjoyed the luxury of scoring a century in a match that Pakistan actually won – but his 103 took over six hours. He fought valiantly in a losing cause at home against Australia in 1959/60, but helped secure a draw in the Third Test at Karachi with a century. The MCC sent a young side to the subcontinent in 1961/62 with a second-string attack apart from the spinners David Allen and Tony Lock. They beat their ultra-defensive hosts 1-0 despite unresponsive pitches. In the drawn Second Test at Lahore, Hanif made two centuries, 111 and 104. It was not exciting stuff. He batted throughout the first day for 64; altogether his innings took eight hours twenty minutes. His second century took over six and a half hours. For a brief while Pakistan appeared to be in trouble against the spinners but there was never any serious possibility of a result. His final century at home was a double, 203 not out against New Zealand in 1964/65, a series Pakistan won 2-0. Hanif had been appointed captain in October 1964. His first assignment was the two one-off Tests against Australia, home and away, and a three-match series in New Zealand. Pakistan had not played any Test cricket since the very disappointing tour of England in 1962. Hanif had had a particularly unrewarding Test series there. It was not entirely clear whether a knee injury that he had picked up against the West Indies at home in 1958/59, which had flared up again in England – and which affects him to this day – would be a problem. So his appointment as captain, in place of Imtiaz Ahmed, was perceived to be a gamble. In fact, the knee was not a handicap. The games against Australia and the three Tests in New Zealand were all drawn. In New Zealand, Hanif developed a strange susceptibility to the left-arm fast-medium bowling of Dick Collinge, who dismissed him five times – three bowled – in five completed innings. In his last innings in the series he made 100 not out.

Hanif's double century came in the drawn Second Test at Lahore. New Zealand put Pakistan in on a rain-affected wicket and soon had them in trouble at 62 for 4, when Hanif came in, and then 121 for 5. He was then joined by Majid Jahangir and they put on 217 for the sixth wicket – a Pakistan record broken by Mohammad Yousuf and Kamran Akmal when they added 259 against England at Lahore in 2005. Hanif batted for eight hours and hit 33 fours.

But for all his worthy rearguard actions at home, it is for an innings away from home that Hanif will always be remembered: one of Test cricket's great defensive innings, his 337 against the West Indies in the First Test at Bridgetown in January 1958. Almost all of the really big Test innings have been played in matches where wicket-taking was generally very difficult: match situation and pitch conditions combine to provide a perfect

You never know when it might come in handy: Hanif Mohammad hits out during a net session at Lord's in 1962.

opportunity on somebody's lucky day. For Hanif, the big occasion was slightly different. This was Pakistan's first visit to the West Indies and it was the first Test of the series. West Indies, mauled in England the previous summer, won the toss and batted, making 579 for 9. Pakistan collapsed in the face of the speed and hostility of Roy Gilchrist and were all out for 106. They had never faced a bowler of Gilchrist's pace before. They began their second innings 473 behind. Hanif forswore the hook: this was serious. At the end of the third day, he was 61 not out. He added exactly a hundred more on the fourth. Returning to his hotel room after dinner, he found a positively Churchillian note from his captain, A.H. Kardar: 'You can save us. They can't get you out. You are our only hope.' He was 270 not out at close of play on the fifth day. He could not do it all on his own of course. There were valuable partnerships with Wazir and with Imtiaz Ahmed and the debutant Saeed Ahmed. But on the final day all attention was on Hanif. Could he break Hutton's record score? He got past Don Bradman's 334 and Wally Hammond's 336. The public address system announced he had passed Hammond's score and almost immediately he was out, caught behind off Denis Atkinson, off a ball that jumped: the wicket was never easy. He was utterly exhausted with bloodshot eyes from the glare. But the game was saved.

Gary Sobers broke Hutton's record a month later at Kingston, when Pakistan lost two front-line bowlers on the first morning. Hanif, however, had a new record all of his own. By the time he was out he had been batting for sixteen hours and thirty-nine minutes (999 minutes). Hanif told Scyld Berry, when they met in Karachi in 1987, that *Wisden* had deprived him of twenty-nine minutes. It remained the longest innings in first-class cricket until 1999/2000. Astonishingly, he was still only just over twenty-four years old. The strain took its toll though. Gilchrist seemed to have his number for much of the rest of the series.

Within a year Hanif had his own record score to go with his supremacy in terms of time. In domestic cricket he had always batted big as well as long. But at the Karachi Parsi Institute ground in January 1959 he scored 499 for Karachi against Bahawalpur in the Quaid-e-azam Trophy. He went in on the first evening after Bahawalpur had been dismissed for 185 on a coir matting pitch and scored 25 in forty minutes. As surely everyone who is reading this already knows, he was run out off the last ball of the third day, having batted for ten hours thirty-five minutes. Karachi made 772 for 7 and bowled Bahawalpur out for 108. Hanif was anxious to impress on Berry that Bahawalpur's attack wasn't half bad.

At times a long innings by Hanif could be as much a test of endurance for the spectators as for the man himself. He twice broke the record for the slowest century in first-class cricket. In his first Test in England, at Lord's in 1954, he spent five hours forty minutes compiling scores of 20 and 39. But it would be wrong to say that he was never good to watch. His stance was tense, legs wide apart and his left shoulder pointing towards the bowler, but his neat and compact style was easy on the eye. He had perfect balance, superb timing and when circumstances allowed him to blossom he had a full range of shots, hooking particularly hard. Berry attributes to him the invention of the reverse sweep, unveiled in a one-day game in England in 1967.

Hanif's record in England seems disappointing: one century and one fifty in three series. The century was a special one though. He was leading the side on a three-Test tour in 1967 in generally awful weather against a very experienced side. The first day of the First Test at Headingley concluded with England on 282 for 2. They were all out for 369 but Pakistan finished the truncated second day on 78 for 4, which soon became 99 for 6. Hanif, batting at number four, then took root. Aided first by Intikhab Alam and then the vibrant Asif Iqbal and the adhesive teenage wicketkeeper Wasim Bari, he was finally left high and dry on 187 with the score on 334. He had been dropped by Colin Milburn on 51. He batted for nine hours and hit 21 fours.

Hanif received both praise and criticism for this innings. The criticism, naturally, concerned the negative aspects of the innings. But it is difficult to see how else Hanif could have played. Was he supposed to go all out for victory from the moment he walked out to bat? Pakistan had won one Test away from home since The Oval in 1954, the consolation win at Port-of-Spain in 1957/58. As it happened, the way the Headingley Test developed meant that Pakistan did have an outside chance of winning on the last day but the fact that the match was drawn owed more to play lost because of rain than to Hanif's frankly match-saving innings.

Hanif only played one Test in Australia, when he captained the side in a one-off Test at Melbourne in December 1964. He made 104 in Pakistan's first innings of 287, scoring a century on the first day after Pakistan were sent in on a green wicket. Robinson called the innings almost perfect. Australia replied with 448. The game ended in a draw. Hanif batted splendidly in the second innings too until he was out in a way he had never been in a Test before and never was to be again. He was stumped by Barry Jarman off Tom Veivers. Imagine: Hanif Mohammad stumped in a Test match! Jarman, ever the gentleman, apologised after appealing. Hanif's score was 93.

HANIF MOHAMMAD
Right-hand bat, off-break, wicketkeeper
Born: 21 December 1934, Junagadh, India
Major Teams: Pakistan, Bahawalpur, Karachi, Pakistan International Airlines

TESTS
(1952/53-1969/70)

	M	I	NO	Runs	HS	Ave	100	50	Ct	St
Batting & Fielding	55	97	8	3,915	337	43.98	12	15	40	0

	Balls	R	W	Ave	BBI	SR	Econ
Bowling	266	95	1	95.00	1/1	206.00	2.76

FIRST-CLASS
(Career: 1952/53-1975/76)

	M	I	NO	Runs	HS	Ave	100	50	Ct	St
Batting & Fielding	238	370	44	17,059	499	52.32	55	66	178	12

	Balls	R	W	Ave	BBI	SR	Econ
Bowling	2,748	1,510	53	28.49	3/4	51.80	3.29

IMRAN KHAN

It is a truism that sport is all about the mind, that the spirit and the will are what single out the champions. When it comes to great cricketers – that narrow band of players who legitimately merit the label – there are few in respect of whom mental strength, the spirit and the will, is demonstrated more clearly than Imran Khan.

There must first be no doubt about the premise. Imran was unquestionably a great player. His record in Test cricket tells us that 3,807 runs at 37.69 and 362 wickets at 22.81 is absolutely outstanding. The best comparison is with his three contemporaries. Ian Botham and Kapil Dev had batting averages comfortably lower (though Imran had twenty-five not outs, to Kapil's fifteen and Botham's six) and bowling averages comfortably higher than Imran's. Richard Hadlee's bowling average was marginally lower at 22.24; Hadlee's batting average was 27.16. Imran scored centuries against India (3), England, Australia and the West Indies. He took 10 wickets in a match against England, Australia, India (twice), Sri Lanka and the West Indies. When a hundred cricketing luminaries were asked to vote for Five Cricketers of the (20th) Century for *Wisden*, Hadlee and Imran came equal tenth, with 13 votes each: Botham was sixteenth and Kapil twentieth.

On figures alone Imran was a highly effective all-rounder. But it goes without saying that Imran's most remarkable achievement as a cricketer was to succeed in the way he did as captain of Pakistan. In that regard, he stands alone. There is no point in comparing him with anybody from elsewhere, contemporary or otherwise. He can only be compared with other captains of Pakistan. And the fact is, there is no comparison. It is a bit like modern French history: a succession of ineffectual leaders presiding over assorted disasters; then a giant, de Gaulle, who shapes the country as he pleases; but once he is gone, chaos rules again. This is how it was with Imran as Pakistan's leader. And the men who came before and after him were not the type of nincompoop or non-entity who headed whichever republic happened to be in place in France on any given day before or after de Gaulle. They were often accomplished and capable men. But none of them received the respect and loyalty of teammates accorded to Imran. As a leader he did not simply inspire his 'boys' to play for each other and for Pakistan;

just as importantly, he raised his own game, and his greatness as a player coincided to a large degree with his period as captain. That goes some way to demonstrating why the mental side of Imran's cricket was so important. But there is more to it than that.

Imran made himself into a great cricketer. The raw materials were there, of course, but he was not a natural. His disciples, Wasim Akram and Waqar Younis, stepped up to the international arena not perhaps as the finished product but as aggressive fast bowlers who could immediately pose problems for experienced batsmen. By the time they emerged, Imran had forgotten more about fast bowling than they knew and his standing, reputation and his need to harness their skills to the national cause meant that they were able to hone their talents and follow in his wake. But it had been very different for him as a youngster. Botham and Kapil had burst upon the international scene as accomplished cricketers almost from the start, racing each other to be the youngest all-rounder to do this or that. Again, it is perhaps Hadlee who provides the most intriguing comparison; reared in a family devoted to cricket, a tearaway fast bowler who had to think his way to cricketing effectiveness, who grew to know exactly what he wanted, and who, in the end, usually got it. Yes – not a bad comparison.

The fact is that, although Imran came from a relatively affluent, privileged and fortunate background in a country where privilege really does mean something, things did not come as easily to him as one might expect. He did not reach his peak as a fast bowler until he was twenty-eight or twenty-nine, when most fast bowlers are thinking of easing up. The captaincy of Pakistan was not handed to him on a plate as a young pup. He became captain as a result of a typical administrative imbroglio. At his belated peak as a fast bowler he suffered an almost-literally crippling injury that cut a couple of years from his bowling life. Imran gritted his teeth and got through it all.

Although affluent upper-middle class rather than the equivalent of royalty, Imran was born in the purple in cricketing terms. His mother, of the Burki clan originally from Afghanistan, had two sisters and each of them had given birth to a child who became an Oxbridge blue who went on to captain Pakistan: Javed Burki and Majid Khan. They were Imran's childhood heroes. Nor did his advantages end there. He went to Aitchison College – the Eton of Lahore – and he had another relative who was chairman of the Lahore selectors. In his boyhood games in Zaman Park in Lahore, Imran thought he was the bee's knees. But he rapidly realised that perhaps he was not. When he discovered a wider world, the Lahore Gymkhana Club and beyond, he also discovered cricketers with far more talent than himself; Wasim Raja, the future middle-order batsman and a contemporary from Lahore, was one who Imran himself admitted was more gifted naturally.

The difference between them was that Imran had the hunger that separates one type of talented player from another. Nothing came easily to him, although by the end of his career it often looked as though everything did, especially when he was batting. Often, but even then not always. In the last innings he played as an international cricketer in the World Cup final against England at Melbourne in 1992, he played in a manner that, if followed today, would have the player concerned installed in a home for the bewildered or alternatively investigated for match-fixing. Imran won the toss and put himself in at number three, as he had done since the penultimate match of the group

Imran Khan with the World Cup after Pakistan's victory over England in the final at Melbourne, 1992.

stage. He came in with the score at 20 for 1. It was soon 24 for 2. Imran and Javed Miandad, his chief lieutenant, then proceeded to settle down. It was extraordinary. At one stage, 3 runs came off the bat in 11 overs. Imran gave a half-chance to England's captain Graham Gooch in the twenty-first over but Gooch could not hold on. At the end of the twenty-fifth over, halfway through their innings, Pakistan were 70 for 2. Then Imran hit Richard Illingworth for six, and gradually the scoring accelerated. Miandad fell for 58: he and Imran had put on 139 in 31 overs. Seventy-nine runs came in the last 10 overs. Imran's 72 occupied 100 balls stretched over 39 overs, with 5 fours and a six. As David Frith said, it was nerveless and probably match-winning. But it was not easy. Imran set out to lay a foundation and that is exactly what he did.

In those early games in Zaman Park, it was his batting that caught the eye but Imran always wanted to be a fast bowler. He made enough of an impression to be selected to tour England with Intikhab Alam's side in 1971. There was no fairytale beginning although, because of a spate of injuries, he did find himself opening the bowling with Salim Altaf in the First Test at Edgbaston. His figures were really rather good in the first innings: 23 overs for 36 runs (England followed on in the wake of Pakistan's massive 608 for 7 and the game was drawn). Imran did not take a wicket and was the first to admit that he was out of his depth.

He stayed on in England after the tour, signing for Worcestershire and continuing his education at the Royal Grammar School, Worcester and later at Keble College, Oxford. It seemed as if he were a batsman who could bowl, rather than an all-rounder; in 1974, however, when he captained Oxford and played in three Tests against England, his first-class figures for the season were 1,016 runs at 36.28 and 60 wickets at 30.13; although only 5 of those wickets, at 51.60, came in the Tests. Glenn Turner, the New Zealand opener who was Imran's county colleague at Worcestershire, told him that he did not have it in him to be a fast bowler. But Imran worked at it. He was constrained by the fact that the 'old pros' at the county, such as Norman Gilford, wanted him to stick to line and length like an English seamer. By 1976, Imran had had enough of this and decided to let off a bit of steam. By now he had filled out and was stronger and faster. Gilford saw the merit of letting him have a go and started giving Imran the new ball. Against Lancashire at Worcester he opened the bowling and dismissed the first four batsmen, to reduce the visitors to 45 for 4, extracting considerable movement from a dry surface. He returned to take 3 of the last 4 wickets, his final figures being 7 for 53. Lancashire were all out for 140. Any doubts they had about the pitch were put in perspective when Worcestershire reached 187 for 2. At that point Imran came in and made a glorious 111 not out in three hours and twenty minutes with 2 sixes and 15 fours. Worcestershire were all out for 383 and then Lancashire capitulated again for 211. Imran took 6 for 46, taking the last 3 wickets in 18 balls. In Championship matches that year, he scored over a thousand runs and took 61 wickets.

Imran's cricketing development took a significant step in 1976/77 when Pakistan went on successive tours of Australia and the West Indies, then the two most formidable outfits in world cricket. Australia, however, were in a transitional period. The magnificent side led by Ian Chappell was beginning to break up and matters were not helped when Jeff Thomson was sidelined by a serious shoulder injury sustained while fielding during the First Test. But, as one great fast bowler departed the scene, albeit temporarily, so another arrived: Imran. Australia went into the final (third) Test at Sydney with a 1-0 lead. Australia batted after Greg Chappell had won the toss but the conditions, warm and humid, turned out to be ideal for Imran and his new-ball partner Sarfraz Nawaz. Before long, Australia were 38 for 4 and ultimately stuttered to 211: Imran took 6 for 102. Pakistan gained a first innings lead of 149 and bowled Australia out for 180. Imran took 6 for 63 and Pakistan levelled the series. Imran's pace – certainly equal to that of Dennis Lillee – and his aggressive intent, with plenty of bouncers, were too much for the Australian batsmen. The great left-arm swing bowler Alan Davidson, presenting Imran with a match award, said it was one of the outstanding achievements he had seen at Sydney. It was Pakistan's first victory in Australia.

There followed an equally interesting and close-fought series in the Caribbean, which the hosts won 2-1. Imran and Sarfraz were outstanding for Pakistan and came close to securing victory for their side in the First Test at Bridgetown, which the West Indies saved with their last pair at the wicket. Imran worked immensely hard: he bowled 60 overs in the match for 5 wickets; overall he took 25 wickets at 31.60. But he knew he was not the complete fast bowler yet. Gary Sobers, one of Imran's cricketing idols, after watching Imran in the nets at Bridgetown, said that if it was true that Imran bowled as fast as Lillee in the series in Australia. Lillee must have been operating at half pace.

While the Pakistanis were in the Caribbean Tony Greig, the England captain, arrived on a recruiting mission for Kerry Packer's still nascent World Series Cricket.

It was a signal to Imran that he had 'arrived' that he was one of several Pakistanis invited to sign for Packer. In general, the battle lines were clearly drawn on the Packer issue. In England, Australia and the West Indies, for example, the players who signed were, sooner or later, banned from Test cricket until 'peace' was declared in 1979. In Pakistan, inevitably, things were more complicated. Initially, the Pakistani players were also banned. Then they were not banned, then they were banned again because England objected to facing Packer players on their tour to Pakistan in 1977/78. But it was likely that there would be civil unrest if Pakistan went into a series against India, scheduled for 1978/79, and the first meeting between the sides since 1960/61, without the Packer players, so they returned once and for all.

Like many of the participants in World Series Cricket, Imran found the games exceedingly challenging. From a personal point of view he felt it was largely ben- eficial, particularly because of technical assistance he was able to pick up from experienced bowlers. Packer cricket was especially challenging for the batsmen because of the formidable battery of pace bowling present in each of the teams. That was why Imran never wavered in his view that, of all the batsmen he played with or against in his career, the greatest was Vivian Richards.

The year 1977 saw another change for Imran. He left Worcestershire, to their consid- erable irritation, and joined Sussex. He did not really enjoy Worcester as a place, and no doubt it was deficient in terms of social 'throb' and the presence of suitably appealing glitterati as Imran's personal horizons expanded. Brighton clearly had more appeal, as of course did Hove, where Maurice Tate and John Snow had held sway. When Garth Le Roux, another Packer player, joined the county in 1980 they really were a considerable force. The following year, 1981, the county came closer to winning the Championship than ever before in their history. Imran scored 857 runs at 40.80 and took 61 wickets at 22.18. His single most telling contribution came during the Eastbourne festival week, in August (25,000 spectators attended during the week). Imran bowled splendidly during Derbyshire's second innings to take 5 for 52 (one bowled, four leg before) including a spell of 4 wickets in 5 balls. 'That was clever bowling,' he said to John Barclay, the Sussex captain as they left the field. 'Now I want to bat!' Sussex needed 233 to win. Imran was number seven on the card. 'I want to bat high in the order, I feel it is my day, we must beat this lot. I think I shall bat at four,' he told Barclay. 'The others won't mind.' 'Why do you always let him have his way?' Barclay was asked. 'Because he says he's going to win the match for us,' he replied. Imran went in at 74 for 2 and made 107 not out, with 3 sixes and 11 fours, reaching his century in eighty-eight minutes. Sussex won by 5 wickets with 5 balls to spare. Overall in first-class cricket for Sussex between 1977 and 1988 Imran averaged 43 with the bat and 19 with the ball.

Imran's main complaint about World Series Cricket was that it lacked the passion and intensity of Test cricket. There was certainly no shortage of those ingredients when India toured Pakistan in 1978/79. Pakistan won the three Test rubber 2-0. Imran and Sarfraz were again dominant figures, establishing a supremacy over the Indian batsmen on the first day of the Second Test at Lahore that they never yielded. Imran took 5 wick- ets in that innings and, as so often, was not shy of using the bouncer, hitting Mohinder

Amarnath on the head and forcing him to retire hurt. In the Third Test, at Karachi, Sarfraz and Imran bowled flat out on an unresponsive wicket to bring Pakistan victory. Imran bowled 60 overs in the match. He also saw Pakistan home in a thrilling run chase, taking them to victory with 2 sixes and a four in the match's penultimate over.

It was all a bit different the following year when Pakistan toured India. India won a six-Test series 2–0. The difference for India was the progress of their opening bowler, Kapil Dev, who took 32 wickets in the series. Pakistan by contrast suffered two set-backs. Sarfraz, the leading wicket-taker in the previous series, was not selected; and Imran was troubled throughout by a muscle strain near his rib cage. He still took 19 wickets at 19.21. The First Test, at Bangalore, was a slow-scoring draw. Imran, despite the unhelpful conditions, was Pakistan's most effective bowler with 4 for 53 in 28.4 overs in India's only innings. In the Second Test at New Delhi he bowled with venomous pace at the start of India's first innings but broke down after 7 overs. Sikander Bakht took 8 wickets and India were dismissed for 126 in reply to Pakistan's 273. India scrambled to a draw but must surely have lost had Imran been fit. He was a passenger in the Third Test and missed the fourth, which India won, on as grassy and green a pitch as can ever have been seen at Kanpur. Imran was back for the Fifth Test at Madras. India won that by 10 wickets, thanks to a big hundred from Sunil Gavaskar, and a fine all-round performance by Kapil Dev. Imran took 5 for 114 in 38.2 overs. The 'dead' Sixth Test, at Calcutta, although drawn, was dominated by Pakistan. On another slow wicket, albeit with uneven bounce, Imran took 9 wickets in the match, including three in a ferocious opening spell in India's second innings. The result of the series was a bitter disappointment to Pakistan's players and their fans. The series was played in an increasingly acrimonious atmosphere, in contrast to the previous year's series in Pakistan. The ever-sagacious Dicky Rutnagur said that Pakistan's players were increasingly distracted by 'commercial and social interests'. 'All of us dreaded returning home,' said Imran.

The West Indies toured Pakistan in the following season, 1980/81. The visitors were well on their way to supremacy in world cricket. They had enjoyed a successful tour of England in 1980, dominated by their cohort of fast bowlers. In Pakistan, they had Joel Garner, Colin Croft, Sylvester Clarke and Malcolm Marshall. Despite the slow, unhelpful pitches, the unremitting pressure brought what seemed to be the inevitable reward. Pakistan fought hard but lost the four-Test series 1–0. The pace quartet shared 54 wickets between them. Imran, playing a predominantly lone hand in an attack dominated by spin, took 17 wickets at 17.84, including 5 for 62 in the final Test at Multan.

In the First Test, at Lahore, he scored his first century. Pakistan had taken a while to remember that Imran was rather a good batsman. Prior to the Lahore Test, he had made two half-centuries in 29 Tests. He usually batted in the middle order in county cricket. He gradually crept up from the tail in Tests and had reached number seven at Lahore. When he went in, Pakistan had slid from 65 for 1 to 95 for 5. His 123 enabled them to reach 376. He completed the Test double of 1,000 runs and 100 wickets in the process. He was twenty-eight in the course of the match. No, nothing came easy. By the time they were twenty-eight Botham and Kapil were well on the way to the 'double double'. But there was one difference between their Test baptisms and Imran's. Much of their early Test cricket coincided with the Packer years. They thus faced sides from Australia, England (in Kapil's case) and Pakistan (in Botham's case) shorn of their Packer players. It was somehow typical that Imran, having honed his skills in World Series Cricket, should have scored his first Test century against the game's most demanding attack.

In 1981/82, Pakistan played series in Australia and at home to Sri Lanka. Imran was Man of the Series in Australia. He took 16 wickets at 19.50, conceding 312 runs in 150.2 overs. He made 70 not out and took 5 wickets in Pakistan's innings victory in the third and final Test at Melbourne; Australia had won the first two Tests, despite some spirited spells of high-class pace bowling in both games from Imran. He missed the first two Tests against Sri Lanka, the first of which was won and the second of which was drawn. Returning for the Third Test at Lahore, he showed what might have been by taking 8 for 58, in what he himself described as one of his better spells in Test cricket, and 6 for 58. Pakistan won by an innings.

The reason Imran (and several other senior players) did not play in the first two games of the series had been because of a bitter row between them and the cricket board in Pakistan regarding Javed Miandad's captaincy. Miandad had been in charge since Asif Iqbal's resignation after the defeat by India in 1979/80. His had been a controversial appointment then and his relative youth and excitable temperament did not make things any easier. The tour of Australia had been an unhappy and contentious episode but the last straw was a statement issued by the board to the effect that senior players had been disloyal to Miandad. This led to a stand-off that resulted in Pakistan fielding what was virtually a second eleven in the first two Tests. When Pakistan only narrowly avoided defeat in the Second Test at Faisalabad (where Arjuna Ranatunga made his Test debut) sanity prevailed. The disgruntled players returned and Miandad was prevailed upon to resign at the end of the series. So a new captain was required. A number of senior players, notably Zaheer Abbas, thought it was their turn. But the job went to Imran.

Aged twenty-nine when he joined his team for the tour of England in 1982, having spent the first part of the summer with Sussex, Imran Khan was – apparently – at the height of his powers as a cricketer. As a bowler, he had reached the stage where genuine pace was allied to a range of skills of the highest quality. He had always possessed the ability to swing the ball into the right-hander: even in his rather embarrassing Test debut eleven years earlier he had at least been able to do that. But at that point, it came out at a pace a little above medium and he had no means of controlling or utilising the swing or of varying either pace or movement. Over the years, he grew and he worked and he studied and he learned. He was always happy to talk cricket and to digest help and he always acknowledged help, which sometimes came from improbable sources; John Parker, the New Zealand batsman who played for Worcestershire, suggested a change to his action that seemed to work – a little jump that later developed into a leap as he went into his delivery stride. Invaluable encouragement and advice regarding his run up and getting more side-on and closer to the stumps came from Mike Procter and John Snow, teammates at World Series Cricket: that aided the development of an out-swinger. But perhaps the greatest assistance came from his Pakistani teammate Sarfraz Nawaz. From early days, Imran found it relatively easy to obtain movement in the air and off the pitch in English conditions, at least with the new ball, but in Faisalabad and Lahore – less so in Karachi, where there was often some humidity – it was a different story. Sarfraz imparted the advantages of shining one side of the ball so that even an old ball would swing. As early as 1976/77 in Australia Ray Robinson was commenting on what an indefatigable shiner of the ball Imran was. It meant that even in the most apparently unhelpful conditions – and many a fast bowler has found conditions in Pakistan exceptionally unhelpful – Imran could conjure up remarkable movement. If one side of the ball were soaked with sweat, and consequently heavier, things got even more interesting. Together, Sarfraz and Imran pioneered the phenomenon of 'reverse' swing.

He was certainly among the most feared fast bowlers of his generation. Six feet tall and perfectly designed for the job, his strict regime that eschewed alcohol and tobacco gave him terrific stamina to go with pace, guile and technique. While the out-swinger came and went, the in-swinger was an ever-present and often vicious threat, whether directed at the toes, the stumps, the ribcage or the helmet.

Imran, in Test matches, and particularly as he got older, batted classically, in the grand manner, and rarely gave vent to flamboyant displays in the manner of Botham or Kapil Dev or Wasim Akram. But that was because being captain of Pakistan was a serious business and if runs were needed from him, it probably meant his team were in trouble. As a youngster, he taught himself to hook, realising he would be on the receiving end of many a retaliatory bouncer. It was always a high-risk shot though and, after getting himself out at a most critical moment in the Edgbaston Test in 1982, he avoided it. In county cricket, he was more of a dasher and had plenty of runs to show for it. On four

Imran Khan bowling against England in the Second Test at Lord's, 1982. Umpire Dickie Bird looks on.

occasions, he made over a thousand runs in a season. There too the demeanour was magisterial, although Barclay said he was invariably nervous and restless before batting.

The question was, as it always is in these situations, how would the captaincy affect his performance as a player? It was a question that had recently been asked regarding Botham, and answered in the remarkable Ashes series of 1981. Imran was older and more mature when the captaincy of Pakistan came to him. And, of course, it transpired that it was a crown he had been born to wear. Imran had four principal ambitions as captain: to beat England, because of the colonial past and the tone of condescension that still dominated relations between the two countries; to beat the West Indies, because they were the best; to beat India, especially in India, because they were India; and to win the World Cup. Everything else was secondary. Imran always enjoyed playing in Australia – he was to spend a season with New South Wales – and there were defeats to be avenged but, as a cricketing power, Australia were in decline. New Zealand sometimes appeared to be beyond Imran's radar screen; he had some slip-ups against Sri Lanka, again not always highly regarded.

The first challenge was England in 1982. England – without their South African rebels – won the one-day series with some ease. They also won the First Test at Edgbaston by 113 runs but the game was closer than the result suggests. Bob Willis won the toss but most of the English batsmen struggled against Imran, who took 7 for 52, and the leg-spinner Abdul Qadir. Whenever the England batsmen seemed on the verge of dominance. Imran would bring himself back on and force a breakthrough. They finished with 272. A number of Pakistan's batsmen got going but too many were out to brainless shots, Imran included; they made 251. Derek Randall's 'lucky' century (Imran) enabled England to set a target of 313. Pakistan subsided for 198. Imran, Man of the Match, made batting look relatively easy in his 65.

Pakistan won an historic victory in the Second Test at Lord's, only their second in England. The individual honours went to Mohsin Khan, who scored a double century in Pakistan's first innings, and to his fellow opening batsman Mudassar Nazar, who rather improbably took 6 for 32 in England's second innings. But Imran was no less central a figure. His bowling was important. He troubled David Gower and Allan Lamb in England's middle order. He gave the first Sunday of Test cricket at Lord's a dramatic start by having England's last man Robin Jackman leg before with the score on 227; the follow on target was 229. But his captaincy was crucial. Until this game nobody was quite sure what sort of a captain he was going to be. By the end of it, nobody had any doubt: his forceful personality was evident in every move. If Gary Sobers was Imran's hero as a player, the captain he regarded most highly was Australia's Ian Chappell. In his early days as a Pakistan cricketer, Imran had seen too much negative captaincy. He was proactive, rather than reactive; he led from the front and he had the respect of his players.

The two sides went to Headingley all square. The game was dramatic and exciting, England winning by 3 wickets. Pakistan won the toss and batted, making 275, Imran top-scoring with 67 not out, which included 2 sixes and 9 fours. England made 256, Imran took 5 for 49 in 25 overs. In a particularly testing spell after lunch on the second day he dismissed Mike Gatting, Lamb and Chris Tavare in 9 balls. There followed a poor batting performance from Pakistan against Willis and Botham. Miandad played well for 52 but the other recognised batsmen failed until Imran came in at 106 for 5. To begin with he was all studious defence but gradually moved to carefully judged aggression, assisted by an adhesive tail. Sikander Bakht hung around for over an hour for 7 before being adjudged caught at short leg by Gatting off Vic Marks: the score was 199 for nine. Imran holed out in the next over.

England needed 219 for victory with the better part of two days left. They seemed to have the game sewn up when debutant Graeme Fowler and Gatting took the score to 168 for 1 but Imran and Mudassar, swinging the old ball extravagantly, reduced them to 199 for 6 and had play carried on that day Pakistan would very likely have won. But the batsmen accepted an offer to go off for bad light and victory for England the next day proved to be a formality.

It was a series that Pakistan should probably have won. They had been unlucky with injuries, Sarfraz and Tahir Naggash missing the final Test. Certainly it was hard not to think that Imran did not deserve to be on the losing side. His discipline, his effort, his aggression as a bowler and his leadership in the field were exemplary. But at this stage, he could not quite get everyone to follow that example. Imran himself conceded that it was undisciplined batting that cost Pakistan the series; he felt they should have won at Edgbaston, let alone Headingley.

And then there was the umpiring. Imran and the manager, Intikhab, had complained about the umpiring at Edgbaston, and the issue became something of a running sore. Commentators at the time suggested that both sides had cause to grumble when it came to poor decisions. The focal point of Pakistan's unhappiness came in the Third Test – where everybody seemed to agree they got the rough end of the stick – when one of the officials was the experienced and respected David Constant. The Indians, who had toured in the earlier part of the summer, had objected to Constant's standing in the Tests because they felt unfairly treated when play had started in a one-day international at Headingley before – they maintained – the pitch had had a chance to recover from the effects of an overnight storm. India lost heavily. The incident was reminiscent of Pakistan's Test at Lord's in 1974 when they had had to face Derek Underwood on a pitch that the covers had failed to protect from overnight rain. Constant had been one of the umpires in charge then too. The bone of contention at Headingley was the dismissal of Sikander in Pakistan's second innings. Imran said the decision was 'truly bizarre'. Even the judicious Christopher Martin-Jenkins suggested England's appeal had been lodged more in hope than expectation. Not that it would have been the first optimistic appeal of the series. While everyone admired Pakistan's cricket under Imran, one common criticism was the apparently orchestrated appealing, especially when Qadir was bowling. As the umpires, according to Imran, had no more idea than the batsmen of what the ball was going to do, the batsmen usually got the benefit of the doubt.

The sense of grievance carried over to Pakistan's next tour of England, in 1987. The genial and popular Intikhab was replaced as manager by the loquacious and combustible Haseeb Ahsan. This was very good for Imran as they made a perfect 'good cop, bad cop' combination. Haseeb could do all the talking and take the flak when people complained about those Pakistanis stirring it again. Imran could look the part and carry on doing what he did best, inspiring his cricket team to victory.

Imran was thirty-four by now, and troubled by a stomach muscle injury at the start of the tour. This was Pakistan's first full, five-Test tour of England since 1962. England had returned from their Ashes victory in 1986/87 and were full of confidence under Gatting. The first two Tests were rain-affected draws. The final Test at The Oval saw a run-glut in which Miandad made 260 and Saleem Malik and Imran made hundreds. The fourth, at Edgbaston looked certain to be a draw after each side made a substantial first innings score, but Pakistan in their second innings collapsed against Neil Foster, Imran holding firm for two hours to make 37. England required 124 from 18 overs. Imran and Wasim Akram bowled through to keep them to 109 for 7.

The only game to reach a positive result was the Third Test at Headingley. Imran, fully fit at last, took charge of the game on the first day and Pakistan never let go. Gatting opted to bat on a fine day with high cloud but before long England were struggling at 31 for 5. In his first spell, Imran took 3 for 16 in 7 overs. He and Wasim bowled at a torrid pace and extracted extravagant swing. It transpired that the pitch also had uncertain bounce. So conditions certainly helped the pace bowlers but Imran and Wasim exploited them perfectly. England were all out for 136. They only managed to take 2 wickets by the close of the first day. Foster in particular bowled well but Pakistan fought hard to make 353. When England batted again, Chris Broad and Tim Robinson were out in Imran's first 2 overs. Television replays, mercilessly repeated at the ground, suggested that Broad had been unlucky to have been adjudged, by umpire David Shepherd, caught behind. Further controversy erupted when wicketkeeper Salim Yousuf claimed to have caught Botham off a ball that he appeared to have caught, dropped and caught again. Imran was swift to reprimand Yousuf. Yousuf had not been alone in appealing and it was the sort of incident that put Pakistan's complaints about the umpiring – and Imran's attempts to claim the moral high ground – in perspective. Anyway, Pakistan were rampant. England were all out for 199 on the fourth morning. Imran had taken 7 for 40, which included his 300th Test wicket.

At the end of the tour, Gatting said he thought England had won the series on points, a laughable comment really. The two series, 1982 and 1987, said a lot about Imran, his captaincy and his relationship with England. In 1982, he was at the start of his reign. But he lost little time in stamping his authority on the side. Almost his first action was to drop the senior player, his cousin, Majid Khan. That was always the way with Imran. He had seen so many captains before him have problems with selection. He always wanted his team and he usually got it. One saw this with his backing of Wasim and, later, Waqar Younis. By the final Test of 1987, many of the senior players thought that Qadir was out of form and should be dropped. Imran did not agree, and insisted on picking him. Qadir took 7 for 96 in England's first innings.

One of the things that Imran was anxious to change was the subservience traditionally shown by Pakistani cricketers to English cricket officials. He had found this irritating even on the 1971 tour when he was an inexperienced eighteen-year-old. This was part of the reason for the business regarding Constant, but it went deeper than that. Today, it is perhaps easier to appreciate his frustrations because there is at least a slightly greater appreciation in cricketing circles of the gulf in culture between England and Pakistan. Back then there was simply incomprehension, certainly on the English side. Martin-Jenkins made an unwittingly droll comment symbolising this in a report on the 1982 Edgbaston Test. England had had a good final session on the Friday: 'The cheese and wine at Bernard Thomas's garden party on Friday night slipped down English throats more easily. Pakistan had let a good chance slip.' Let's hope Bernard had ordered some chapattis.

If Imran had had a complaint about Bernard's party, other than the wine, and possibly the cheese, it would probably have been that the guest list was not grand enough, unless Emma Sergeant or – heaven forbid – Jeffrey Archer had strolled in. Of course, in 1982, Imran's social horizons had not reached the stratospheric levels they were to attain in later years. But as an Oxford-educated scion of Lahore's upper echelons, blessed by almost indecent good looks, he had a lifestyle that was considerably more exotic and exalted than that of the average county professional. With a base in south Kensington – where else? – as well as Lahore it seemed as though he had a foot in both camps. He was too shrewd to follow in the footsteps of Paul Scott's Hri Kumar in The Raj Quartet: too English for the Indians and too Indian for the English. And he was too proud. Imran liked the cosmopolitan feel of London; but the Punjab was home. He spent many enjoyable and successful years as a professional cricketer in England. He was a popular figure at Sussex and got on well with the old Etonian skipper, Barclay. His increasingly patrician air and rather haughty demeanour undoubtedly rubbed some people up the wrong way; his slightly drawling voice, instantly recognisable, became the subject of continued mimicry by the slightly tiresome Dermot Reeve. But Ivo Tennant's biography mentions only one English cricketer whom Imran actually disliked: surprisingly Hampshire's dashing leader, Mark Nicholas. Outside the tiny and inward-looking cricket community, the English admired his aquiline features and rippling torso and wondered, vaguely, where they had seen them before. Then they remembered: the Greek Antiquities Department at the British Museum. That was the men; the women just fell in love with him.

Imran featured prominently in two of the great dramas that have periodically convulsed cricketing relations between England and Pakistan. The first was umpiring. The disgruntlement over David Constant has been mentioned. Pakistan wanted both him and Ken Palmer withdrawn from the panel for the 1987 series but the Test and County Cricket Board refused and their attitude irritated Imran. He sometimes got carried away, as at The Oval in 1987, when he and Mudassar openly fulminated against Constant when he turned down an appeal against Botham. But it would be wrong to regard this as an anti-English campaign: indeed, Imran conceded that English umpires were the most professional in the world. He criticised umpires wherever he went. Pakistan would have beaten New Zealand in Auckland in 1978/79 but for some 'dubious umpiring decisions'. In Sri Lanka, in 1985/86, the Pakistanis discovered that 'biased umpiring was part of a plan'. Umpiring mistakes in the closing stages of the Third Test in the Caribbean in 1987/88 contrasted so starkly with the generally high standard encountered earlier that he could only conclude that 'patriotism had taken over'. And then, of course, there was Pakistan. Imran missed the series between Pakistan and England in 1987/88, which was memorable — notorious would perhaps be better — for the appalling confrontation between Gatting and the umpire Shakoor Rana that somehow encapsulated English grievances about umpiring on the subcontinent. Whatever the rights and winnings of the Faisalabad incident, this was the sort of attitude Imran found frustrating. When David Constant made a mistake, it was one of the best umpires in the world (because he was English) making a rare, if human error; when Shakoor Rana did, it was another 'Paki cheat'. Imran felt that the standards of umpiring in Pakistan were getting better — a comment that seems almost laughable given that it was written after the England tour. Imran's point was wherever the game was played, visiting teams operated at a potential disadvantage. Talking of patriotism, though, there is a wonderful picture in Scyld Berry's book about England's 1987/88 tour of Pakistan of Shakoor Rana proudly wearing Mudassar's Pakistan cap while umpiring a Test. Imran first advocated neutral umpires as long ago as 1978.

The second controversy, not unrelated, was ball-tampering. Allegations thereof became something of a Pakistani specialty. There were quite a few formidable swing bowlers around in the 1980s and 1990s: Dennis Lillee, Kapil Dev, Ian Botham, Terry Alderman, Bruce Reid. But see Imran Khan, Wasim Akram or Waqar Younis unleashed and there seemed to be something fishy going on. Complaints only started to be made once Pakistan began winning; in 1982 it was suggested after their victory at Lord's that their bowlers had used some kind of illegal polish to make the ball swing more. Imran was indignant. Similar sorts of allegations were made after the Headingley victory in 1987. Tongues really started wagging in the early 1990s and reached a crescendo during Pakistan's tour of England in 1992. Imran had retired by this time but he added his own not inconsiderable shovel of fuel to the flames in 1994 by admitting that he had once — and once only — used a bottle top to 'rough up' a ball in a county match back in 1981.

Imran was always stout in his defence of Wasim and Waqar. His main points were that when they played in England, balls they used were regularly inspected by the umpires and that, almost parenthetically, 'interfering with' the ball, in the widest sense, was a tradition in English cricket almost as hallowed as the tea interval. It was this second general assertion, no doubt casually uttered to a journalist, that brought Imran nose to nose, as it were, with Botham in the High Court in London in 1996. Botham (and Lamb) sued for defamation because, he claimed, Imran had accused him of ball-tampering and of being ill-educated and 'low-class'. Similar comments were made in Ivo Tennant's biography of Imran; after its publication Imran wrote a curious letter to Botham, saying that he thought Botham was a worthy opponent and an outstanding sportsman and that he just wanted to 'put the record straight'. The jury found in favour of Imran. If the case established anything at all it was that Imran's point about interfering with the ball being widespread in English cricket was not without merit (he had not suggested in the original article that Botham had interfered with a cricket ball; the issue was raised by way of a defence of justification brought up at the last moment and subsequently withdrawn). There was much inconclusive discussion about where to draw the line between accepted custom, sharp practice and downright illegality. Incidentally Botham, in his autobiography, leaves no room for doubt regarding his views about the methods sometimes employed by Pakistan's pace bowlers. The end result surprised many observers. Imran had, after all, apologised to Botham for alleging, in his plea of justification, that Botham had interfered with the ball in Test matches against India and Pakistan in 1982. Had it been a cricket match, the trial would probably have been a draw.

The case showed what an enigmatic relationship Imran had with the English. He was never going to be as popular as Botham, an authentic English hero. But he had a touch of 'celebrity' glamour, enhanced by his marriage – subsequently dissolved – to the fragrant and fabulously wealthy Jemima Goldsmith that even Botham could hardly match. At the same time, he was a citizen of what was to all intents and purposes an Islamic state and a friend of one of its most disagreeable leaders, the genuinely despotic General Zia-ul-Haq. In recent years, Imran has withdrawn somewhat from British life, trying to forge for himself a political career at home with his own party, Movement for Justice. In March 2006 he earned what must have been regarded as a signal badge of honour by many people, being detained in his home in Islamabad during the visit to Pakistan of President George W. Bush.

Back to 1982, and more challenges for Pakistan's new captain. Australia toured in September and October. Lacking most of their big names, apart from Rod Marsh and Jeff Thomson, they lost all three Tests, the only baggy-green-wash of the century. Qadir posed imponderable queries to the batsmen; Zaheer and Mohsin made untroubled runs. Imran commanded operations and took 4 for 45 and 4 for 35 in 44 overs in the Third Test at Lahore. Then came the Indians, led by Gavaskar for a six-Test series. Pakistani sensitivities were still smarting from Asif Iqbal's disastrous tour of 1979/80. Revenge was sweet. Pakistan won three Tests; the others were drawn. Imran was indomitable. He took 40 wickets at 13.95; four times he took 5 wickets in an innings, twice he took 10 in a match. At Faisalabad in the Third Test he emulated Botham by becoming only the second man to make a century and take 10 wickets in a Test: 6 for 94 and 5 for 82 (55.5 overs in all) and 117, one of four centuries in Pakistan's first innings. In the Second Test at Karachi he had taken 8 for 60 in India's second innings; they collapsed from 102 for 1 to 197 all out.

But a heavy price was paid. Imran was playing through pain for much of the series and he was eventually diagnosed as suffering from a stress fracture of the left shin – essentially what you or I would call a broken leg. He could not bowl for a couple of years. He led Pakistan in the World Cup in England in 1983 playing solely as a batsman. He played for Sussex predominantly as a batsman in 1983 and scored 1,262 Championship runs at 57.27. He did bowl in a couple of matches, albeit virtually at half pace. Against Warwickshire at Edgbaston he bowled only 5 overs in the home side's first innings of 300 for 4. He scored 94 in Sussex's reply, 300 for 7. At one point in Warwickshire's second innings, they were 173 for 4, Alvin Kallicharran having made a second century in the match; Imran came on and took 6 for 6 (five bowled, one leg before), including a hat-trick, in 4.3 overs. Warwickshire were all out for 218. Sussex could only manage 197 in the fourth innings, Imran top-scoring with 64.

To beat India in Pakistan was of course very satisfying; but to beat them in India was the dream. The two sides had got into their familiar stalemate routine by the time Imran was fully fit again and ready to lead his side to India in 1986/87 after five successive draws in 1983/84 and 1984/85. The first four matches in 1986/87 were drawn, on slow turning pitches, prepared principally to blunt the pace of Imran and Wasim. Imran played splendidly in the First Test at Madras. Pakistan had started well with a century from Miandad but had collapsed from 215 for 2 to 257 for 6 when Imran came in. He put on 112 for the eighth wicket with Wasim. When last man Tauseef Ahmed came in, Imran's score was 68. Batting with the tail had become one of the strongest features of his play since England in 1982, one of the tenets of his self-imposed responsibility. He reached his century with a six and made 135 not out, out of a total of 487 for 9.

The teams went to Bangalore for the Fifth Test and found a pitch that was turning significantly from the first day. Imran won the toss and batted. Kapil Dev, after an unproductive series, made the initial breakthrough but it was the left-arm spinner Maninder Singh who caused panic in the Pakistani ranks; they were all out for 116, an exceptionally meagre total for the first innings of a Test. India did not do a lot better making 145. When Pakistan batted again, Imran sent Miandad in to open with Rameez Raja and the lead was soon wiped out. The middle order batted soundly, Imran making 41. India needed 221 to win. Gavaskar played magnificently for 96 but the Pakistani spinners prevailed. Imran said it was the most difficult match he had ever had to captain. He was named Man of the Series.

It is difficult for an outsider to appreciate all the singular nuances of a series between Pakistan and India. Encounters with the West Indies in the 1970s and 1980s were rather different. Essentially the cricket was something like a blood sport; not much was left to the imagination. Fear was central. Vivian Richards intimidated the opposition bowlers. The pace quartet terrorized the batsmen. And they just kept winning. The West Indies and England played six series between 1980 and 1989/90. Poor old England: why did they agree to play so often? West Indies won them all; England won one match (out of twenty-eight), in the last of those series. The next series, in England in 1991, was drawn 2-2. Between 1979/80 and 1990/91, Australia and West Indies played six series. West Indies won them all. Australia won four matches (out of twenty-six).

Pakistan had won one series against West Indies, at home back in 1958/59. Clive Lloyd's side had beaten them 1-0 in 1980/81 and they did not meet again until a three-Test series in Pakistan in 1986/87 that preceded Pakistan's trip to India. The series was drawn, each side winning a Test and the third being drawn. The series got off to a sensational start at Faisalabad with the Pakistanis sliding to 37 for 5 when Imran came in. Once again he batted exceptionally well with the tail, putting on 39 for the last wicket with Tauseef Ahmed. Imran was out for 61, the total 159. West Indies found the going tough too against Wasim Akram, who took 6 for 91 but they gained a first innings lead of 84. Pakistan's middle order dug in and Wasim and, again, Tauseef batted heroically. The

West Indies needed 240 to win. Imran bundled out the openers and Qadir did much of the rest; the unofficial world champions were all out for 53. Imran took 4 for 30.

Those were the days when West Indies did not take a humiliation lying down. They won the Second Test at Lahore by an innings and 10 runs. Their own score, only 218, (Imran 5 for 59 in 30.5 overs) is an eloquent comment on the difficulties faced by the batsmen of both sides throughout the series. Nobody made a hundred.

Imran Khan.

Karachi, where (as one gets tired of noting) Pakistan had yet to lose a Test, was the venue for the final match. West Indies won the toss and made 240, Pakistan responding with 239. Rameez made Test cricket's third-slowest fifty. The game came alive on the fourth day when Imran produced one of his inspired spells of pace bowling, causing the West Indies to collapse spectacularly from 171 for 4 to 211 all out. Twice he was on a hat-trick, taking 5 for 10 in a 6-over spell. Mohsin Khan and Qasim Omar were out before the close of play and Pakistan were always struggling on the final day. At tea they were 97 for 7 and it looked as if the Karachi ramparts were about to be stormed. But Imran and the redoubtable Tauseef stood firm until bad light finally stopped play.

In 1987/88, Pakistan made their first trip to the Caribbean since 1976/77. Imran had not originally intended to tour but was prevailed upon to change his mind. It was an enthralling and dramatic series. Pakistan won the First Test at Georgetown by 9 wickets. Their veterans, Imran and Miandad, led the way. Gordon Greenidge, deputising for the absent Richards, won the toss and batted but Imran dismissed Desmond Haynes in his first over and bowled a series of magnificent spells to take 7 for 80. Miandad made his first century against the West Indies and Pakistan established a lead of 143. When West Indies went in again an infected toe restricted Imran but he recovered on the rest day and took 4 more wickets, including the two batsmen who threatened most, Greenidge and Gus Logie. Pakistan only needed 32 to win. It was West Indies' first home defeat since 1977/78.

The Second Test at Port-of-Spain saw fluctuating fortunes and a gripping climax ending in a draw, with West Indies needing 1 wicket and Pakistan 30 runs short of a demanding target of 371. There were heroic individual performances from both sides. The bowlers held sway in each side's first innings, only Saleem Malik passing fifty, but in the West Indies' second innings, Richards and Jeffrey Dujon made hundreds while Miandad got Pakistan's response under way with his second century in consecutive matches. Imran, once again, was the leading wicket taker in the match. He took 4 for 38 in the first innings. By the close of the second day he had dismissed Greenidge and Logie. In the West Indies' second innings total of 391 he took 5 for 115 in 45 overs.

So, if the West Indies failed to win the final Test at Bridgetown (their equivalent of Karachi) they would have lost their first series at home since – well, nobody could quite remember – a man with a long grey beard told a television reporter it was when Colin Cowdrey's England side won after a rather generous declaration by Gary Sobers in 1967/68. There were unlikely to be any generous declarations in this match. Pakistan were put in and made 309. On the second morning, West Indies started poorly, recovered to 198 for 3 and finished the day on 288 for 6. Aggressive batting by Malcolm Marshall enabled them to reach 306. At the close of the third day Pakistan were 177 for 6. Imran, who had come in at 167 for 5, batted through to the end to make 43 not out, out of 262. The West Indies needed 266 to win. When they were 207 for 8 it seemed to be all over but Dujon and Winston Benjamin, not without a slice of luck, saw them home. Imran was Man of the Series.

The two sides met again in 1990/91 in Pakistan. Another three-Test series saw another drawn one with each side winning a match. Imran had entered a new phase in his career. He topped the bowling averages for Pakistan but he only bowled 19 overs – all in the drawn Third Test at Lahore – and took 4 wickets: Greenidge and Haynes in the first innings, Richie Richardson and Brian Lara in the second. The bulk of Pakistan's bowling in the series was done by Waqar and Wasim, who provided several bursts of devastating pace and swing. Pakistan won the First Test at Karachi by 8 wickets. Wasim and Waqar shared 15 wickets and Saleem Malik scored a hundred in Pakistan's first innings. Pakistan had made 201 for 4 in response to the West Indies' 261 (Haynes 117) when Imran joined Shoaib Mohammad. They put on 80 and Imran batted through the remainder of the innings, scoring 73 not out out of 345.

Yet again, the West Indies came back strongly in the Second Test at Faisalabad, winning a low-scoring match by 7 wickets. At Karachi, in the Third Test, the West Indies made all the running, scoring 294 in their first innings and bowling Pakistan out for 122. Imran, coming in at 48 for 5, stayed in an hour and a half for 17. In the fourth innings, Pakistan needed a notional 346 to win and they started the final morning on 110 for 4. Imran joined the nightwatchman Masood Anwar and they added 67. Imran had added another 55 runs with Wasim before Haynes called an end to proceedings. Imran's 58 not out occupied over four hours and he faced 196 balls. He hit 3 fours.

So, three drawn series against the undisputed Test world champions. Two of them were in Pakistan where conditions are always hard. But it was no longer the case, as it used to be, that visiting teams excused their leading players from going. If anything, it was the other way round. Imran himself sat out more than one series in the 1980s and 1990s for reasons other than injury. But he would never have voluntarily missed a series against the West Indies.

There was one ambition left – Imran's final frontier: the World Cup. He was sure that Pakistan's best chance of winning it was when the competition was held in the subcontinent in 1987. Defeat in the semi-final against Australia at Lahore by 18 runs (Imran 3 for 36 and 58) prompted his decision to retire. The persuasive powers of General Zia – and the thought of another go at the West Indies in the Caribbean in 1987/88 – brought about a change of mind. He came back – and he just carried on. The enforced lay-off in the mid-1980s caused by the stress fracture turned out to be a blessing in disguise.

By the time of the World Cup in Australasia in early 1992 he was thirty-nine. His bowling, inevitably, was not what it had been but it hardly mattered. Even if his batting had declined as well his would still have been the first name on the team sheet. In fact, his batting improved if anything. He himself said he had never batted better than in the drawn home series against India in 1989/90, when he averaged 87.33 in the series. In the first innings of the First Test at Karachi he injected some much-needed life into Pakistan's batting, scoring 105 not out in 201 minutes with a six and 17 fours. He headed the batting averages in the series in Australia that followed and, in the drawn Test at Adelaide, shared a magnificent match-saving partnership of 191 with Wasim for the sixth wicket in Pakistan's second innings. Imran scored 136 in 485 minutes with 10 fours. The team of course was generally much younger. Miandad was a survivor from the old days but even he was almost five years younger and the two men were never exactly soul mates.

Imran now had another passion apart from winning cricket matches. His mother had died of cancer in early 1985 and he became involved in a project to build a cancer hospital bearing her name in Lahore. Imran's profile as a cricketer and a charismatic personality made him an ideal fund-raiser and he devoted large amounts of his time to the project.

The World Cup campaign started rather inauspiciously. Waqar was ruled out of the tournament with a stress fracture of the back. Imran injured his shoulder and missed the opening game against West Indies, which Pakistan lost. He played in the second game, against Zimbabwe, but needed neither to bat nor bowl. He missed the next game, against England at Adelaide, because of his shoulder. England bowled Pakistan out for 74 but rain aborted the match. Next, Pakistan faced India, surprisingly for the first time in a World Cup. India made 216 – Imran 0 for 25 in eight overs – and Pakistan were 105 for 2 in the thirty-first over but collapsed to 173 all out: Imran was run out for 0 in a mix-up with Miandad. They lost the next game too, against South Africa at Brisbane by 20 runs: Imran 2 for 34 in 10 overs and 34. After five games, only Zimbabwe were below them in the qualifying table; the top four were to qualify for the semi-finals.

Things started to improve at this point. Australia, who had started well but seemed to have peaked too soon, were comprehensively defeated in a day-night match at Perth (Imran 2 for 32 in 10 overs). Saleem Malik, on whom many hopes were placed, made a duck batting at number three, the latest of a number of failures there and, for the next game against Sri Lanka, also at Perth, Imran promoted himself to number three. He made 22 as Pakistan successfully chased a target of 213. Victory by 7 wickets over New Zealand at Christchurch effectively guaranteed Pakistan a semi-final place, an extraordinary turnaround.

The semi-final, also against New Zealand, at Auckland was one of the higher scoring games in the competition. New Zealand – the team of the tournament so far – made 262 for 7. Pakistan's 4-wicket victory owed much to the twenty-one-year old Inzamam-ul-Haq, who made an apparently nerveless 60 not out. But Imran, batting again at number three, laid a solid platform at the start of the innings, combining seemingly somnolent defence with sudden bursts of aggression: 93 balls, 44 runs, a four and 2 sixes.

And so to Melbourne. As we have seen, he played a similar hand there. Pakistan made 249. Then, for the last time, Imran marshalled his brilliant and variegated bowling resources: the versatile, almost demonic Wasim Akram (3 for 49); his opening partner Aqib Javed, pacy and accurate (2 for 27); the cherubic but devious leg-spinner Mushtaq Ahmed (3 for 47) and Imran himself, the old warhorse with his respectable medium-pace in-swingers, almost reminiscent of his Test debut at Edgbaston all those years ago (1 for 43). It was all too much for Gooch's valiant Englishmen; they too had peaked a bit early.

It was indeed a famous victory. At the height – or depth – of the crisis, when it seemed that Pakistan could not possibly qualify, Imran had famously told his players to play like 'cornered tigers'. Wasim was told not to worry about wides and no-balls but to concentrate on getting people out. That was Imran's way, the Pathan way. Why defend when you can attack?

'I would just like to say I want to give my commiserations to the English team. But I want them to know that by winning this World Cup, personally it means that one of my greatest obsessions in life, which is to build a cancer hospital… I'm sure that this World Cup will go a long way towards completion of this obsession. I would also like to say that I feel very proud that at the twilight of my career, finally, I have managed to win the World Cup. Thank you.'

It could almost have been de Gaulle himself (apart from the 'Thank you'). Imran was standing on a podium at the MCG in front of 87,000 spectators and a small group of exultant but slightly bemused Pakistani cricketers. Somehow, he had forgotten to mention 'the boys'. All too soon, the team was squabbling about prize money. Was this or that sum meant for the players, or was it meant for the cancer hospital?

It was time to move on.

IMRAN Ahmed KHAN Niazi
Right-hand bat, right-arm fast
Born: 25 November 1952, Lahore
Major Teams: Pakistan, Lahore, Dawood Industries, Pakistan International Airlines, Worcestershire, Oxford University, Sussex, New South Wales

TESTS
(1971-1991/92)

	M	I	NO	Runs	HS	Ave	100	50	Ct
Batting & Fielding	88	126	25	3,807	136	37.69	6	18	28

	Balls	R	W	Ave	BBI	5	10	SR	Econ
Bowling	19,458	8,258	362	22.81	8/58	23	6	53.75	2.54

ONE-DAY INTERNATIONALS

	M	I	NO	Runs	HS	Ave	SR	100	50	Ct
Batting & Fielding	175	151	40	3,709	102★	33.41	72.64	1	19	36

	Balls	R	W	Ave	BBI	5	10	SR	Econ
Bowling	7,461	4,844	182	26.61	6/14	1	0	40.99	3.89

FIRST-CLASS
(Career: 1969/70-1991/92)

	M	I	NO	Runs	HS	Ave	100	50	Ct
Batting & Fielding	382	582	89	17,771	170	36.79	30	93	117

	Balls	R	W	Ave	BBI	5	10	SR	Econ
Bowling	65,224	28,726	1,287	22.32	8/34	70	13	50.67	2.64

LIST A

	M	I	NO	Runs	HS	Ave	100	50	Ct
Batting & Fielding	425	384	80	10,100	114★	33.22	5	66	84

	Balls	R	W	Ave	BBI	5	10	SR	Econ
Bowling	19,122	11,312	507	22.31	6/14	6	0	37.71	3.54

INTIKHAB ALAM

The Third Test between Pakistan and Australia at Karachi in 1959/60 was a draw of quite staggering dullness. The series had been an intriguing one, a triumph for Richie Benaud's Australians, Pakistan losing their first series at home. Hanif Mohammad's century made the Karachi match safe but it was dreary fare.

The game contained two notable incidents, however. First, for a period on the fourth day, the cricket was watched – with what one suspects must have been a sense of profound bewilderment – by President Eisenhower of the United States. Although he may well have come across cricket in his time spent in Britain during the Second World War, that would probably not have prepared him for the experience of watching the second-slowest scoring day in Test match history.

If 'Ike' had been there on the second day instead, he would have seen something that might have been worth a footnote in his memoirs. Pakistan had occupied almost nine hours on the first and second days in getting to 287. Colin McDonald and Gavin Stevens opened for Australia. Pakistan's captain Fazal Mahmood shared the new ball with Munir Malik. After a few overs Fazal called up the burly Punjabi Intikhab Alam. 'Inti' set his field, licked his fingers and trotted up to deliver his first ball in Test cricket. McDonald moved back to cut what he expected to be a leg-break. But it was not a leg-break. Benaud has said it was a googly; Scyld Berry, presumably after consulting Inti himself, has said it was a front of the hand ball that hurried on, a top spinner. Whatever it was, it deceived McDonald and bowled him.

McDonald was not the first distinguished batsman to have fallen to a tyro. The same fate had befallen Archie Maclaren and Victor Trumper, no less. Nobody had taken a wicket with his first ball in Test cricket since Dick Howorth, the Worcestershire slow left-armer, who dismissed Dennis Dyer of South Africa at The Oval in 1947. No one was to do it again until Richard Illingworth, the Worcestershire slow left-armer, bowled Phil Simmons of the West Indies at Trent Bridge in 1991. Thirteen bowlers have done it altogether, and Inti was by no means the only one not to have passed what might be thought to be the necessary pre-condition of being a slow left-armer from Worcestershire christened Richard and with a surname ending 'worth'. Several of them are only remembered as cricketers for the essentially fluky achievement of securing a wicket with their first delivery. Matthew Henderson of New Zealand, for example, who achieved the feat in New Zealand's first ever Test, never played again. Easily the most distinguished of the club is the great English medium-pacer Maurice Tate. But Intikhab vies with the Yorkshireman George Macauley to take second place.

Among non-English bowlers only the Australian Albert Trott and Malcolm Marshall took more first-class wickets than Intikhab. All three played much of their cricket in England. Of the eighty-two bowlers who have taken 1,500 or more first-class wickets none has secured his victims at a higher cost than Intikhab. But, as Scyld Berry has cogently argued, the odds were stacked against him. How he must envy Saqlain Mushtaq and Ian Salisbury bowling on the relaid Oval strip. In his day – and he spent many of them as an overseas player with Surrey, his round and beaming face cheering up many a county game – it was a batsman's paradise. Nor were things much better at home where, before the era of Imran Khan, not losing was generally the limit of ambition, and keeping the runs down was Intikhab's main job. Of these eighty-two bowlers, however, there can have been few who were more cheerful and enthusiastic.

He also gave sterling service as his country's captain. He was first appointed to lead Pakistan in the home series against New Zealand in 1969/70, replacing Saeed Ahmed. The series was not an especially happy one for the new captain or his team; they lost 1-0 to a team against whom they had always enjoyed some success. Intikhab took 10 wickets in the rubber, all of them coming in the third and final game at Dacca. He took 5 for 91 in each innings on a pitch of baked mud. New Zealand had been struggling at 25 for 4 in their second innings but a brilliant hundred from Mark Burgess – dropped twice off absolute sitters by Aftab Gul – helped them to safety. Minor rioting brought the game to an early conclusion. It was Pakistan's last Test in Dacca: within months East and West Pakistan were at war.

Despite the disarray at the start of his reign it was a settled side that Intikhab led in England in 1971 and the tour was a successful one. The visitors made all the running in the drawn First Test at Edgbaston, forcing England to follow on. The Lord's Test was ruined by rain but the final game at Headingley was a magnificent match that England won by 25 runs: Intikhab took 3 wickets in each innings. On the tour as a whole Intikhab took 72 wickets at 26 apiece; Asif Masood was the next highest wicket-taker with 27. He took 13 wickets in 63 overs against Glamorgan at Swansea but could not prevent the Welsh county's victory. In the final match of the tour, at The Oval, he bowled his county colleagues out for 166 in the first innings, taking 7 for 55; Pakistan won by 8 wickets.

Intikhab then rejoined Surrey, who went on to win the Championship for the first time since their seven-year run in the 1950s. Surrey lost their three-day match against Pakistan on 16 July. On 17 July, Intikhab was bowling for them against Middlesex. The match was won by a leg-spinner – Middlesex's Harry Latchman, who took 6 for 39 in the fourth innings. But Intikhab soon got into his stride. In three games at The Oval at the end of August he and the off-spinner Pat Pocock took 40 wickets between them. Surrey lost the final game of the season – in which Intikhab bagged a pair and took one wicket – against Hampshire at Southampton, but obtained the bonus points that secured the title. Intikhab finished the season with 104 first-class wickets.

An indication of Intikhab's growing stature in the game came when he was picked as Gary Sobers' vice-captain on the Rest of the World tour of Australia in 1971/72. But nobody has ever found the captaincy of Pakistan an easy ride and the 1972/73 season proved problematical for Intikhab. The main event was a long tour of Australia and New Zealand. Pakistan lost all three Tests on the Australian leg of the tour. That was not really a fair reflection. Pakistan were demoralised in the first game, at Adelaide, which they lost by an innings, but they gave a good account of themselves in the other two Tests, which Australia won by 92 and 52 runs respectively, after Pakistan had got themselves into good positions: it was almost as if they thought they could not win. Intikhab played hard-hitting innings of 68 and 48 in the Second Test at Melbourne. The tour was marred by disciplinary problems involving Saeed Ahmed and the opener Mohammad Ilyas, who were sent home. This combination of circumstances probably meant that Intikhab's days as leader were numbered, whatever happened in New Zealand. In fact, Pakistan won the series there 1-0, an historic achievement in that it was their first overseas series victory. In the innings victory at Christchurch Intikhab took 7 for 52 and 4 for 78. A.H. Kardar's telegram informing Intikhab and the tour management that he had been relieved of his duties arrived, with impeccable timing, in the middle of the final Test at Auckland, in which he took 6 for 127 in the first innings. Majid Khan then led the side in a drawn series at home against England; Intikhab had a splendid series with bat and ball, scoring 202 runs at an average of 50 and taking 15 wickets at 28.33.

He had an excellent summer with Surrey in 1973, when the county came third in the Championship. He took 72 wickets and made 600 runs with two centuries. In 1974 he was back in charge of the national side, Majid having been removed as suddenly and mysteriously as he had been appointed.

The tour of England in 1974 was even more successful than that in 1971. Intikhab's Pakistanis became the first side since Bradman's Australians in 1948 to go through a tour of England undefeated. Intikhab was again the leading wicket-taker on the tour and took 5 for 116 in the high-scoring draw at The Oval. The fact was, though, that England were the better side. Intikhab was not positive enough as a leader. For instance, he should probably have declared earlier at The Oval when Pakistan made over 600. He led Pakistan in a drawn series against the West Indies at home in 1974/75. He was not even in the squad for the inaugural World Cup in 1975, strangely, given his experience of English conditions and all the one-day cricket he played for Surrey and Mushtaq Mohammad replaced him as captain for the series against New Zealand in 1976/77. Intikhab was the leading wicket-taker with 15 wickets. At this point there was a dispute between the Pakistan board and the leading professionals – Mushtaq, Majid and Asif Iqbal – over pay and conditions. Intikhab, an establishment figure by instinct, stood aside from the dispute. Asif and the others got their way. After that, it seemed that they would not let Inti play with their ball and he was a sad and peripheral figure on the eventful tours of Australia and the West Indies that followed the New Zealand series, barely getting a game. He announced his retirement from international cricket after the West Indies tour but carried on playing for Surrey.

Intikhab was always a useful performer in the lower-middle order. He batted splendidly in the one-off Test against Australia at Karachi in October 1964, scoring 53. English spectators (if not Scottish – he had three seasons as a professional in Scotland in the 1960s) had their first real opportunity to appreciate his worth on the 1967 tour; Intikhab had come on the 1962 tour but had not done much. In 1967, he took 35 wickets on the tour at 18.20, being the leading wicket-taker and heading the averages. But it was his batting that made the most impact. In one of the most memorable passages of play of the whole summer, he and Asif put on 190 for the ninth wicket in Pakistan's second innings at The Oval in 170 minutes. Intikhab made 51, with 6 fours.

Although he could be obdurate and was always conscientious, it was his power as a hitter that was the most memorable aspect of Intikhab's batting. In that 1972/73 series against England, he made his only Test century, 138 at Hyderabad. He batted in all for four and a half hours but his first fifty came in forty-five minutes and he hit 4 sixes and 15 fours. He hit Pocock, who had taken 4 wickets, out of the attack. In the 90s, he had to go into the crowd and plead with them to stop running onto the field; Hyderabad was staging its first Test.

At the end of Pakistan's innings in the Third Test at The Oval in 1974, he launched into Chris Old with two massive blows for six. In the 1970s the general view was that only Gordon Greenidge hit the ball harder.

A youthful – and hirsute – Intikhab Alam on the tour of England in 1962.

After cricket there was – well, more cricket: Inti is addicted. He was a popular manager of Imran Khan's team that toured England in 1982, captaining the side in his final first-class appearance against D.B. Close's XI at Scarborough. He resigned the managership after the unhappy tour of Australia in 1983/84. He had several subsequent spells in charge, including the tour of New Zealand in 1988/89 where he upset the locals by accusing the umpires of cheating. He became embroiled in the match-fixing controversies of the mid-1990s when he was manager of Saleem Malik's ill-fated expedition to southern Africa in 1994/95.

Intikhab's most recent appointment has been as coach to the Punjab state cricket team. Not Punjab in Pakistan, Punjab in India. That seems right, somehow. After all, Inti had been born there back in pre-Partition days. As relations improve between the two neighbours it is good to have people like Intikhab Alam – genuine, conscientious, enthusiastic and cheerful – on the front line.

INTIKHAB ALAM KHAN
Right-hand bat, leg-break & googly
Born: 28 December 1941, Hoshjarpur, India
Major Teams: Pakistan, Karachi, Pakistan International Airlines, Public Works Department, Sind, Punjab, Surrey

TESTS
(1959/60-1976/77)

	M	I	NO	Runs	HS	Ave	100	50	Ct
Batting & Fielding	47	77	10	1,493	138	22.28	1	8	20

	Balls	R	W	Ave	BBI	5	10	SR	Econ
Bowling	10,474	4,494	125	35.95	7/52	5	2	83.79	2.57

ONE-DAY INTERNATIONALS

	M	I	NO	Runs	HS	Ave	SR	Ct
Batting & Fielding	4	2	0	17	10	8.50	37.77	0

	Balls	R	W	Ave	BBI	SR	Econ
Bowling	158	116	4	29.50	2/36	39.50	4.48

FIRST-CLASS
(Career: 1957/58-1982)

	M	I	NO	Runs	HS	Ave	100	Ct	Ct
Batting & Fielding	489	725	78	14,331	182	22.94	9	227	227

	R	W	Ave	BBI	5	10
Bowling	43,474	1571	27.67	8/54	85	13

LIST A

	M	I	NO	Runs	HS	Ave	50	Ct
Batting & Fielding	199	169	29	2,548	62	18.19	5	40

	Balls	R	W	Ave	BBI	5	SR	Econ
Bowling	6,419	4,392	151	29.08	6/25	2	42.50	4.10

INZAMAM-UL-HAQ

As 2005 moved into 2006, the perennial cricketing debate as to the identity of the best batsman in the world also moved on. The tumbrils appeared to be rolling in Mumbai as Sachin Tendulkar, the nation's darling, struggled against Pakistan and then England. A magnificent double century by Brian Lara against Australia could not disguise the fact that getting a start was becoming increasingly difficult for Test cricket's leading run scorer – although it may be that his reappointment as captain will herald more great deeds. It was the turn of the next cricketing generation, batsmen who had come to prominence in the mid-1990s, to assert their dominance. The slightly dull but massively acquisitive Jacques Kallis, the new Indian captain Rahul Dravid – many people had been saying for years that he was the best technically equipped player around – and, above all, the remarkable Australian Ricky Ponting appeared to have the stage to themselves.

But one of the veterans refused to go quietly. In Pakistan, big Inzi, the Lion of Multan, rolled out the hundreds at a greater rate than ever. The 2005/06 home season was one of Pakistan's best for years as Inzamam and the coach, Bob Woolmer, masterminded the dismantling of England, fresh from a glorious triumph in the Ashes. Pakistan then defeated arch-rivals India 1-0 in the Tests and, although Inzamam missed the decisive victory at Karachi, he scored a hundred at Faisalabad and his influence could not be discounted.

The series against England was particularly important. England's attack was being talked up as the best in the world following the defeat of Australia. More to the point, perhaps, Pakistan as a nation was still reeling from the apocalyptic catastrophe of the earthquake in Kashmir. Success at cricket might at least provide some consolation. Imran Khan was scathing about what he perceived to be negative comments by Inzamam at the start of England's tour. On the field, however, Inzamam led from the front. Without being demonstrative or effusive as a leader, he clearly had the respect of his talented side and he handled his bowlers skillfully, especially on the final afternoon of the First Test at Multan when England appeared to be moving towards victory before Danish Kaneria and Shoaib Akhtar struck. He never failed to reach fifty in the three Tests and, in the draw at Faisalabad, he made two centuries, becoming the fifth Pakistani to achieve this feat. Each was a great innings in its own very different way. His 109 in the first innings was a monumental display. England were bowling well and Inzamam was simply determined to thwart them, to stay in. The fireworks were provided by Shahid Afridi and, to a lesser extent, Mohammad Yousuf. In the second innings, the other senior batsmen failed. On the morning of the fifth day, Pakistan were 163 for 6 with Inzamam on 41 not out. He did not try to protect the tail but concentrated on scoring: Steve Harmison was hit for a straight six in the second over of the day. Inzamam declared just before lunch on 268 for 9 when he had reached his twenty-fourth Test match hundred, overtaking Javed Miandad as Pakistan's leading centurion. His 97 – run out – in the innings victory at Karachi was a different sort of innings again. It was made in two parts, separated by an injury to his wrist and a massive partnership between Yousuf and Kamran Akmal. By the time Inzamam got back in the English attack was wilting and he took merciless toll as the field was spread far and wide.

Inzamam's path to the captaincy had not been straightforward, although by the time he got it his talismanic presence as senior player made any other choice seem very far-fetched. But he had had a dreadful World Cup in Southern Africa in 2002/03 – 19 runs in 6 matches – and was left out of the side for a while. The turning point came in the improbable context of a Test match against Bangladesh in, happily enough, Multan in September 2003. He was back in the side, and it was just as well. Pakistan had won the first two Tests with relative ease but the third looked like turning into an embarrassment. On a pitch giving an unusual amount of help to the seamers, Bangladesh established a more-than-useful first innings lead of 106. Pakistan fought back though, through Umar Gul and Shabbir Ahmed, bowling Bangladesh out for 154. Pakistan needed 261; midway through the third afternoon they were 132 for 6 with only Inzamam of the recognized batsmen left.

Pakistan could hardly have cut it finer. They won in the end by 1 wicket, a couple of dropped catches and some dogged partnerships doing the trick. It really did go down to the wire. The number eleven, Yasir Ali, was a seventeen-year-old making his first-class debut. Bangladesh were going to have to wait a bit longer for their maiden Test victory: they are, of course, still waiting, Ponting having done an Inzi at Fatullah in April 2006 (Sorry, the win against mugabe's blighted Zimbabwe really should not count).

Inzamam made 138 not out in five hours seventeen minutes. The opener Salman Butt made 37; nobody else got more than 18. Rameez Raja called it one of the great Test innings of modern times, which is a bit much. But it was very good. It was the tenth 1-wicket victory in Tests and Pakistan's second. Inzamam had been at the heart of the first one too. It was at Karachi in 1994/95, a match that subsequently became notorious because it was at the centre of match-fixing allegations against the Pakistan captain Saleem Malik. Pakistan, chasing 314 for victory in the First Test against Australia, had scored 258 for 9 when Mushtaq Ahmed joined Inzamam. Inzamam on that occasion made 58 not out in two hours thirty-five minutes. Both innings showed that he had a terrific temperament. But back to Multan, and that Test against Bangladesh. The captain was Rashid Latif, who had replaced Waqar Younis after the World Cup. During Bangladesh's second innings, Latif appealed

Inzamam powers his way towards a second hundred in the Second Test against England at Faisalabad, 2005.

successfully after diving for a catch. TV replays showed the ball dropping out of Latif's gloves onto the ground and bouncing back again. He was suspended for five one-day internationals after complaints from the Bangladeshis and the stand-in captain was Inzamam. Within two months he was the official captain of the team touring New Zealand.

Pakistan won the two Test series 1-0. The match winner at Wellington was Shoaib Akhtar but Inzamam did his bit. The fourth innings run chase saw him at his most indomitable and his most infuriating. New Zealand had established a first innings lead of 170 and, even after Shoaib's stunning performance (5 for 48 and 6 for 30), Pakistan's target was a challenging 274. They proceeded steadily and needed only 26 to win when the fourth day reached its scheduled close on a beautiful sunlit evening. Inzamam, who was batting at the time, chose not to claim the extra half-hour, preferring, presumably, an early dinner. Anyone who knew anything about Wellington's weather was amazed at the decision and sure enough the next day dawned grey and overcast, though it did not get bad enough to thwart Pakistan. Inzamam made 72 not out.

Those three innings, at Karachi, Multan and Wellington, showed something that has been demonstrated time and time again; namely that Inzamam makes his big innings count. Pakistan's victories – not as frequent as they should have been over the last dozen years or so – have more often than not coincided with a big or important innings from Inzamam. There have been several examples since he became captain. One was his century against India at Lahore in April 2004. India had overwhelmed Pakistan in the First Test at – oh dear – Multan and Pakistan needed to fight back, and Inzamam led the way with a patient 118. India won the decider at Rawalpindi when Inzamam failed in both innings. In the return series in India in March 2005, the team's fortunes followed his; 57 and 86 in the draw at Mohali; 30 and 13 in the defeat at Kolkata; and 184 (Younis Khan got 267) – and 31 not out – in the victory at Bangalore where he also out-captained Sourav Ganguly. Aggressive field-placings pressurised India into a second innings decline against Shahid Afridi and Danish Kaneria. Again, in the Caribbean in 2005, he showed that he was close to indispensable. He missed the First Test at Barbados because of a one-match ban for dissent in the Test at Bangalore; West Indies won. Returning for the second and final game at Kingston, he made 50 in the first innings and 117 not out in the second: Pakistan won by 136 runs.

This phenomenon, however, was not something that started when Inzamam became captain. Right from the beginning his big innings seemed to count, to make a difference to the result of a game. This certainly sets him apart from Tendulkar and Dravid if not, to the same extent, Lara – when the West Indies were still capable of winning – and Ponting. Inzamam's first Test century was made in a losing cause, against the West Indies in 1992/93. But his second, against New Zealand, his third, against Sri Lanka, his fourth, against Zimbabwe, his fifth, against England, his sixth, against the West Indies (his first at home, in 1997/98) and his seventh, against Sri Lanka (in the final of the Asian Test Championship at Dhaka – it was a double, and Ijaz Ahmed got one as well) all came in matches that Pakistan won. So did his ninth, against Sri Lanka (two match-winning innings at Karachi in March 2000; 86 and 138).

He has made two significant, imperious and arguably decisive Test hundreds in England. In 1996, at Lord's, he set up an emphatic Pakistan victory with a magnificent 148 (his fifth Test century) off 218 balls on the first day, reaching his hundred with an on-driven six off Graeme Hick. His 114 on the opening day of the Old Trafford Test in 2001 was, if anything, even better. England were one-up in a two-Test series. As at Lord's five years earlier, Pakistan were in trouble when Inzamam arrived (this time it was 39 for 2 as opposed to 12 for 2). Two more wickets fell before the score reached 100 and then Inzamam was caught off a Dominic Cork no-ball, on 31. The bowling deteriorated as the day wore on and Inzamam did more or less as he pleased, milking the bowling, especially off his legs through mid-wicket. He was well supported

Inzamam acknowledges the applause for his century against England in the Second Test at Old Trafford, 2001.

by Younis Khan and Latif and Pakistan finished that first day on 392 for 7. England
went from 15 for 2 to 282 for 2 to 357 all out in response to Pakistan's 403. Then
another master class from Inzamam: dropped on 31, he made 85. England crumbled
to defeat after tea on the last day. The editor of *Wisden* must be hoping Inzi gets a few
runs in 2006 too. How many Test batsmen can you think of with an average of over
50 and twenty-four centuries who have not been one of *Wisden's* Five Cricketers of
the Year? Of modern cricketing personalities, perhaps only Mark Nicholas has been
similarly slighted.

Australia, after that masterly display at Karachi in 1994/95, proved difficult: he
only averages 31 against them. But Pakistan generally have performed surprisingly
poorly against the modern era's greatest Test match power. Indeed, since 1995/96,
the two countries have met fifteen times. Australia have won twelve of those, including the last nine on the trot. Pakistan have won one. That victory came at Sydney
in 1995/96 when Mushtaq Ahmed was the match-winner. Inzamam top scored in
Pakistan's second innings of 204 with 59. Of the nine losses in a row – five of which
Inzamam missed through injury – one should certainly have been won by Pakistan.
This was the Hobart Test in 1999/2000, which Australia won thanks to an amazing
sixth-wicket stand between Justin Langer and Adam Gilchrist. The Australian target
was 369. Pakistan's second innings was built around Inzamam's 118, which contained
12 fours and, rather improbably, 9 threes. That was the eighth Test century, missing
from the list above.

At Lahore, in May 2002, against New Zealand, he became the second Pakistani, after
Hanif Mohammad, to score a triple century, making 329 with 38 fours and 9 sixes, a
display that was at once flamboyant and magisterial. He was suffering from cramp on
the second day and, although he was allowed a runner for a while, that privilege was
withdrawn. His third hundred came at a run a ball, with 7 fours and 4 sixes. The game
was over in three days, Pakistan winning by an innings and 324 runs.

'Magisterial' suits Inzi nicely. He stands tall and big, impassive, imperturbable,
almost motionless. And that's just when he's fielding. No, really – he is a calming
influence and that has been a good thing in a volatile dressing room. Being in charge
of characters like Shoaib Akhtar and Shahid Afridi cannot be easy. Pakistan have had
plenty of 'up and at 'em' captains since the retirement of Imran Khan: Javed Miandad,
Wasim Akram, Waqar Younis, Moin Khan. It was time to go for the strong silent
type. Still, Inzamam has had his detractors. They did not take long to emerge after
the hugely disappointing tour of Australia in 2004/05. Pakistan lost all three Tests. A
back injury ruled Inzamam out of the last two Tests. In the first, at Perth, he scored
1 and 0; Australia won by the little matter of 491 runs. There were other team problems because of injury and discipline. Inzamam said it was the toughest tour he had
been on. Even after the 2005/06 domestic season some commentators were saying
he should be replaced at least as one-day captain, by Younis Khan. Inzamam's 'body
language' was said to be too negative.

It is true that he has always been laid back. That has in part been the key to his
success, the ability to remain calm in high-pressure situations. Not that he cannot be

riled: hence the bizarre incident during a meaningless one-day international against India in, of all places, Toronto, when he sought out and hit a spectator who had insulted him and his country. It was his amazing maturity and unflappability that first made Inzamam a star as long ago as 1992 in the World Cup in Australia and New Zealand. He was the baby of the Pakistan squad, having gained selection with some brilliant batting in a one-day series against Sri Lanka earlier in 1992. He first caught the eye in the World Cup in a match against South Africa at Brisbane when, batting at number three, he orchestrated a vigorous if unavailing run chase: he top-scored with 48. But his most memorable contribution came in the semi-final against New Zealand at Auckland. New Zealand made 262 for 7, one of the highest scores of the tournament. At the final drinks break Pakistan had 6 wickets standing but were still 109 runs adrift with only 13 overs left. The hugely experienced Javed Miandad was still in but the hero of the hour turned out to be Inzamam, now batting at number six. He made 60 off 37 balls, reaching his half-century in a record-equalling 31 balls. Inzamam pummelled the bowling to all parts. With Miandad urging him on the pair put on 82 in 10 overs. Pakistan won by 4 wickets. Inzamam also made 42 off 35 balls in the final against England at Melbourne.

In two of those three tremendous innings – against South Africa and New Zealand – Inzamam was run out. Indeed, the stunning photograph of the great South African fielder Jonty Rhodes flying vertically through the air before shying at the stumps is one of many abiding images of that memorable World Cup. Now, anybody can be run out by Jonty Rhodes: nothing to be ashamed of there. So nobody really appreciated back in those early days that being run out – or perhaps rather more frequently being a bystander, and not an innocent bystander, when somebody else was run out – was to become something of an Inzi speciality. One example will suffice. It was another World Cup, this time in England in 1999, Pakistan *v.* Australia at Headingley. Pakistan won convincingly and Inzamam was Man of the Match, scoring 81 before he was run out. He was hit on the foot by a ball from Damien Fleming. Looking up he was startled to see his partner and captain, Wasim Akram, charging towards his end. Instead of following his leader's example and hot-footing it to the non-striker's end Inzi collapsed into a disconsolate heap at or rather just outside the batting crease. Even Wasim couldn't help laughing.

The run-outs have added fuel to the theory that Inzamam is not so much laid back as lazy, that he likes a good feed and that he prefers whacking a few boundaries to running up and down between the wickets. He had the misfortune to be run out in a rather strange way to end his first century at Faisalabad against England when Steve Harmison, the bowler, shied at the stumps and Inzamam moved to avoid being hit: he was clearly not attempting a run and he was mistakenly given out. His rather lumbering gait does appear to make him a natural for run outs. That suggests, though, that he is leaden footed and ponderous. It is true that, insofar as it is possible these days, he has to find somewhere relatively quiet to field. But when he is batting, it is different. Then all is not simply power but also ease and grace. He hits with immense force, particularly square of the wicket with cuts and pulls and hooks. He loves to drive too, with the lofted drive a particular joy; and like all the best players he will drill anything on his pads through the gaps on the on-side, barely moving a muscle: that is the Inzamam way. Sometimes he pilfers runs cutting delicately and late; more often though it is a case of smash and grab. On his day, he can tear any attack apart and Inzamam in full flight is genuinely awe-inspiring. He is brilliant against pace – Imran has said he is one of the best players of fast bowling he has ever seen – but, once he is 'in', he is highly effective against spin too, advancing swiftly down the wicket to drive over the top: he has had some memorable duels with the great Indian leg-spinner Anil Kumble. At the start of an innings, he can be a bit leaden-footed, and is always vulnerable. But to see this imposing, powerful man – he has been compared to a great, but warm and almost cuddly, bear – move rapidly and easily and send the ball skimming to the boundary almost effortlessly or smite it hither and yon as if armed with a giant club, is one of the great sights of the modern game.

INZAMAM-UL-HAQ
Right-hand bat, left-arm slow
Born: 3 March 1970, Multan
Major Teams: Pakistan, Faisalabad, Multan, National Bank of Pakistan, Rawalpindi, United Bank Limited

TESTS
(1992-2006)

	M	I	NO	Runs	HS	Ave	100	50	Ct
Batting & Fielding	108	178	19	8,265	329	51.98	25	42	79

	Balls	R	W	Ave	Econ
Bowling	9	8	0	–	5.33

ONE-DAY INTERNATIONALS

	M	Runs	HS	Ave	100	50	Ct
Batting & Fielding	358	11,369	137★	39.75	10	83	104

	Balls	I	NO	R	W	Ave	BBI	SR	Econ
Bowling	58	334	48	64	3	21.33	1/0	19.33	6.62

FIRST-CLASS
(Career: 1985/86-1982)

	M	I	NO	Runs	HS	Ave	100	50	Ct
Batting & Fielding	229	365	53	15,085	329	51.55	45	82	165

	Balls	R	W	Ave	BBI	5	SR	Econ
Bowling	2,704	1,295	38	34.07	5/80	2	71.15	2.87

LIST A

	M	I	NO	Runs	HS	Ave	100	50	Ct
Batting & Fielding	436	411	65	13,265	157★	38.33	12	95	118

	Balls	R	W	Ave	BBI	5	SR	Econ
Bowling	896	740	30	24.66	3/18	0	29.86	4.95

JAVED MIANDAD

It was always thought that the Pakistan tour of England in 1992 was going to be a tricky one. The previous tour, under Imran Khan, had been problematical in terms of umpiring. That had been followed by a series in Pakistan rarely exceeded in terms of fractiousness and controversy. Most recently the two sides had met in an emotion-shredding World Cup final, which Pakistan had won, in the end, quite convincingly. Imran had now gone and Pakistan were led by the streetwise and mercurial Javed Miandad.

Just before the Third Test, an incident occurred which it would not be too far-fetched to describe as absolutely shocking. That the captain of a first-class cricket team should have been allowed to behave in such a manner and get away with it seems quite extraordinary. It happened in the tourists' match against Hampshire at Southampton. Pakistan had batted first and made 406 for 1 (two batsmen retired hurt). Miandad made 142 and Asif Mujtaba 154 not out. Pakistan won the match by an innings and 14 runs, a overwhelming victory. That, in a way, made the incident all the stranger. David Gower and Hampshire's captain Mark Nicholas were rebuilding Hampshire's first innings after the loss of 2 early wickets when Nicholas was given out, caught at short leg off Mushtaq Ahmed. The bowler's umpire, Jeffrey Tolchard, had not been sure the ball had carried and consulted his colleague at square leg, Roy Palmer, before raising his finger. Nicholas instead of striding to the pavilion in the manner of a Bradfield boy dispatched in the heat of a house match, deviated from the path of righteousness to discuss the matter with Palmer. The result of their negotiations was that the decision was rescinded, to the undisguised and understandable fury of the Pakistanis. The distinguished scribe John Woodcock, who was sitting just behind a rather more humble scribe, namely me, at the time, was disgusted. The event gets a couple of lines in the match report in *Wisden*. It is not even mentioned in the *Hampshire Handbook*. Nor is it mentioned in Scyld Berry's thorough and objective account of the campaign as a whole in *Wisden*, which dissects all the controversies of the tour, including ball-tampering. Berry does discuss an incident that took place only a few days later and generated much more excitement. At Old Trafford in the Third Test, England's first innings and the fourth day's play were both drawing to a close. The pace bowler Aqib Javed was bowling to England's hapless number eleven Devon Malcolm. Aqib bowled some short stuff and got a warning from the umpire for intimidation. Aqib appeared to disagree with the umpire's interpretation and a heated discussion ensued. At the end of the over, the way in which Aqib's sweater was returned to him made it look as if it was being chucked at him dismissively; in fact it seems more likely that it got caught in some other item, but appearance can be important and at the end of a long day this was enough to get the fielding captain involved. Miandad was soon in the thick of it expostulating and gesturing with vigour in a manner that reminded Berry of the Mike Gatting-Shakoor Rana face-off at Faisalabad in 1987/88. At Old Trafford, the umpire concerned was Roy Palmer.

In his autobiography, Miandad does not mention the Nicholas 'dismissal' at all and deals with the Aqib Javed furore in half a page, insisting that Palmer was being unfair to the bowler and that he was simply explaining the position to him. This and other controversies in which he was involved during his career are explained away as examples of a 'cultural clash' between East and West – although many people would maintain that, wherever cricket is played, the umpire is the arbiter of what goes on on the field (a point Miandad himself makes in his discussion of the Gatting-Shakoor Rana incident). The fact is though that, with regard to Old Trafford 1992, it is easy to feel some sympathy for Miandad. In the five Tests, seven different umpires – all English of course – were used. Dickie Bird, probably the most respected umpire in the world, stood once, in the final Test; David Shepherd stood twice. Ken Palmer, Roy's brother, had been the cause of unhappiness to the Pakistanis in 1982 and 1987. Brother Roy was standing in his first Test at Old Trafford and, given what had happened at Southampton, it would have been a miracle if the Pakistanis had had full confidence in him.

But the focus was all on Miandad with his 'reputation for waywardness' (Berry). In fact, as Berry was the first to admit, Miandad was an admirable leader on that tour. His magnificent team won the Test series 2-1 and went into the county games with a positive attitude rarely displayed by touring sides. Miandad led from the front with a masterful century in the First Test at Edgbaston.

A more striking example of a culture clash was his contretemps with Dennis Lillee at Perth in 1981/82. It was Miandad's first overseas Test as captain of Pakistan. It was a nightmarish overture. Pakistan seemed reasonably well placed after a turgid first day in which only 74 (eight-ball) overs were bowled. Imran and Sarfraz Nawaz kept Australia to 154 for 7 and they did not last much longer the next day, being all out for 180. That total soon looked commanding, however. Pakistan collapsed sensationally to 26 for 8 to Lillee and Terry Alderman. They finally managed 63 and then Australia piled on the runs, making 424 for 8 in their second innings. Their margin of victory was 286 runs. Miandad top-scored with 74 in Pakistan's second attempt, and the clash with Lillee occurred during that innings. The photograph that has immortalised this confrontation really doesn't do Miandad any favours. It must surely be the most dramatic cricket picture of a batsman using a bat for something other than hitting a ball. Of course, it is a limited field. There is Ken Kelly's wonderful shot of Ron Headley's bat splitting in two – it captures a marvellous look of incredulity on Headley's face. But that may have to be disqualified as there was obviously a ball involved. The only real challenger

Javed Miandad.

is the picture of England's poacher turned game-keeper, Chris Broad, in the one-off Bicentennial Test at Sydney in 1987/88. The distinguished match referee, as he now is, is shown expressing his disgruntlement at an umpire having the temerity to give him out by smashing the stumps down. It's good, but it doesn't really hold a candle to the Miandad shot. My rather old copy of *Treasure Island* has a picture of Billy Bones raising his cutlass and preparing to aim a mortal blow at his fellow pirate Black Dog. The Miandad photo always reminds me of that picture although Lillee, fists clenched, standing tall with a very aggressive bearing, looks much more menacing than Black Dog (he, you may recall, had lost a couple of fingers, so his leg cutter was probably not much good either). Miandad with his bat raised over his shoulder looks almost homicidal.

As with many such events it is not easy to establish precisely what happened. Miandad turned a ball from Lillee to leg and moved to take what seemed an easy single. This is where accounts start to differ. Miandad says Lillee, having finished his follow through, suddenly moved across so that he was blocking the batsman's path. Miandad concedes that at this point he pushed Lillee out of his way and made his ground but that Lillee kicked him on the back of the leg as he went past. Miandad raised his bat in retaliation and umpire Tony Crafter separated the pair. Miandad says that the background to the whole thing was constant abusive sledging by the Australian.

Lillee's account is a bit different. He says that he had for some years been the subject of sledging from Miandad (Miandad concedes that he would retaliate if the subject of sledging himself: anecdotal evidence suggests that the Pakistanis sledge like champions). Lillee says that as Miandad ran past him to the bowler's end he whacked him in the back with his bat when Lillee made a comment to him. The so-called kick was a reflex action as he was off balance. In Lillee's account though, he also gives Richie Benaud's version, which appears to coincide almost exactly with Miandad's. In the end, Lillee was punished and Miandad wasn't, which simply gave more cause for friction. Strangely, bizarrely even, it seems that not only the Australian players but some of the senior Pakistanis thought Miandad should have been penalised as well. The thing with Lillee was important because it gave Miandad a lasting reputation as a 'bad boy'. Fast bowlers had a certain licence to misbehave but international captains did not.

Reading Miandad's own account of these various unhappy events, it is sometimes difficult to restrain a grin, if not outright laughter. There comes a time when the argument that he was the callow innocent from the Third World begins to wear a bit thin. The fact is that Miandad loved nothing more than winding the opposition up. Occasionally he comes close to admitting this. It is true that there was an element of standing up for his country; one saw a similar thing with Arjuna Ranatunga of Sri Lanka. Writing about the Lillee incident, he said that one could not imagine Lillee kicking the captain of England and getting away with a rap on the knuckles and a fine, but that perhaps said more about Lillee's Australia than about Miandad's Pakistan. The fact is, though, that it was part of Miandad's make up to irritate and provoke and always will be. As Berry put it, 'Nobody becomes the most hated man in cricket just like that.'

The Australian tour effectively put an end to Miandad's first spell as captain of Pakistan, as a players' revolt led ultimately to the appointment of Imran. Javed returned to the helm for several spells when Imran was injured or not interested and, ultimately, when he retired. Perhaps inevitably Miandad was in charge at the time of the fracas in Faisalabad, although he was not on the field when the actual confrontation took place. In Berry's view, Miandad and Haseeb Ahsan, Pakistan's chief selector at the time, were the evil geniuses of the debacle.

Miandad's record as captain of Pakistan was actually very good. He captained in thirty-four Tests, of which fourteen were won and six lost; Imran also led Pakistan to victory fourteen times, with eight losses, but in forty-eight Tests. Interestingly the difference numerically is accounted for almost exclusively by India, against whom Imran led Pakistan fifteen times to Miandad's none. Miandad acknowledged Imran's indispensability as a fast bowler but felt he was a lucky captain in some ways. He also felt that Imran did not always offer his full support when Miandad was captain: he particularly felt so in the series against Sri Lanka in 1985/86, the last time Imran played under his captaincy. Imran was scathing about Miandad's first spell as captain and felt that he made no attempt to build relationships with players. Whatever the rights and wrongs of the situation, the relationship between these two great players, the Lahori sophisticate and the street fighter from Karachi, dominated Pakistani cricket for the best part of thirty years.

He was undoubtedly one of the outstanding batsmen of his day. Pakistan certainly had no finer one between Hanif Mohammad and Inzamam-ul-Haq and posterity may well judge that he was a greater player than either of them. His versatility and inventiveness as a strokemaker, his instinctively aggressive intent and his pugnacity and adroitness in all conditions marked him out as special from the day he started in Test cricket with a century in his first innings until the day he finished some seventeen years later.

Agile as an alley-cat, keen-eyed and a born improviser, he had a technique all his own. Miandad could sense and pilfer a run like the Artful Dodger snaffling a handkerchief.

Peter Roebuck famously compared the crafting of an innings by Miandad to a rickshaw journey through the turbulent streets of downtown Karachi: Miandad liked that. The remark was made in the context of what was probably Miandad's most brilliant innings in England, his 200 not out for Glamorgan against Essex at Colchester in 1981. It was his eighth century of the season, beating Gilbert Parkhouse's county record, set in 1950. By this time, Miandad was very well versed in English conditions. He had become a county cricketer before he became a Test cricketer, joining Sussex in 1976. He enjoyed Sussex and initially did well there – their then captain, Tony Greig, was an early believer – but competition for overseas places got tighter and, when an opportunity presented itself at Glamorgan, Miandad seized it. 1981 was his second season there.

Keith Fletcher, the Essex captain, had set Glamorgan an improbable 325 to win in 323 minutes, on a pitch that was offering a lot of assistance to the spinners Ray East and David Acfield (Acfield had taken 6 wickets in Glamorgan's first innings, in which Miandad top-scored with 87). John Lever and Stuart Turner reduced Glamorgan to 7 for 2 and then 44 for 4. The Joneses, Alan Lewis and Eifion gave doughty support with 36 and 26 respectively in the middle order. The opener John Hopkins made 16. Nobody else got double figures. The captain, Robin Hobbs, himself a former Essex spinner, was out first ball: while he was 'in' the score advanced from 227 for 7 to 270 for 8. Graham Gooch, playing for Essex, said it was the best batting he had ever seen in the company of a tail-ender. When last man Simon Daniels was out in the thirteenth over of the last twenty, Glamorgan were 13 runs short. Miandad had batted for 315 minutes. Umpire Ken Palmer, no less, said it was the best innings he had ever seen because the conditions were so difficult.

Before the tour of England in 1982, Miandad had a Test average in excess of 56, significantly higher than any other Pakistani batsman had ever attained. Indeed, uniquely, his Test average was never lower than 50 throughout his career. He had started his Test career with a terrific bang against New Zealand at home in 1976/77, not only making a century on debut (163, the first victim of a hat-trick by Peter Petherick, and 25 not out) at Lahore in the First Test but also following it up with 206 and 85 at Karachi in the Third. A moderate series in Australia and a poor one in the West Indies on the arduous tour that followed the New Zealand series led to an impression being formed that he was only really effective at home. He averaged 61.38 in Pakistan, where he hit fourteen of his twenty-three Test hundreds. But away from home he averaged 45.80 – and most Test batsmen of any generation would settle for that as a Test career average.

Many of his most prolific displays were at home, none move so than the 1982/83 series against India. In the Fourth Test at Hyderabad he put on 451 with Mudassar Nazar, equalling the then record partnership for any Test wicket, set by Don Bradman and Bill Ponsford in 1934. Imran declared with Miandad on 280, a decision that rankles to this day. He averaged 118.80 in the series. Against New Zealand, at home, in 1984/85, he averaged 84.25 in the series and at Hyderabad became the second Pakistani, after Hanif, to score two centuries in a Test match. But against the same opposition – this time including Richard Hadlee – in New Zealand in 1988/89, he did even better, averaging 194.50. This was an acrimonies series marred by more disputes about umpiring. All three Tests were drawn. In the second, at Wellington, Miandad made 118; in the third, at Auckland, he made 271, with 5 sixes (all off slow left-armer Stephen Boock) and 28 fours. A couple of months earlier, he had scored a double century against Australia at Karachi, building a platform upon which Pakistan constructed a series-deciding victory. Allan Border's Australians were furious about the umpiring. The remaining Tests were drawn; in the second, at Faisalabad, Miandad was out leg before – for the fourth time in Tests in Pakistan.

It did not help the perceived imbalance between his home and away records that, despite his outstanding achievements in county cricket, he did little in Tests in England on his first two tours, in 1978 and 1982. Miandad himself said that success and recognition in England were essential if one was to be regarded as a world-class player. That specific goal was certainly attained by the end of the 1987 English season; in the Oval Test he made a massive, untroubled and domineering 260.

In any event, by the late 1980s he had been universally acknowledged to be one of the world's leading batsmen. There had been various contributory factors. Unquestionably one of them was his performances against the West Indies in 1987/88. His record against the best team in Test cricket had raised a question mark about his real quality. The 1976/77 tour did not really count; he was still very young and had been dropped after a couple of failures. He had led Pakistan in a close-fought series in 1980/81 but had only averaged 32 with the bat and had performed even more modestly in the home series in 1986/87.

In the series in the West Indies in 1987/88, however, under Imran, he finally came good. He scored consistently in the one-day games that preceded the three-Test series, making a century – Pakistan's first in one-day games against the West Indies – in the fifth match at Georgetown. Then, at the same venue, he made 114 in the First Test. A

Javed Miandad batting for the Pakistan tourists against the MCC in 1978.

dedicated display lasting six and three quarter hours, it enabled Pakistan to establish a first innings lead of 142. Inspired fast bowling by Imran helped Pakistan to secure a 9-wicket victory. His hundred in the Second Test, at Port-of-Spain, was, if anything, even better. There were only 10 runs between the sides on first innings and when West Indies were all out just before lunch on the fourth day Pakistan's target was 372, a tall order by any standards, particularly with Malcolm Marshall, who had missed the First Test, back to lead the attack. By close of play, Pakistan were 107 for 3, with Miandad on 19 not out. He added 83 with Saleem Malik and then 113 with the belligerent eighteen-year-old Ijaz Ahmed. Gradually it appeared that Pakistan might actually win but Miandad was finally out after batting for over seven hours. Unlike at Georgetown, it was a chanceless innings. The tail-enders held on for a well-deserved draw. Miandad finished the series with an average of 56.40. But his career average against the West Indies remained under 30.

Another factor that bolstered Miandad's global reputation was his World Cup record. His achievement in appearing in six – the first six – World Cups is unique and surely unchallengeable. In the first, in England in 1975, he was a precocious leg-spinning all rounder, a young pretender. In the last, on the subcontinent in 1996, he had almost got beyond the veteran stage: an old pretender. Wasim Akram did not seem to know how best to use him. In between there were days – and nights – of triumph and disappointment. The 1987 tournament, staged in India and Pakistan, was arguably the single most significant cricket competition in the history of the game. It revolutionised the way cricket, and in particular one-day cricket, was perceived on the subcontinent and laid the foundations for a shift in the balance of world cricket power from St John's Wood to Mumbai. Miandad scored a century in the first game against Sri Lanka at Hyderabad (Pakistan) and a valiant 70 as Pakistan lost by 18 runs to Australia in the semi-final at Lahore.

Then there was the glory of victory in Australasia in 1992. Miandad was Imran's trusted lieutenant, the dominant batsman in the competition with absolutely crucial innings both in the semi-final against New Zealand at Auckland and in the final against England at Melbourne. And Miandad also provided the most memorable image of the tournament. It was a typical Miandad moment. It occurred in the game against India at Sydney – the first time the two countries had played each other in a World Cup. Pakistan were chasing, ultimately in vain, a target of 217. Miandad became increasingly irritated by the incessant chatter and exuberant and frequent appealing of the Indian wicketkeeper Kiran More. All of a sudden, in a break between overs, Miandad suddenly leapt up and down and squawked in a remarkable way, clearly mimicking More's distinctive appealing style. You had to be there…

The innings that, in Miandad's own mind, and to many of his countrymen, was genuinely special and set him as a man apart, was played in a one-day match but not in a World Cup. It was played in what to the neutral observer might be regarded as an instantly forgettable competition, the Austral-Asia Cup (who makes up these names?). It was held in April 1986, in Sharjah, in the United Arab Emirates. The final, neatly following the script, was between India and Pakistan, thousands of whose expatriate supporters were there to watch. Pakistan won the match by 1 wicket. It was the manner of the victory that earned Miandad cricketing immortality. Jack Bannister wrote about it in his book on great innings. Bannister, himself a former bookmaker, was highly impressed by the facilities at Sharjah. 'What adds to the atmosphere is the fact that more betting takes place on the Sharjah ground than anywhere else I have seen.'

India, captained by Kapil Dev, made 245 for 7 in their 50 overs. 'An interesting shuffle of the batting order failed,' said Bannister, 'as 6 wickets fell for 29, and, even though Mohammad Azharuddin had then been in Test cricket for only two years, it seems unbelievable that, with quick runs the priority, he did not bat after being relegated behind Chetan Sharman, Ravi Shastri and Chandu Pandit.'

Pakistan got off to a shaky start, losing 3 wickets for 61 ('The Indian supporters must have been counting their rupees.') Miandad and Malik then added 49 but when Malik was run out half the overs had gone. There were useful stands with Abdul Qadir and Imran but, when Imran was out, the initial required rate of 5 an over had risen to 8.

But Miandad was still there. At this stage, he just wanted to salvage some honour. But 51 from 30 balls became 31 from 18 and, for the first time, he began to think that Pakistan could win. Mansoor Elahi was out to the first ball of the forty-eighth over, caught off Sharma ('Indian supporters pressed their international dial numbers like touch typists.').

Wasim Akram came in to join Miandad in a frantic eighth-wicket stand of 20: Miandad reached his century in that Sharma over. Eleven were still needed off the final over. Although he had completely dominated the scoring – his last five partners had scored 15 between them – Miandad had only hit 1 six and 2 fours: his innings had been marked by brilliant running. Now something different was needed. For that reason, as Tony Lewis told Bannister, 'the odds were with Sharma'.

Off the first ball, Wasim was run out going for a second run. Off the second ball Miandad hit a four to mid-on and then got a single. That brought wicketkeeper Zulqarmain to face Sharma. Lewis was sitting with Sharjah's technical director Asif Iqbal – 'he hardly dared to look as Sharma ran in for death or glory'. Zulqarmain was bowled by the fourth ball. Last man Tauseef Ahmed came in. Miandad told him he had to get a single. Tauseef pushed the ball into the covers and they took off. But Tauseef had managed to find the best fielder in the Indian side, Azharuddin. But, as Miandad put it, 'a bizarre thing happened. Azharuddin's throw at the non-striker's end missed its mark. Had Azhar hit, Tauseef would have been out by yards. It was an uncharacteristic miss from Azhar, who wasn't even side-on, but had a straight shot.' One ball to go, 4 runs to win.

Sharma tried for a yorker. Miandad had anticipated that and was standing out of his crease. The ball must have slipped. It arrived as a knee-high full toss on or just outside leg. It finished over the fence behind mid-on. The crowd scenes were astonishing. Miandad could see that many of the spectators were in tears. Bannister could understand it: 'a coup at 5-1 can do that – even to hard-bitten gamblers!' One hundred and sixteen off 114 balls. It was classic Miandad. Clever, opportunistic batting, the vital blow coming when it was needed. Like Colchester in 1981 and Port-of-Spain in 1987/88 it – even though they were in vain – was an object lesson in how to bat one's way to victory, dare one say it, against the odds.

Miandad's century at Edgbaston in 1992 turned out to be his last in Tests, and it had been his first since 1989/90. He was eased out of the captaincy, much against his will, in favour of Wasim Akram after leading the side to victory in a one-off Test in New Zealand in 1992/93. Inevitably – maybe correctly – Miandad suspected that Imran was behind it. He was dropped after a series against Zimbabwe in 1993/94 and he announced his retirement from Test cricket at a press conference soon afterwards.

After he stopped playing, Miandad had several spells coaching Pakistan. His first assignment ended in a controversial resignation just before the 1999 World Cup. He felt he was not getting the best out of the players, and he was particularly concerned about under-performance in a one-day tournament in Sharjah just before that. Wasim Akram, captain for part of the time Miandad was in charge, felt that one problem was that Miandad wanted to do everything. Interestingly, Wasim made the same observation about Bob Woolmer, Pakistan's current coach. His last stint – to date – ended with Pakistan's defeat at home to India in 2003/04.

Mohammad JAVED MIANDAD Khan
Right-hand bat, leg-break & googly
Born: 12 June 1957, Karachi
Major Teams: Pakistan, Karachi, Sind, Habib Bank, Sussex, Glamorgan

TESTS
(1976/77–1993/94)

	M	I	NO	Runs	HS	Ave	100	50	Ct	St
Batting & Fielding	124	189	21	8,832	280★	52.27	23	43	93	1

	Balls	R	W	Ave	BBI	5	10	SR	Econ
Bowling	1,470	682	17	40.11	3/74	0	0	86.47	2.78

ONE-DAY INTERNATIONALS

	M	I	NO	Runs	HS	Ave	SR	100	50	Ct	St
Batting & Fielding	233	218	41	7,381	119★	41.70	66.99	8	50	71	2

	Balls	R	W	Ave	BBI	SR	Econ
Bowling	436	297	7	42.42	2/22	62.28	4.08

FIRST-CLASS
(Career: 1973/74–1993/94)

	M	I	NO	Runs	HS	Ave	100	50	Ct	St
Batting & Fielding	402	632	95	28,663	311	53.37	80	138	341	3

	Balls	R	W	Ave	BBI	5	10	SR	Econ
Bowling	12,690	6,507	191	34.09	7/39	6	0	66.43	3.07

LIST A

	M	I	NO	Runs	HS	Ave	100	50	Ct	St
Batting & Fielding	439	407	79	13,973	152★	42.60	13	101	142	2

	Balls	R	W	Ave	BBI	SR	Econ
Bowling	830	613	18	34.05	3/20	46.11	4.43

MAJID KHAN

Majid Khan's batting oozed class. When he was 'in the zone' he could tear the best attack in the world apart. Of his contemporaries, only the matchless South African Barry Richards, Lawrence Rowe, the unfulfilled genius from Jamaica, and Greg Chappell could make batting look as deceptively simple and as aesthetically pleasing as Majid. With his faded sunhat and off-white pads and his air of nonchalant ease, he looked as if he had strolled out of a sepia-tinted partnership with C.B. Fry or K.S. Ranjitsinhji.

'Strolled' is the word all right. Majid never seemed in much of a hurry – except when it came to his scoring rate. Nor was he fixated with technique. His footwork was positive and decisive when he felt it needed to be, but that was not always the case. Peter Walker, his Glamorgan teammate, told a story, corroborated by Tony Lewis their captain, of a team discussion about technique that Majid concluded by saying, 'You don't need any footwork in batting, just hand and eye.' He then challenged the capable and experienced Glamorgan attack to bowl at him in an unprepared net on a filthy day at Derby, his feet remaining rooted to the spot. Walker said he had never seen such a memorable exhibition of batsmanship.

Blessed with great natural talent, Majid was an imperious stroke-player, driving, hooking, sweeping and cutting with power and style. Honing his skills on uncovered wickets in England at an early age – he had three years at Glamorgan before he went up to Cambridge – he could cope with varied bowling attacks in all sorts of conditions: five of his eight Test centuries were scored outside Pakistan. Dennis Lillee was a great admirer. He has said that he thought Majid was one of the best batsmen he bowled to, because of his elegance and his brilliance when attacking. Majid had some great battles with the famous Australian, scoring 158 in the Melbourne Test of 1972/73. Lillee was intrigued by the sunhat. It was like the proverbial red rag. Majid said he could have it if he ever knocked it off. Four years later, at Adelaide, Lillee managed it. He followed through right to the other end. Majid was as cool as ever. He bent down, picked up the hat and handed it over, 'As promised.'

He was a flexible and unselfish batsman too. He began and finished his international career in the middle order but much of his success as a Test cricketer came

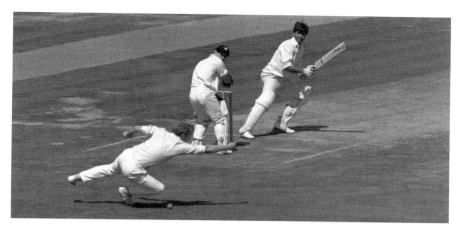

Majid Khan batting in the University match in 1970.

when he opened the innings, usually with the left-hander Sadiq Mohammad. This started in England in 1974: Majid played a magnificent innings of 98 in the Third Test at The Oval. For a while in the mid-1970s Majid could fairly claim to be one of the most successful openers in Test cricket as well as one of the best to watch.

If any season can be cited in support of this claim it must be that of 1976/77. He had just resigned from Glamorgan as captain and player after a deeply depressing final campaign. This may have released something in him because he played with a freedom of expression that he had rarely allowed himself at Test level before. Pakistan began their season with a home series against New Zealand. After a quiet First Test, Majid was in irresistible form. He made 98 in the innings victory at Hyderabad, putting on 164 with Sadiq for the first wicket. Majid was stumped off David O'Sullivan. He did even better in the Third Test at Karachi. He became only the fourth man to score a hundred before lunch on the first day of a Test match, a dazzling assault that demoralised the New Zealand attack. Pakistan made 565 for 9, but the game was drawn. He made a number of useful scores in the series against Australia that followed. He hit the winning runs in the famous victory at Sydney.

But he was seen at his best in the Caribbean a few weeks later when he scored 530 runs in the five Tests. Wasim Raja also made over 500 runs but no other Pakistani batsman averaged more than 31. All struggled against the challenging bouncy pace of Colin Croft (33 wickets at 20.48) and Joel Garner (25 wickets at 27.52). Majid began the tour in prime form, scoring 143 against the Leeward Islands and got the intriguing First Test at Bridgetown off to an entertaining start with a commanding 88. West Indies won the Second Test at Port-of-Spain thanks largely to a devastating spell of fast bowling from Croft (8 for 29) on the first day. Only Majid (47) and Raja (65) offered much resistance. In the second innings Majid (54) put on 123 for the first wicket with Sadiq (81) and Raja again top-scored, with 84, but it was not enough. At Georgetown, Pakistan went into their second innings facing a deficit of 254 and with two days' play left. Majid and Sadiq refused to be bogged down, putting on a brisk 60 before Sadiq had his jaw broken by Andy Roberts. Zaheer Abbas joined Majid and they added 159 in two and a half hours. Majid, who gave one chance at 74, made 167 in six hours with 25 fours. The game was drawn. Pakistan won the Fourth Test, at Port-of-Spain, by 266 runs, thanks in large part to a splendid all-round display from their captain Mushtaq Mohammad, but Majid played with magnificent assurance on the first morning when Sadiq, Zaheer and Haroon Rashid all fell cheaply, making 92 out of 159 for 4 with a six and 14 fours. The West Indies won the decider at Kingston comfortably. Majid scored 11 and 4 and by this time the constant barrage of short-pitched bowling was beginning to pall. He took time off before joining World Series Cricket and his cousin Imran Khan thought that he was not the player he should have been in that intensely competitive environment.

After Packer, he returned to Test cricket for another four years or so, but he never quite touched the heights scaled during that tour of the West Indies. He was very consistent against India in 1978/79 and scored centuries against New Zealand and Australia in the tour that followed. But Rodney Hogg got him for a pair at Perth in the second and last Test of the Australian series. After that it was rather a mixed bag. There were renewed jousts with Lillee. Majid had much the better of it in Pakistan in 1979/80 when he made 89 at Lahore and 110 not out – batting at number seven – at Karachi. Lillee took 3 for 114 in the latter innings, the sum total of his wickets in Pakistan. It was even-stevens in Australia in 1981/82, low scores in the first two Tests being compensated for by 74 at Melbourne, including an unusual, if not unique, all-run seven off Lillee.

Like many of his compatriots, Majid was something of an infant prodigy and his promise as a youngster was such that there was even talk of his touring England in 1962, when his cousin Javed Burki was captain. He made his Test debut in 1964/65 against Australia in Karachi, in the same match as Asif Iqbal. In fact, they opened the bowling together; Majid was a useful pace bowler in those days. Indeed, he dismissed Bill Lawry in both innings of that game. It is doubtful whether Lawry shrieked 'What a ripper!' at the top of his voice, as he has done for a living over the last twenty years or so. It seems more likely that he or the skipper, Bob Simpson, had a quiet word – a word, anyway – in somebody's ear about the legality of Majid's bouncer; so he opted to concentrate on batting and, now and again, essentially harmless off-spin.

He appeared in that first Test match as Majid Jahangir and occasionally afterwards as Majid Jahangir Khan. His father had been a famous cricketer before him. Jahangir Khan appeared in India's first Test against England at Lord's in 1932, in the second innings dismissing Hobbs, Woolley, Hammond and Paynter – as distinguished a quartet as one can imagine. He also played in the three Tests in 1936, in between representing Cambridge University. In a game against the MCC at Lord's in 1936 a dead sparrow was found by the stumps at the striker's end while he was bowling; the bird was stuffed and put in a glass case in the Memorial Gallery and Jahangir Khan has been immortalised as the man who bowled the ball that killed a sparrow, though nobody involved could actually recall ball hitting bird.

Majid followed in his father's footsteps – not as an accidental if clinical threat to bird life but as a Cambridge blue. Indeed, he was one of Cambridge's most successful batsmen and captains. In 1971, with Dudley Owen-Thomas to help him score runs and Mike Selvey, Phil Edmonds and John Spencer to take wickets, Majid led Cambridge to three victories in their ten first-class matches. One of those victories came, oddly enough, against the Pakistan tourists; Majid made 94. He played in the first two Tests against England that summer but missed the third because he was captaining Cambridge in the Varsity match. Nobody thought this at all unusual or absurd. In fact, there was a lot more press comment eleven years later when Derek Pringle, then captain of Cambridge, opted to play for England against India rather than appear in the Varsity match.

Majid's Test career, although quite advanced in terms of years, had still not really got going in 1971. By the end of that series, he had scored just under 400 Test runs at an average of 24 with two half-centuries. Yet he was recognised as being a rare talent. He had made some prodigious scores at home: he had scored an unbeaten double century for Punjab University against Karachi after his side had been 5 for 4. But his wider reputation had been made in England – or rather, Wales.

Majid had toured England in 1967 and played in all three Tests, making 38 runs in six attempts. But he was the leading run-scorer on the tour, making almost a thousand runs in fourteen matches, and against Glamorgan at Swansea in August he played one of the innings of the season. In Pakistan's second innings Majid scored 147 in eighty-nine minutes, with 13 sixes – then a record for a match in Britain – with 5 coming in an over from off-spinner Roger Davis, all in an arc between the sight-screen and midwicket. He reached his century in sixty-one minutes. Glamorgan lost no time in signing him. It did no harm that Jahangir Khan had been a contemporary at Cambridge of Glamorgan's domineering and energetic secretary, Wilf Wooller. The next three years saw heady days for the county and their overseas star. In 1968 they came third in the Championship – rising from fourteenth. Majid took a while to find his touch but gave some dazzling displays in the second half of the summer. On a rain-affected pitch at Neath, Surrey won the toss and were bowled out for 86. When Majid went in, Glamorgan were 9 for 3 but he made 85 in two hours with 13 fours, and his fourth-wicket partnership of 133 with Walker effectively settled the match.

The following year Glamorgan won the Championship for the first time since 1948. Majid added a touch of individual brilliance to what was essentially a team effort. His slip fielding was a factor too. Glamorgan went into the final match, against Worcestershire at Cardiff, knowing that if they won the game the title was theirs. Majid's innings of 156 out of 214 scored while he was in was the decisive innings of the match. He reached his hundred before lunch and batted for three hours twenty minutes. Alan Jones made 37, Walker 27, Eifion Jones 16: nobody else got into double figures. Glamorgan won by 147 runs. The innings ensured his heroic status among Welsh cricket lovers. He had also scored a hundred before lunch – on the third day – against the West Indian tourists at Swansea, making 147 with 5 sixes and 19 fours.

Glamorgan were runners-up in 1970. Majid made 1,800 runs in the season: over a thousand of these were for Cambridge, for whom he scored a double century in the Varsity match. In 1972 Majid was the leading run-scorer in the country, with over 2,000 runs. Cambridge was an important stage in Majid's life, as a person and as a cricketer, and his captaincy of the university must have played a part in his rather surprising appointment as captain of Pakistan against Lewis's England side in 1972/73. He had had a successful tour of Australia and New Zealand, scoring centuries at Melbourne and Auckland, but there were times, particularly in the Test at Sydney, when his casual approach to fielding hardly suggested that he had leadership potential.

The England series did little to alter that impression. All three games were high-scoring draws. In each of them to some degree there was a feeling that Pakistan had an advantage that could have been exploited with more adventurous and dynamic captaincy. Curiously, in the Third Test, at Karachi, Majid, Mushtaq and Dennis Amiss each scored 99. In Pakistan's next Test series, also against England, in 1974, Majid was back in the ranks but opening the batting. He captained Pakistan in one more game the following year. It was the World Cup game against the West Indies at Edgbaston, which was one of the most memorable one-day games of the decade although Pakistan, and perhaps their stand-in captain above all, would probably like to erase it. Majid batted with sumptuous authority to help Pakistan to a very good total of 266 for 7. Sarfraz Nawaz reduced the West Indies to 36 for 3. When last man Andy Roberts joined Deryck Murray in the forty-sixth over the score was 209 (these matches were 60 overs then). Famously the West Indies won – and went on to win the tournament. Majid's sums went wrong somewhere: the last over, off which the West Indies needed 5 to win, had to be bowled by Wasim Raja – hardly a front-line bowler, and it was his third over of the tournament.

His stewardship of Glamorgan was not a great success either. He took over from Lewis in 1974 when the county rose from thirteenth to eleventh in the Championship. They were ninth in 1975 but bottom the next year, Majid's last.

Despite his success at Cambridge, Majid was probably too detached and enigmatic a figure to be a consistently successful captain at a higher level. He stares out of team photographs of the 1970s with an air of studied indifference, as though he has been

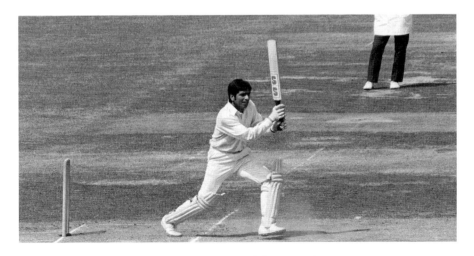

Majid Khan batting for Glamorgan against Middlesex in 1975.

dragged there, forced to abandon something more interesting. But he was always a dignified and cordial figure and, in difficult times in the 1990s, he was a safe pair of hands at the helm of the Pakistan Cricket Board and as a tour manager.

Majid's final tour of England in 1982 was a profound disappointment. It was, perhaps, a mistake to go. He struggled against the counties and, although he was in the twelve for the First Test, Imran left him out on the morning of the match. Relations were permanently soured. He played in the Third Test at Headingley, batting at number six and scoring 21 and 16. For a brief moment, though, the metaphorical clouds parted and the sun broke through. It was a short ball from Bob Willis on the off stump; Majid pulled it, hardly seeming to move his feet. A swivel of the hips, a turn of the wrists. Minimal effort brought maximum velocity, as the ball flew past square leg to the boundary.

Sheer class.

MAJID Jahangir KHAN
Right-hand bat, right-arm fast medium-pace/off-break
Born: 28 September 1946, Ludhiana, India
Major Teams: Pakistan, Lahore, Universities, Pakistan International Airlines, Punjab, Rawalpindi, Glamorgan, Cambridge University, Queensland
Also known as Majid Jahangir

TESTS
(1964/65-1982/83)

	M	I	NO	Runs	HS	Ave	100	50	Ct
Batting & Fielding	63	106	5	3,931	167	38.92	8	19	70

	Balls	R	W	Ave	BBI	SR	Econ
Bowling	3,584	1,456	27	53.92	4/45	132.74	2.43

ONE-DAY INTERNATIONALS

	M	I	NO	Runs	HS	Ave	SR	100	50	Ct
Batting & Fielding	23	22	1	786	109	37.42	74.71	1	7	3

	Balls	R	W	Ave	BBI	SR	Econ
Bowling	658	374	13	28.76	3/27	50.61	3.41

FIRST-CLASS
(Career: 1961/62-1984/85)

	M	I	NO	Runs	HS	Ave	100	50	Ct
Batting & Fielding	410	700	62	27,444	241	43.01	73	128	410

	Balls	R	W	Ave	BBI	5	10
Bowling	410	7168	223	32.14	6/67	4	0

LIST A

	M	I	NO	Runs	HS	Ave	100	50	Ct
Batting & Fielding	168	166	9	4,441	115	28.28	2	31	43

	Balls	R	W	Ave	BBI	5	SR	Econ
Bowling	2,817	1,610	71	22.67	5/24	1	39.67	3.42

MOHAMMAD YOUSUF

Mohammad Yousuf is the Tom Graveney of Pakistan. A batsman of considerable natural talent and a sublime gift of timing, he looks, when in form, as good as any player in the world. Yet home supporters have been as much infuriated as enchanted by his performances over the years. He has often flattered to deceive with bewitching cameos when a serious-minded century was called for. Opinion has been divided about Yousuf. Some have said that he, with Inzamam-ul-Haq, is the bedrock of the Pakistan batting line-up. He has compiled a statistical record that many would envy, a genuine class act. Others, though, have said he is a dilettante who rarely succeeds when the pressure is on.

For a long time it was the same with Graveney. Nobody doubted his talent: he was an England player at an early age. But did he really have that extra something that marked out the great player from the rest? Len Hutton, captain of England at their best in the mid-1950s, was never convinced. After Graveney's third unsuccessful tour of Australia, in 1962/63, most people who mattered seemed to agree. Even Alan Ross, who seemed a natural supporter of a player of Graveney's lustre as a batsman, had expressed doubts back in 1954/55 when Graveney made his first tour Down Under. 'What good net batsmen these players are!' wrote Ross about Graveney and Reg Simpson, the two underachievers of that tour. In 1964, Graveney became the first entirely post-war player to make a hundred first-class centuries. Neville Cardus, in his generous tribute in *Wisden*, was prepared to excuse Graveney's disappointing Test career as an irrelevance in the context of his prowess as an exponent of style and the grand manner in an age of mean and mechanical batsmanship. His Test career seemed over: he was content to help his new county, Worcestershire, win more championships.

But his Test career was not over. In 1966, at the age of thirty-nine, he was summoned for the umpteenth time in a genuine crisis after England's calamitous defeat in the First Test against Gary Sobers' West Indians and was not found wanting. In his maturity, Graveney at last fulfilled his destiny as not just England's most glorious strokemaker but one of her heaviest run-scorers too. Twilight became a glowing sunset in the last three years of Graveney's Test career.

One cannot take this analogy too far. Yousuf has been an ever-present in the Pakistan side, except when injured, pretty well since he first played in 1998. Nor is it likely that he will make a century of centuries. Currently he has twenty, sixteen of those were made in Tests. Yousuf is very much a twenty-first-century cricketer. There is simply no time or space for non-international cricket. His figures would look different if he had played in English cricket but, unusually for such a notable player, he has not. There was talk of his playing for Derbyshire in 2006 but some arcane qualification rule barred him from doing so. It might surprise some people that there are rules that prevent overseas cricketers from playing in county cricket. In the old days, it was very unusual for an overseas player to represent more than one county in his career. Now, with short-term engagements, it is all very different. Shoaib Akhtar seems to be trying to break some sort of record for the number of counties he has signed up for, although he rarely actually plays. It is surely only a matter of time before an overseas player is allowed to play for two counties in the same season, if not the same match.

There is another curious thing about Yousuf's record. In all his professional career, whether in Test, first-class or one-day cricket, he has bowled only 32 balls. Most wicketkeepers manage more than that in a couple of seasons. It is not worth doing the research but it is hard to believe that any non-wicketkeeper in the history of the game has bowled less.

But I digress. There has been a feeling that too many of Yousuf's big innings were agreeable but slightly pointless. At the beginning of his career he was patient and circumspect. His first hundred, in 1998/99, against a not bad Zimbabwe side, who had won the First Test at Peshawar, was a five-hour affair that gave much-needed substance to Pakistan's innings. It was his eighth score of 50 or more in eleven innings in Test or one-day matches against Zimbabwe. He scored two fluent hundreds in the Caribbean in 1999/2000. At Bridgetown in the Second Test, Moin Khan won the toss and batted but saw his side reduced to 37 for 5 by Courtney Walsh. Yousuf rescued them with 115 out of a total of 253. The match was drawn. West Indies won the third and decisive Test at St John's after another first-day hundred from Yousuf. He continued to make polished runs in large quantities but they did not often lead to victory for Pakistan. He tucked into England's bowling when they toured Pakistan in 2000/01. At Lahore, he made 124 having been 37 not out at the fall of the eighth wicket: he batted for over six hours. At Faisalabad, he top-scored in the first innings with 77. At Karachi, he put on a magnificent display with Inzamam as they added 259 for the fourth wicket on the first day and seemed to have batted England out of the game. Yousuf's 117 occupied 311 minutes and he hit 14 fours and a six. The games at Lahore and Faisalabad were drawn. England won at Karachi; it was Pakistan's first defeat there. He scored solidly when Pakistan routed the West Indies in Sharjah in 2001/02. In 2003/04, he played a decisive role in the Second Test against New Zealand at Wellington, which Pakistan won to take the series 1-0, top scoring in both innings with 60 and 88 not out.

More typical, however, was in the Boxing Day Test at Melbourne in the 2004/05 series. Pakistan had been massacred in the First Test at Perth, losing by 491 runs. The captain, Inzamam, retired with a bad back and to lick his wounds. Yousuf, the official

Mohammad Yousuf shows his style during the Faisalabad Test against India at
Faisalabad, 2006.

vice-captain, took over in Melbourne. Pakistan lost again – they lost 3-0 in the end – but Yousuf led from the front, scoring a brilliant hundred on the first day. Salman Butt had got Pakistan off to a great start but they had lost 3 wickets for 9 runs when Yousuf was joined by Younis Khan with the score on 94. In 46 overs they put on 192, a fourth-wicket record for Pakistan against Australia. Yousuf's 113 occupied a mere 134 balls: three times he lofted balls from Shane Warne into the crowd. But it was another beautiful hundred in a losing cause, like the one at Multan a few months earlier, when Yousuf had made 112 in the second innings and India had won by an innings and 57 runs.

Yousuf and Younis seem locked together as partners and rivals. They are very different types of player. Yousuf is the aesthete, driving with a silky flourish but more than happy to clobber the ball when the opportunity arises. He likes to deal in boundaries. Younis is more of an artisan. He has to work harder for his runs. In the early days, he would sometimes lose patience and concentration. Now he seems to have put foolish things behind him. It will be interesting to see who emerges as the stronger player. Younis may be hungrier but his record against bowlers of genuine pace is patchier than Yousuf's.

By the time of Pakistan's next engagement after Australia, the tour of India in March 2005, Younis, younger by more than three years, had replaced Yousuf as vice-captain. Both got hundreds in the Second Test at Kolkata, which India won with Rahul Dravid making twin centuries and Anil Kumble taking 7 for 63 in Pakistan's second innings. But Younis went one better in the next Test at Bangalore, where Pakistan squared the series. He made a massive 267, and 84 not out; Inzamam made 184 and 31 not out. Yousuf got 37. When the series against England started in November 2005 it seemed to be the same old story. In the First Test at Multan, Yousuf made 5 and 16. No batsman can succeed all the time. Yousuf has maintained a Test average in the high forties – at least – throughout his career; and is clearly a quality player. But there was something about that 16 that got his critics' teeth grinding. Butt and Inzamam had worked hard to keep Pakistan in the game after England had taken a substantial first-innings lead. When Andrew Flintoff demolished the middle order with the second new ball, that hard work looked in danger of being wasted. Yousuf's brief and breezy innings, which included three boundaries, seemed willfully out of keeping with the context of the match. It reminded some of his bizarre second innings against South Africa at Cape Town in 2002/03. On the third afternoon Pakistan were following on 378 behind. Yousuf went in at 130 for 3 and opener Taufeeq Umar, who had played a lone hand in the first innings to make 135 out of 252, fell at the same score for 67. Yousuf proceeded to smash 50 off 27 balls – now the third-fastest fifty in Tests in terms of balls faced – with 6 fours and 2 sixes. 'I will not speak of that,' said Taufeeq after the match. 'I have no comment.' South Africa's margin of victory was an innings and 142 runs.

But at Multan, in November 2005, Pakistan did not lose. They won, or rather England lost. It was the first time in six series that Pakistan had taken the lead in the opening Test of a series and they were determined not to concede it. Inzamam won the toss and batted in the Second Test at Faisalabad and this time Yousuf played his

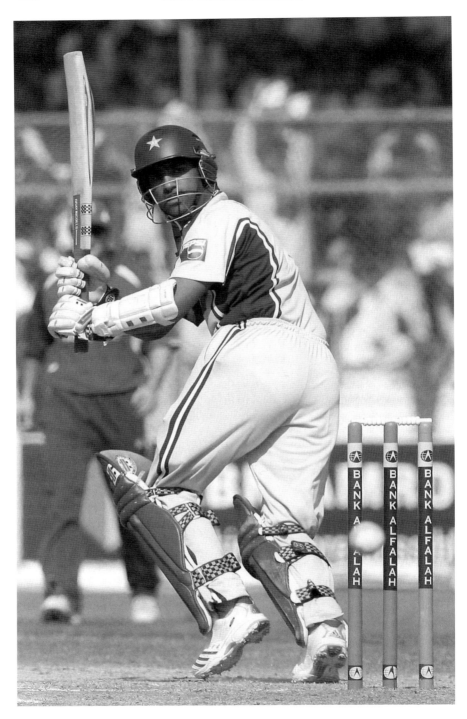

Mohammad Yousuf batting against England in the one-day international at Karachi,
December 2005.

part properly. Inzamam joined him at 73 for 3 and together they wore the England attack down, adding 128 for the fourth wicket. Yousuf's 78 took over three hours. He was out to a rather dubious caught and bowled by Ian Bell. That magnificent game at Faisalabad, illuminated by Inzamam's two centuries, ended in a draw and the teams moved on to Lahore with the series still in the balance. England batted into the second day to make a below-par 288. Matthew Hoggard struck two early blows and this time it was 68 for 3 when Inzamam joined Yousuf. Inzamam retired hurt at 148 and Hasan Raza did not last long. At the close of play Pakistan were 185 for 4 with Yousuf on 84. Nightwatchman Shoaib Akhtar kept him company while a further 62 were added on the third morning and then Yousuf and Kamran Akmal embarked on a stand that finally broke the back of England's determined and talented attack. By the close of the third day, Pakistan were 446 for 5 and when Yousuf was finally out for 223 the score was 516. They had added 269, a Pakistan record for the sixth wicket. Inzamam then returned and bludgeoned the bowlers into total submission. Pakistan won by an innings and 100 runs. Man of the Match Yousuf batted for over ten hours, hitting 2 sixes and 26 fours. It was his third Test double-century. The first had come in a forgettable draw against New Zealand at Christchurch in 2000/01. The second was against Bangladesh at Chittagong in 2001/02: enough said. The Lahore innings was an altogether more meritorious performance. It came against an attack that, despite the difficult conditions, never gave up. Just as importantly, it was an innings that mattered.

He carried that form into the one-day series, making three fifties in the five matches, and then into the run-fest against India. Most of the top batsmen gorged themselves but Yousuf and Younis were perhaps the most self-indulgent. Each of them made hundreds at Lahore and Faisalabad and each, rather implausibly, was a victim of Irfan Pathan's first-over hat-trick at Karachi. Yousuf top-scored with 97 in the second innings, helping build a platform from which Pakistan stormed to victory in the only game of the series to produce a positive result. By the end of the campaign Yousuf was comfortably in the top ten of both the Test and one-day rankings.

That double century at Lahore had been his third in Tests, as noted. But it was his first as Mohammad Yousuf. He played his first 59 Tests as Yousuf Youhana, one of only four Christians to have played for Pakistan. The others were the Anglo-Pakistani Duncan Sharpe, the talented middle-order batsman Wallis Mathias and the pace bowler Antao D'Souza. It is probably not far-fetched to predict that Yousuf was the last. He announced his conversion to Islam – hence the name change – at the start of the England series. It is not known exactly when the conversion took place but it is known that it is a very sensitive matter within his family. The Pakistan Cricket Board felt constrained to issue a statement to the effect that it was an entirely personal matter and that no pressure whatsoever had been put on Yousuf to persuade him to convert. Whereas previously he had celebrated a landmark like a century by crossing himself, at Lahore he prostrated himself on the pitch in the Islamic manner. His conversion will deprive reporters of the odd extra line about him – 'Pakistan's first Christian captain' and the like. His career has been headline-free apart from his actual playing. Waqar Younis sent him home from a tour of Sri Lanka for not practicing hard enough. He was involved in a nasty incident with the belligerent South African Andrew Hall in a one-day international at Lahore in October 2003. Hall appeared to obstruct Yousuf when taking a single – Yousuf raised his bat and the umpires had to intervene. The match referee's inquiry resulted in much heavier penalties being imposed on Hall and the South African captain Graeme Smith – inevitably involved too – than on Yousuf.

Otherwise the stories have all been about polished and easeful runs. With Inzamam and Younis, he makes up an exceptionally talented and commanding middle order. It may well be that Yousuf has passed through some invisible barrier, much as Graveney appeared to do in that 1966 series, and finally established himself as a Test batsman of the highest rank. Yousuf has yet to do himself justice in a World Cup. 2007 could be his year.

MOHAMMAD YOUSUF
Right-hand bat
Born: 27 August 1974
Major Teams: Lahore, Pakistan, Bahawalpur, Lahore, Pakistan International Airlines
Also known as Yousuf Youhana

TESTS
(1997/98-2006)

	M	I	NO	Runs	HS	Ave	100	50	Ct
Batting & Fielding	66	110	9	5,106	223	50.55	16	25	57

	Balls	R	W	Econ
Bowling	6	3	0	3.00

ONE-DAY INTERNATIONALS

	M	I	NO	Runs	HS	Ave	100	50	Ct
Batting & Fielding	213	203	28	7,126	141★	41.00	11	48	48

	Balls	R	W
Bowling	1	1	0

FIRST-CLASS
(Career: 1996/97-2006)

	M	I	NO	Runs	HS	Ave	100	50	Ct
Batting & Fielding	104	170	15	7,342	223	47.36	20	40	73

	Balls	R	W
Bowling	18	24	0

LIST A

	M	I	NO	Runs	HS	Ave	100	50	Ct
Batting & Fielding	242	230	33	7,774	141★	39.46	11	51	57

	Balls	R	W	Ave
Bowling	7	13	0	–

MUDASSAR NAZAR

Could they do it? Surely there would never be a better chance.

Pakistan had not beaten England in a Test match in England since The Oval in 1954, nearly thirty years before. But at Lord's in 1982, Imran Khan's side had an opportunity. Pakistan, winning the toss, scored 428, the opener Mohsin Khan stroking a magnificent double century. England were all out for 227 and had to follow on. Pakistan's varied and challenging attack shared the wickets: 4 for the imponderable legspin of Abdul Qadir, 3 for the fast-medium swing bowler Sarfraz Nawaz, 2 – acting captain David Gower and last man Robin Jackman, to secure the follow-on – for Imran himself, and 1 for pace bowler Tahir Naqqash.

Jackman had been dismissed in the first over on the Sunday morning and makeshift openers Derek Randall and Chris Tavare came out to start England's second innings. Sarfraz opened the bowling with Imran but limped off with a strain. Tahir was also incapacitated so Imran's options were limited. He turned to his trusted opening bats-man, Mudassar Nazar: current Test bowling record 11 wickets at 43 apiece. But he was not a complete novice with the ball. It was classic dibbly-dobbly stuff really, but Dennis Lillee no less had taught him how to bowl the leg-cutter and Mudassar was a crafty and intelligent cricketer, varying his line of attack cleverly. Anyway, to cut a short story shorter, within a few minutes England were 9 for 3. Randall went almost immediately, bowled for 9. Within the space of ten balls Mudassar had also had Allan Lamb leg before and Gower caught behind, both for ducks. Rain came to England's rescue temporarily, wiping out the afternoon session. Then Tavare and Ian Botham rebuilt the innings and England closed the day at 95 for 3.

Tavare was positively – or rather negatively – Tavaresque: even Botham, because of the situation, was relatively subdued. Botham was the first to go on the Monday, caught in the deep by Sarfraz off Mudassar for 69. Mudassar quickly removed Mike Gatting and Ian Greig too. Imran ended Tavare's 406-minute vigil (82) and Qadir did the rest. Mudassar, who swung the old ball prodigiously, took 6 for 32 in 19 overs. The sub-editors were quick to dub him 'The Man with the Golden Arm'. More importantly, Pakistan won by 10 wickets.

It was far from being a one-off for the cheerful and popular Mudassar. He picked up quite a few wickets in the one-day games against Australia and the West Indies in Australia in 1981/82. In the First Test against New Zealand at Lahore in 1984/85, he took the new ball and bowled 11 overs, taking 3 for 8. But his day job, as it were, was at the top of the order. In that capacity he gave diligent service as an opening batsman, predominantly in the company of Mohsin to begin with and subsequently Rameez Raja. Always an agreeable character, Mudassar was utterly professional and committed in everything he did. He played for many years for the English minor county Cheshire, and there cannot have been many more popular overseas players in that competition.

The phrase 'he played within his limitations' could almost have been coined with Mudassar's batting in mind. He had no little skill but it was of a particular and distinctive type, not remotely flashy. He hardly ever drove the ball in front of square, getting his runs by nudges and deflections and horizontal bat shots. He was a very good hooker. He was also very much an apple-crumble cricketer: always better at home. The low, slow bounce of doctored wickets in Pakistan suited him perfectly. In Pakistan, he averaged a rudely healthy 53.63, making eight centuries. Away, it was a humble 26.53, with two centuries, and one of those was in India, against whose suffering bowlers he scored six hundreds altogether.

As a fledgling opener in the 1970s, Mudassar seemed to operate on the principle that if you hung around for long enough – and with his technique on a dead track, that was not a problem – the runs would come. He took the formula to its logical conclusion as early as his third Test innings, against England at Lahore in 1977/78, when he made the slowest-ever century in Test cricket. He reached his hundred, which contained 9 boundaries, in nine hours seventeen minutes. The 50,000 spectators seem to have enjoyed it, because the match was interrupted by a small riot when some of them invaded the pitch to celebrate his hundred – although he was only on 99 at the time. Once order was restored Mudassar got the necessary single and then, apparently infected by the air of popular revelry, hit three more fours before being dismissed for 114, made in nine minutes under ten hours. If Mudassar cared about such things, he might have begun to worry whether his hard-fought-for record was going to be one of the shortest-lived in cricket history. For his counterpart as England's opening batsman was one G. Boycott, who got the bit between his teeth as England began their reply to Pakistan's 407 for 9. It was by now the third afternoon of the match. Despite the distraction of another more serious riot – prompted by the presence at the ground of the wife of imprisoned former Prime Minister Zulfiqar Ali Bhutto and their daughter Benazir, rather than excitement in the face of the Yorkshireman's classical forward defensive – Boycott proceeded to a half-century that was actually slower than Mudassar's. He was then bowled by an absolute beauty from Iqbal Qasim. Mudassar hit fifties in each of the remaining Tests and, although his batting did not compare with the attractive strokeplay of Haroon Rashid and Javed Miandad, he had established himself in the sheet-anchor role.

Mudassar's most successful series was against India in 1982/83. At Karachi, in the Second Test, batting at number six, he made 119, putting on 313 for the fifth wicket with Zaheer Abbas. He finished with a smorgasbord of uninhibited run-gluttony. He made

Mudassar Nazar batting against England in the First Test at Lord's, 1978.

231 in the Fourth Test at Hyderabad, putting on 451 for the third wicket with Miandad and equalling the Test partnership record for any wicket. He carried his bat for 152 not out out of 323 in the next Test, the Fifth, at Lahore and in the final Test made another 152. He finished with an aggregate of 761 runs at an average of 126.83. When Mudassar carried his bat at Lahore, he became only the second Pakistani to do so. The first, remarkably, had been his father, Nazar Mohammad, who made 124 not out out of 331 in Pakistan's first Test win, an innings victory over India at Lucknow in 1952/53. He batted for eight hours thirty-five minutes, so perhaps one should call Mudassar a chip off the old blocker (sorry). That was his only Test series: he suffered a serious injury and retired in 1953. He opened in all five Tests against India with Hanif Mohammad and another curious double occurred when, on more than one occasion in the mid and late 1980s, their sons, Mudassar and Shoaib, opened together for Pakistan. By yet further coincidence, Nazar was national coach when Mudassar made that slowest-ever Test century.

Mudassar's one Test century outside the subcontinent was in England. England was very much a second home – his wife is English – so that is not surprising. In 1982, he did little with the bat in the Tests: he got a pair at Edgbaston, the victim of a dubious leg-before decision and that seemed to affect his confidence. But he averaged over 80 on the tour as a whole, making four centuries, including 211 not out against Sussex. The century came on the next tour, in 1987, at Edgbaston. Pakistan were 1-0 up in the five-match series. This was the Fourth Test and England had to have a go at winning it. Mike Gatting put Pakistan in but at the end of the first day they were 250 for 3, Mudassar 101 not out. He eventually made 124; as David Lemmon rightly said, there was never a dull moment in his innings of nearly seven hours at the crease.

More than any other game cricket exposes character and personality: Mudassar had both in abundance.

His final Test century was also against England, at Lahore in 1987/88. It was a series racked with acrimony and mistrust but, as Scyld Berry in his superb account of the series noted, the senior Pakistani batsmen, Mudassar, Rameez and Saleem Malik, always maintained cordial relations with the visitors and did their best to try to ensure that everybody kept things in perspective. The Lahore Test was a nightmare for England, Abdul Qadir and Shakeel Khan (the latter being an umpire) combining to seal their fate. England made 175 in their first innings, and Mudassar and Miandad took Pakistan well past that with their second-wicket stand of 142. Mudassar batted for 252 minutes and hit 18 fours.

He fell to Neil Foster with the second new ball. He did something not many batsmen do. He had moved back and across to a short one and was struck on the pad. As the Englishmen appealed Mudassar looked up, saw Shakeel Khan about to shake his head, grinned, and walked off. Leg before wicket Foster, 124.

MUDASSAR NAZAR
Right-hand bat, right-arm medium-pace
Born: 6 April 1956, Lahore
Major Teams: Pakistan, Lahore, Punjab, Universities, Habib Bank, Pakistan International Airlines, United Bank

TESTS
(1976/77–1988/89)

	M	I	NO	Runs	HS	Ave	100	50	Ct
Batting & Fielding	76	116	8	4,114	231	38.09	10	17	48

	Balls	R	W	Ave	BBI	5	10	SR	Econ
Bowling	5,967	2,532	66	38.36	6/32	1	0	90.40	2.54

ONE-DAY INTERNATIONALS

	M	I	NO	Runs	HS	Ave	SR	100	50	Ct
Batting & Fielding	122	115	10	2,653	95	25.26	51.71	0	16	21

	Balls	R	W	Ave	BBI	5	SR	Econ
Bowling	4,855	3,432	111	30.91	5/28	1	43.73	4.24

FIRST-CLASS
(Career: 1971/72–1993)

	M	I	NO	Runs	HS	Ave	100	50	Ct
Batting & Fielding	220	355	34	14,080	241	43.86	42	59	143

	Balls	R	W	Ave	BBI	5	10	SR	Econ
Bowling	12,465	5,281	153	34.51	6/32	2	0	81.47	2.54

LIST A

	M	I	NO	Runs	HS	Ave	100	50	Ct
Batting & Fielding	181	172	16	4,437	122*	28.44	2	26	42

	Balls	R	W	Ave	BBI	5	SR	Econ
Bowling	6,792	4,628	149	31.06	5/28	1	45.58	4.08

MUSHTAQ AHMED

Mushtaq Ahmed is a survivor. For the best part of twenty years he has whirled and twirled away around the cricketing world, deceiving the very best batsmen with his leg-breaks and googlies. Most unusually, he has forged for himself two quite separate cricketing careers. First, he was one of three outstanding leg-spinners operating simultaneously in Test cricket; an almost unprecedented cornucopia. Together with Shane Warne and Anil Kumble he was a genuine match-winner at the highest level. Gradually though he was eased out of the national side and disappeared from view. But he resurfaced with Sussex in the county championship in 2003. In that first season his brilliant bowling was crucial in the county winning the Championship for the first time ever. While Sussex have not been able to repeat that wonderful achievement, Mushtaq has continued to shine, being the leading wicket-taker in the English season again in 2004 and 2005, emulating Hampshire's Derek Shackleton back in the 1960s in achieving that in three successive seasons.

The England team that toured Pakistan in 1987/88 had already had an overdose of leg-spin by the time they went to Sahiwal – Mushtaq's birthplace – to play the Punjab Chief Minister's XI. Dr Evil – in the form of the masterly Abdul Qadir – had lured them to destruction in the First Test at Lahore. If that wasn't bad enough, they now had to deal with Mini-Me at Sahiwal. Shorter, chubbier but in terms of style very similar with that same curious bouncy run up, the seventeen-year-old Mushtaq produced some surprises of his own for the shell-shocked England XI batsmen. In the first innings, they made 279 and he took 6 for 81 including a spell of 5 for 28 in 75 balls. A heel injury suffered by Qadir at Lahore meant there was a possibility of Mushtaq replacing him at Faisalabad. In fact, Qadir recovered in time.

The run-up was shorter than Qadir's, three or four paces, but Mushtaq had clearly modelled himself on the master, as one would expect. He eventually developed a leg-break that was much harder spun than Kumble's and a googly that was much harder to spot than Warne's. He bowled a classic spell of leg-spin on the final day of the Lord's Test in 1996. England had to bat out the day to secure a draw and, after the loss of Nick Knight on the fourth evening, Mike Atherton and Alec Stewart seemed to be taking

Mushtaq Ahmed bowling for
Sussex against Surrey, 2004.

them to safety. Mushtaq had not caused many problems in England's first innings, largely because he was concentrating his line on and outside the leg stump and, without a really big-spinning leg-break like Warne, it was easy to defend. But in the second innings, all of a sudden, he changed his line to off stump and started giving the ball more air. It was at once obvious that Stewart, in particular, was having problems reading him and spotting the googly. After lunch, he switched to round the wicket and started pitching in the rough outside the right-hander's leg stump and the breakthrough came. Atherton was caught at slip off a leg-break and Stewart was caught off the glove. A collapse followed, with 7 wickets falling in 75 balls for just 18 runs. Mushtaq seemed rather lucky to get Graham Thorpe leg before – it was one of those afternoons when there was a lot of appealing – but he bowled Mark Ealham round his legs with a beauty. Mushtaq took 5 for 57 in 38 overs as England subsided to a 164-run defeat. At The Oval in the Third Test, England found themselves in a similar position and again the middle order and the tail were found wanting. This time Mushtaq took 6 for 78 and was Man of the Match. In the series, he took more wickets than anyone else, 17, at a lower average, 26.29.

He was in a purple patch. In November 1995, Pakistan had played three Test matches in Australia, losing the first two Tests heavily but winning the Third, at Sydney by 74 runs. Mushtaq was omitted for the First Test at Brisbane but at Hobart in the Second Test he took 5 for 115 and 4 for 83, and he was Man of the Match at Sydney with 5 for 95 and 4 for 91. Then the Pakistanis went to New Zealand and Mushtaq picked up another match award in the one-off Test at Christchurch, which Pakistan won by 161 runs. Mushtaq took 10 wickets in the match, including 7 for 56 in the second innings. In all three series 'Mushy' worked his magic with a smile on his face and he was always a popular figure.

Back home in Pakistan for the 1996/97 season, his fine form continued. He took 18 wickets in the two Test series against New Zealand, 10 for 143 in the defeat at Lahore, and 8 (6 for 87 in the first innings) in the victory at Rawalpindi. He bowled well in Sri Lanka in 1996/97 but for the first time the off-spinner Saqlain Mushtaq was the leading slow bowler. Mushtaq was back to his best when South Africa played their first Test series in Pakistan in 1997/98. South Africa won the series 1-0 thanks to a victory at Faisalabad, the hero of which, with bat and ball, was the off-spinner Pat Symcox. Mushtaq took 7 wickets in that match and had the unusual and frustrating experience in South Africa's first innings of beating Symcox with a googly that passed between off and middle stumps. Symcox, batting at number nine, made 81 off 94 balls.

Two more match-winning performances followed within a couple of months. A lumbering West Indian batting line-up capitulated to an ignominious defeat by an innings and 19 runs at Peshawar; Mushtaq took 5 for 35 and 5 for 71. Then, in the return series against South Africa, he took 3 for 71 and 6 for 78 in the victory at Durban, Pakistan's first in Tests against South Africa.

After that the pickings, unlike Mushtaq, got slimmer. He was mentioned non-incriminatingly in the wrong sort of dispatches, the Qayyum inquiry report into match-fixing, and he gradually faded from the scene, although he did make a brief return in the home series against South Africa in 2003/04.

He had made his Test debut in Australia back in 1989/90. He played in one Test after Qadir returned home early. He had been selected for the tour of New Zealand a year earlier, but Imran Khan, appointed to lead the side at the last moment in place of Javed Miandad, insisted on Qadir's selection. At this time Mushtaq was bowling almost exclusively googlies and top-spinners and the Australians played him as an off-spinner. He was rather unexpectedly one of the stars of the World Cup in Australia and New Zealand early in 1992. He took 16 wickets, 3 of them in the final against England at Melbourne, including Graeme Hick, classically deceived and bowled by a googly. He had a highly successful tour of England in 1992, picking up 66 first-class wickets including Mark Nicholas twice in the match against Hampshire. In the Test series, which Pakistan won 2-1, his guile and spin were, as in 1996, the perfect accessories to the speed and swing of Wasim Akram and Waqar Younis. He played a vital part in the victory at Lord's, dismissing Hick, Robin Smith and Allan Lamb in 22 deliveries in England's second innings.

Somerset signed him for 1993 and he did not disappoint, reveling in English county batsmen's traditional incompetence against high-class leg-spin. Only Steve Watkin of Glamorgan took more than his 85 first-class wickets at 20.85: on eight occasions he took 5 or more in an innings. He had a great match against Sussex at Taunton at the beginning of July, making an energetic 90 in Somerset's first innings and then taking 12 for 175 despite suffering a blow to his bowling hand. In 1995, he took 95 first-class wickets at 29.69, including another 10 against Sussex at Bath.

He took 50 wickets in over 500 overs in 1997 but he really struggled in 1998, having problems with a knee injury and seeming tired and distracted, very different from his normal self. That was his last year with Somerset. 'Mushtaq Ahmed: The

Wilderness Years' seemed to have no happy ending in sight until, all of a sudden, Sussex announced that they had signed him for 2003.

Has there ever been a shrewder and more successful overseas signing in county cricket? Of course there have been greater players. But Sussex, sixth in the First Division in 2002, just above the relegation zone, won the Championship for the first time in 164 years. And there is no doubt whatsoever that without Mushtaq they would not have done it. He was on a cash incentive for every wicket he took over 50. Chris Adams, the captain, said he could hardly get the ball out of Mushtaq's hand. Five times he took 10 wickets or more in a match: each one of those matches was won.

He was back to his best. Irrepressibly cheerful and enthusiastic, it is impossible not to warm to Mushtaq Ahmed, still, at thirty-six, with the look of a naughty schoolboy. His international career may be over – although he was in the squad to face England in 2005 and is helping out as a bowling coach – but he could still spring a few surprises in county cricket.

MUSHTAQ AHMED
Right-hand bat, leg-break & googly
Born: 28 June 1970, Sahiwal
Major Teams: Pakistan, Multan, United Bank, Islamabad, Lahore, Peshawar, National Bank, Redco, Somerset, Surrey, Sussex

TESTS
(1989/90-2006)

	M	I	NO	Runs	HS	Ave	50	Ct
Batting & Fielding	52	72	18	656	59	11.71	2	23

	Balls	R	W	Ave	BBI	5	10	SR	Econ
Bowling	12,532	6,100	185	32.97	7/56	10	3	67.74	2.92

ONE-DAY INTERNATIONALS

	M	I	NO	Runs	HS	Ave	SR	Ct
Batting & Fielding	144	76	34	399	34★	9.50	57.24	30

	Balls	R	W	Ave	BBI	5	SR	Econ
Bowling	7,543	5,361	161	33.29	5/36	1	46.85	4.26

FIRST-CLASS
(Career: 1986/87-2006)

	M	I	NO	Runs	HS	Ave	50	Ct
Batting & Fielding	274	344	47	4,708	90★	15.85	10	110

	Balls	R	W	Ave	BBI	5	10	SR	Econ
Bowling	62,098	31,229	1,201	26.00	9/93	84	24	51.70	3.01

LIST A

	M	I	NO	Runs	HS	Ave	Ct
Batting & Fielding	361	210	73	1,555	41	11.35	57

	Balls	R	W	Ave	BBI	5	SR	Econ
Bowling	18,013	12,547	437	28.71	7/24	3	41.21	4.17

MUSHTAQ MOHAMMAD

If you have thought about the matter hard enough to have a favourite Mohammad brother – and let's face it, there are enough to choose from – then the chances are, particularly if you live in England, that it is Mushtaq. This busy, chubby, multi-talented cricketer was always fun to watch, especially away from the stress of Test cricket. A pioneer among the Pakistani county cricketers of his generation, he was an outstanding performer for Northamptonshire for many years. A first-class record of over 31,000 runs at an average of 42 – only Zaheer Abbas among Asian batsmen has scored more – and over 900 wickets at 24 apiece with his leg-breaks and googlies, is ample demonstration of his prowess, his versatility and his longevity as a player.

His longevity as a Test cricketer owed something to the fact that he was famously and astonishingly young when he started – 15 years and 124 days old on his debut at Lahore against the West Indies in 1958/59. He had been only 13 years and 41 days old when he made his first-class debut. These recorded dates of birth are notoriously unreliable. The current holder of the Test record, also a Pakistani, Hasan Raza, is widely thought to be at least a bit older than the cricket almanacks suggest. In Mushtaq's case – and in Hanif's and Sadiq's for that matter – there is the fact of Partition to help explain any inaccuracies – their parents left home in a bit of a hurry.

Mushtaq's youthfulness as a debutant is scarcely more extraordinary than the duration of his Test career. He played his last Test match, against Australia, in March 1979, twenty years almost to the day after playing his first. Of course, they played a lot less in those days. Mushtaq was pretty much a regular from beginning to end, except for the brief period of World Series Cricket, and he played in 'only' 57 Tests. The twenty-year span, though, has rarely been approached by purely post-war players. Brian Close played for England remarkably between 1949 and 1976 but he was hardly a regular. Gary Sobers, Colin Cowdrey and Imran Khan are Mushtaq's closest rivals. These days, you are doing well if you get a dozen years: who knows, perhaps Shane Warne will break another record?

He was also the youngest player to make a Test century, 101 against India at Delhi in 1960/61 when he was 17 years and 82 days old. It has often been described as a match-saving innings, although the cynic might ask how could a match be saved where the sole concern of both sides was not to lose? In fact, this Test, the Fourth, was probably the only one played by India and Pakistan between 1955 and 1978 that came close not to being drawn. In the end, Pakistan only narrowly avoided defeat, and Mushtaq's first-innings hundred certainly contributed to that.

His next Test century was played in similarly dire circumstances. Pakistan's tour of England in 1962 was bitterly disappointing. They played a full tour of five Tests, the first three of which were lost comprehensively. The Fourth, at Trent Bridge, was drawn after England had made yet another big total: the veteran Fazal Mahmood, who had just flown in as a replacement, bowled 60 overs – 45 of them in a single day – for 130 runs. Mushtaq batted at number three and scored 55 and, when Pakistan followed on, 101 not out out of 216 for 6, both grittily determined efforts. At The Oval, where England also won, he made 43 and 82. He averaged 44 in the Tests and was the leading run-scorer on the tour. He was surely the youngest ever *Wisden* Cricketer of the Year.

That tour probably did Mushtaq a power of good. These were very different conditions from home, although he had played in England before, with the Pakistan Eaglets in 1958. This time, though, he had Brian Statham and Fred Trueman to contend with. They were England's leading wicket takers. More importantly though, Hanif had a poor series. The great opening batsman was troubled by a knee injury and, although he scored over a thousand runs on the tour – coming second to Mushtaq in the averages – he could not get going at all in the Tests. Sadiq, whose career coincided with Hanif's for just one Test, said that he often felt he was playing under Hanif's shadow. One gets the same feeling about Shoaib, Hanif's very talented but slightly unfulfilled son. Mushtaq had his bowling to fall back on but it may be that his considerable success in England in 1962 enabled him to plough his own furrow.

Soon he was a full-time professional in England. While touring with the Pakistan Eaglets in 1963, he signed for Northamptonshire, which meant serving a two-year qualification period as an overseas player. In his first season, 1966, he made 1,000 runs at just under 24 and took 45 wickets at 18. Gradually he got used to the rigours and rhythms of the county season and became an outstanding county cricketer. As he had shown in the county matches in 1962, he may have lacked Hanif's technical soundness and composure and balance at the crease, but he could be a superb entertainer. By the early 1970s, he was emerging as a leading batsman at both Test and county level. In Test cricket, Pakistan were one of the most talented batting sides in the world and Mushtaq was no longer being forced to play purely defensively. At Edgbaston in 1971, he and Zaheer Abbas ground England into the dust on the first day of the series, finishing the day on 270 for 1, having made 82 in the hour after tea: Mushtaq scored 100. He was very much a senior player on that tour and exerted a stabilising influence in the batting order. His most rewarding county season came in 1972 when he came fourth in the national batting averages, scoring 1,949 runs at 59.96, with six hundreds. He and the redoubtable David Steele were always rescuing the innings. He also came twelfth in the bowling with 57 wickets at 19.82. Teammates Bob Cottam and John Dye were among those above him in the bowling ranks and Bishan Bedi was not far behind.

Mushtaq Mohammad batting during his century against England in the First Test at Edgbaston in 1971.

Figures though, were not what people found interesting about 'Mushy'. What people liked about him was that he was busy and interested and always in the game, a lively close fielder to add to his other talents. He was a particularly busy batsman. As a bat-twiddler, he was in the Alec Stewart class. In fact that is not fair: Stewart was in the Mushtaq class. Slightly crouched at the crease with his backside jutting out, he was a brilliant attacking batsman, cutting and hooking pace bowlers in particular with relish. It was he who brought the reverse sweep, played usually against left-arm spinners, into the public domain. His chubby features and ready smile gave the impression, early on, that he was a rather jolly little chap. That was true but only up to a point. Essentially Mushtaq was a serious, tough-minded professional cricketer.

His bowling was a very good second suit. Late in his career against New Zealand, in 1978/79 when he had left the Packer circus, he bowled Pakistan to a comprehensive win in the First Test at Christchurch, taking 4 for 60 and 5 for 59. Were he playing today it is probable that he would be an outstanding all-rounder. As a leg-spinner, he was accurate, relatively inexpensive and had decent variations. At the time he became captain of Pakistan only two current wrist-spinners, his predecessor as captain, Intikhab Alam, and the Indian Bhagwat Chandrasekhar, had taken more Test wickets than Mushtaq. Surprisingly though, he is not among that group of Test cricketers, growing larger almost by the month, who have scored over 1,000 runs and taken over 100 wickets; he finished with 79 wickets at just under 30 apiece. Leg-spin, in the years between Richie Benaud and Abdul Qadir, was very much a minority interest. Also, he would almost certainly have got many more wickets if his career had not coincided with Intikhab's. As captain, Intikhab tended to overbowl himself and sometimes seemed to forget Mushtaq was there.

Nonetheless Mushtaq gave two particularly remarkable all-round performances in Test cricket. The first was against New Zealand at Dunedin in 1972/73. Pakistan won by an innings, the only decisive result in a three-match series. Their innings of 567 for 6 was built around a magnificent fourth-wicket partnership of 350 between Mushtaq (201) and Asif Iqbal (175). Mushtaq started slowly and carefully but by the end he and Asif were in rampant form against New Zealand's predominantly medium-paced attack. The home-side's batsmen were routed by the Pakistani wrist-spinners, Intikhab and Mushtaq, totalling 156 and 185. In the first innings Intikhab took 7 for 52 and Mushtaq 2 for 15. In the second, Mushtaq took 5 for 49 in 18 overs, and became the second Test player, after Denis Atkinson of the West Indies, to score a double century and take a 5-wicket haul in the same Test. The second was in the Caribbean in 1976/77, when Mushtaq was leading Pakistan on their first tour there since 1957/58. The series was a tough one for the Pakistani batsmen. Mushtaq himself only passed 20 twice in the first three Tests, as Andy Roberts and Colin Croft targeted the captain. The West Indies were 1-0 up as the teams moved to Port-of-Spain for the Fourth Test. There, it was like a different game, played on a slow wicket that gave help to the spinners and had nothing in it for the fast men.

Clive Lloyd won the toss and, doubtless sensing a psychological advantage that might outweigh the condition of the wicket, sent Pakistan in. The decision seemed to have been justified when Pakistan were 51 for 3 after 80 minutes. Then Mushtaq joined Majid Khan and the pair put on 109 as conditions eased. At the end of a rain-interrupted first day Pakistan were 225 for 5 with Mushtaq on 70 not out. Wasim Raja and Imran Khan fell early the next morning but Sarfraz Nawaz helped Mushtaq put on 68 for the eighth wicket. Pakistan made 348, Mushtaq scoring 121 in 370 minutes. Roy Fredericks and Gordon Greenidge got off to a brisk start with an opening stand of 73 but, after Imran had broken through with a couple of quick wickets, the innings subsided spectacularly: 107 for 5 at close of play and 154 all out. Mushtaq gave a splendid display of controlled leg-spin to take 5 for 28 in 10.5 overs. The West Indies' fast bowlers were soon at the Pakistanis again. The visitors were 95 for 5, with the game in the balance. But Mushtaq and Raja, having the series of his life, put on 116 (Raja 70, Mustaq 56) and there were more useful runs from Sarfraz and Imran. The West Indies' eventual target was an academic one of 489. They closed the fourth day on 146 for 4. Two of those wickets fell to Mushtaq, including the crucial one, that of Vivian Richards, stumped off a leg-break. Next morning he dismissed Alvin Kallicharan in his first over and, although there was determined resistence from Deryck Murray and the tail, it was only a matter of time. Mushtaq finished with 3 for 69. The winning captain, he thus had a hundred, a fifty and 8 wickets in the match.

It was a rude re-awakening at Kingston in the Fifth Test, however. The West Indies won by 140 runs and Mushtaq scored 24 and 17, twice dismissed by Joel Garner. The West Indies series came at the end of what had been a hectic 1976/77 season for

Mushtaq Mohammad bowling during the Second Test against England at Lord's 1971.

Pakistan. Mushtaq was appointed in place of Intikhab for the home series against New Zealand. Pakistan were far too good for the visitors, winning the series 2–0. All the batsmen prospered. Mushtaq scored two centuries, although he was bowled cheaply by the hostile Richard Hadlee in the First Test at Lahore. Then the Pakistanis were off to Australia, where Intikhab's team had lost 3–0 four years earlier. This time it was 1–1. Mushtaq led his team to their first Test win in Australia, at Sydney in the Third Test. With the bat, though, he had a torrid time, scoring 77 runs in five completed innings: Dennis Lillee got him four times. Jeff Thomson – who only bowled in one innings in the series because of injury – got him once. He was manifestly uncomfortable against the short-pitched ball. There was more to come in the West Indies.

In his autobiography, written in the late 1980s, Imran was highly critical — it would hardly be an exaggeration to say disparaging — of Mushtaq. One loses count of the number of times he says Mushtaq was frightened of pace bowling, particularly in the West Indies series and during World Series Cricket, in which both Imran and Mushtaq played. The judgment seems unduly harsh, although it is undoubtedly true that, by the end of his long career, pace was causing problems as Lillee was able to show. Mushtaq's batting average was well over the benchmark figure of 40 when he took over as captain and he relished playing pace in his youth. He slipped down the order when he returned to lead Pakistan after the spell with Packer.

Imran was also curiously dismissive of Mushtaq's abilities as a captain; describing him as inflexible and defensive. Mushtaq's record was certainly as good as that of any Pakistani captain before Imran himself. He led his team to victories against New Zealand at home (the first series win at home for over a decade) and away, and against India at home — a highly significant result in the first series between the teams for almost two decades — and to two drawn series in Australia. The only defeat came in the Caribbean. Javed Miandad, in contrast to Imran, thought that Mushtaq was a brilliant and imaginative leader, and particularly admired the way he handled the side in the historic victory over India in the Karachi Test in November 1978. Mushtaq stepped aside from the leadership for the World Cup in 1979 in favour of Asif, while making it clear that he wanted to retain the job in Test matches. But when the side to tour Indian in 1979/80 was picked he was not even in it as a player.

Mushtaq also had a brief spell in charge of Northamptonshire. He took over in August 1975 after a troubled year in which there had already been three captains. The move worked. The last month of the season was easily the best and, at Chelmsford, he shared a record fourth-wicket stand of 273 against Essex with a young batsman then averaging 9 for the season, Wayne Larkins. The county finished thirteenth in the table, poor reward for all the talent at their disposal. He was captain for the whole of 1976 and the county had what was arguably their best season ever, coming second in the Championship and winning the Gillette Cup, their first ever trophy. In the Championship, they won nine games out of twenty, two fewer than Middlesex but all by dint of bowling the opposition out twice. Mushtaq was eighth in the national batting averages, making 1,620 runs at an average of over 50. Zaheer was top, Miandad fourth and Sadiq thirteenth. He also took 37 Championship wickets at 27.51. Not that Mushtaq's captaincy was without its critics. There was consternation when he omitted Steele, still a cult figure after his success against Australia in 1975, from the team to play Hampshire in the Gillette Cup semi-final. Northants' target was a modest one of 217 and at one stage they were 142 for 2. But Roy Virgin was run out by the brilliant cover fielder David Turner and they panicked unaccountably, only just scraping home in the end. Ken Turner, Northants' secretary-manager for many years, was seething.

The celebrations of 1976 did not last long. By July 1977 Turner was dismantling the side. Leading players including Virgin, Dye and Bedi were sacked and Mushtaq was relieved of the captaincy and left the club at the end of the season. It was a bitter end, not so unusual in those days and understandable from the point of view of a small and far from wealthy club needing to build for the future. Wounds have been healed. Mushtaq has coached at the county's academy. He has also coached Pakistan. He remains devoted to the great game.

MUSHTAQ MOHAMMAD
Right-hand bat, leg-break & googly
Born: 22 November 1943, Junagadh, India
Major Teams: Pakistan, Karachi, Pakistan International Airlines, Northamptonshire

TESTS
(1958/59–1978/79)

	M	I	NO	Runs	HS	Ave	100	50	Ct
Batting & Fielding	57	100	7	3,643	201	39.17	10	19	42

	Balls	R	W	Ave	BBI	5	10	SR	Econ
Bowling	5,260	2,309	79	29.22	5/28	3	0	68.58	2.63

ONE-DAY INTERNATIONALS

	M	I	NO	Runs	HS	Ave	SR	100	50	Ct
Batting & Fielding	10	9	3	209	55	34.83	59.20	0	1	3

	Balls	R	W	Ave	Econ
Bowling	42	23	0	–	3.28

FIRST-CLASS
(Career: 1956/57–1984)

	M	I	NO	Runs	HS	Ave	100	50	Ct
Batting & Fielding	502	843	104	31,091	303★	42.07	72	–	349

	R	W	Ave	BBI	5	10
Bowling	22,789	936	24.34	7/18	39.00	2

LIST A

	M	I	NO	Runs	HS	Ave	100	50	Ct
Batting & Fielding	180	169	16	4,471	131	29.22	1	24	48

	Balls	R	W	Ave	BBI	SR	Econ
Bowling	2,090	1,482	49	30.24	4/30	42.65	4.25

SADIQ MOHAMMAD

Did they force Sadiq to bat left-handed? It is not unreasonable to ask. My father was the oldest of five brothers, all good cricketers. All natural right-handers. When the youngest, Leslie, now a robust eighty-five-year-old, came along, he was required to bat left-handed, 'for the good of the team'. Sadiq too was the youngest of five, in what was surely the most famous and accomplished cricketing family of the twentieth century. Wazir, Raees, – who did not play in a Test – Hanif and Mushtaq were all right-handers. Is it not possible that as soon as little Sadiq – two years Mushtaq's junior and sixteen years younger than Wazir – was old enough to twiddle a bat, he was gently taken aside and given some intensively sinister coaching?

That is not to say that Sadiq did not look the part. On the contrary, he was an instinctively ebullient and free-scoring batsman. Compact and well-organised like his older brothers, Sadiq had a wristy ebullience that was all his own. Like many small left-handers he was a deft cutter and glancer and Ray Robinson said that his square-cutting at Melbourne in 1972/73 put him in mind of a miniature Gary Sobers. He drove sweetly square on the off-side, although he was always perceived to be vulnerable outside the off stump.

Wasim, Hanif, Mushtaq and Sadiq collectively represented Pakistan in a virtually unbroken line of succession from 1952 to 1980. When Sadiq was not picked for the Third Test against England in January 1978, and Mushtaq – along with Zaheer Abbas and Imran Khan – was withdrawn from the team because the England management refused to allow their team to play against anyone contracted to World Series Cricket, it was the first time in ninety-six Tests that there had not been a Mohammad brother in the side.

Like Hanif, Sadiq was an opening batsman. He came into the team at a time when Pakistan were having difficulties finding a settled opening combination. He made his Test debut ten years after having made his first-class debut, against New Zealand at Karachi in 1969/70. To say it was the end of one era and the beginning of another may be both clichéd and tautological but in terms of human resource management it was a significant game for Pakistan. Sadiq was not the only debutant. There was the Surrey left-hander Younis Ahmed, half-brother of the experienced former captain Saeed Ahmed: he played in the next Test at Lahore but then had to wait a record seventeen years for another try. Also making his first appearance, more significantly, was Sadiq's future county colleague at Gloucestershire, Zaheer Abbas. More notably still, Sadiq's opening partner was making what turned out to be his final Test appearance. This was the great Hanif. Mushtaq was batting at number four, so the Mohammad family emulated the Graces – W.G., E.M. and G.F. – in having three representatives in a Test match team. Wazir was a selector, and a few eyebrows were raised when Sadiq was picked.

Sadiq Mohammad batting against England in the Second Test at Lord's, 1971.

Sadiq made five Test centuries, three of them coming in 1972/73. Pakistan lost all three Tests to Australia on an unhappy tour where they failed to do themselves justice as a team, but Sadiq personally had a productive series, playing with panache and determination. In the First Test at Adelaide, he made a gutsy 81 as Pakistan fought in vain to stave off an innings defeat. Ashley Mallett took 8 wickets. In the Second Test, at Melbourne, Pakistan put up a better fight, making 574 for 8 in their first innings and getting a lead of over 100. Sadiq made a highly impressive 137. He had a fine series in New Zealand. He made 166 and 68 in the draw at Wellington, in each innings sharing a substantial stand with Majid Khan after Talat Ali and Zaheer had fallen early. His third century of the season came in the First Test against England at Lahore, where he made 119; he scored 89 at Karachi.

Sadiq's other two Test centuries came as much as four years later, again in a short burst. In the 10-wicket victory over New Zealand at Hyderabad he scored 103, putting on 164 for the first wicket with the imperious Majid, who made 98 of them. His final Test century came at Melbourne a couple of months later. Australia inflicted a heavy defeat on Pakistan, mainly through very hostile bowling from Dennis Lillee. Sadiq withstood the fire for five hours in the first innings making 103.

It was strange that Sadiq never scored a Test century in England. He had three reasonably successful tours there and was a reliable performer for many years with Gloucestershire. But he played some of his most memorable Test innings in England. None was better than his fighting 91 in the final innings of the Leeds Test in 1971. The first two Tests had been drawn, the first dominated by Pakistan, the second ruined by rain. The Leeds Test was a curious mix of some very exciting cricket, especially on the last day, and some excruciatingly dull passages. Geoffrey Boycott made a century on the first day: no, that was not the excruciating part – it was really rather good. Zaheer and Mushtaq batted brightly for Pakistan but the lower-middle order were desperately slow on the Saturday as Pakistan crept to a lead of 34. There were solid contributions all down the order for England on the Monday but Saleem Altaf swept the tail away, with the last 5 wickets falling in less than an hour.

Pakistan needed 231 to win and Sadiq and Aftab Gul took them to 25 for no wicket by close of play. The wicket had been expected to help the spinners and England had three: the captain, Ray Illingworth, Norman Gilford the slow left-armer and Robin Hobbs, the leg-spinner, making one of his rare appearances in Test cricket. The pressure was on immediately on the final day, Illingworth taking 2 wickets in his first over. Neither of Pakistan's most experienced batsmen, Saeed and Mushtaq, lasted long and they slumped to 65 for 4. Then Asif Iqbal joined Sadiq and slowly they repaired the damage and began to take control of the game. Asif was stumped off Gilford with the score on 160 but Pakistan still seemed to be favourites. Sadiq was in total command, treating Hobbs, trying to pitch into the rough outside the left-hander's off-stump, with particular disdain. But Basil d'Oliveira, so often a partnership breaker, dismissed Sadiq and Intikhab Alam in rapid succession: England won by 25 runs with twenty minutes to spare.

Although he did not make any big scores in the Tests in 1974 he had a splendid tour, making over a thousand runs. He and Majid played brilliant cameos at Lord's in a game marred by heavy rain that leaked under the covers. He and Majid became an attractive and effective opening pair; Sadiq lacked his partner's polish but he was an admirable foil.

Sadiq's final tour of England, in 1978 was demanding and difficult. He was now the senior batsman, by dint of Majid. Mushtaq, Zaheer and Asif having signed for Kerry Packer. Nonetheless, Sadiq bore the responsibility well. The team was hopelessly disadvantaged, not only by their inexperience but also by the appalling weather that marred the start of the tour and made preparation almost impossible. England overwhelmed them in the first two Tests. The weather ruined the third, in which Pakistan at least appeared more competitive. No Pakistani batsman apart from Sadiq reached fifty in the series. At Edgbaston – many English people will remember the match as David Gower's debut – Sadiq made a defiant 79 in Pakistan's second innings. At Headingley in the final Test, he made 97 in over five hours, an innings interrupted by rain seven times. It was poor reward for Sadiq to be dropped after one Test when the Packer players returned to the side for the series against India in 1978/79. He returned for the World Cup in 1979 but was then dropped again. Recalled in the middle of Pakistan's unhappy tour of India in 1979/80, he made a sparkling 46, with 10 fours, on the first day at Madras.

None of his other innings saw Sadiq display as much courage as his 98 not out against the West Indies in the second (and final) Test at Karachi in 1974/75. He missed the First Test because he was playing for Tasmania (where he coached after retirement). In the Second the West Indies made 493 in response to Pakistan's 406, the left-handed all-rounder Bernard Julien scoring an aggressive century. A full-blooded pull from him whacked Sadiq, fielding at short leg, on the left ear. His neck swelled up and he could hardly turn his head. Pakistan were soon in trouble against Andy Roberts and Keith Boyce. They recovered through Asif and Wasim Bari to finish the fourth day on 148 for 4. Sadiq came in in the first over of the final day when Bari was run out. Still in considerable pain, he batted through the remainder of the innings, shepherding the tail and resisting a long and persistent spell by Lance Gibbs. When the ninth wicket fell, Wasim Raja, himself injured, came out to try to get Sadiq to his century but Raja was out with Sadiq on 98. The draw had been secured.

Injury came to be a bit of a problem for Sadiq in the latter part of his Test career. His Hyderabad century against New Zealand was interrupted by injury. He missed the First Test against Australia in 1976/77 because of an injury picked up in the game against Western Australia. He had to retire hurt before scoring when hit on the forearm by a short ball from Colin Croft in the Second Test, at Port-of-Spain, in 1976/77. Croft took 8 for 29 in that innings and West Indies won comfortably. In the second innings of the next Test, at Georgetown, he retired hurt at 22, hit in the face by a bouncer from Roberts. He returned to make 48 and help Majid to take Pakistan to safety. He was at the non-striker's end – wearing one of the earliest batting helmets (his exuberant moustache sometimes made one feel he should have been wearing a sombrero) – when one of the most infamous cricketing injuries of the 1970s took place, nightwatchman Iqbal Qasim being hit in the face by a bouncer from Bob Willis at Edgbaston in 1978.

Having done the rounds of the leagues, and played a solitary match for Essex in 1970, Sadiq settled down for a decade with Gloucestershire, opening the innings first with the veteran Ron Nicholls and then with Andy Stovold and finally Chris Broad. He scored half his fifty first-class centuries for the county, four of them in successive innings in 1975. In 1980 he was fifth in the national averages, scoring 1,595 runs at 56.95, with eight centuries, including two in the match against Glamorgan at Bristol: even Zaheer was eclipsed. He had hoped to remain with the county in an administrative capacity after retiring but the Home Office would only give him a visa if he played. Yes, the fight against mass immigration had begun in earnest. His son, Imraan, born the day before his father's second Melbourne century, and a Cambridge blue, also played for the county.

SADIQ MOHAMMAD
Left-hand bat, leg-break & googly
Born: 5 May 1945, Junagadh, India
Major Teams: Pakistan, Karachi, Pakistan International Airlines, United Bank, Essex, Gloucestershire, Tasmania

TESTS
(1969/70-1980/81)

	M	I	NO	Runs	HS	Ave	100	50	Ct
Batting & Fielding	41	74	2	2,579	166	35.81	5	10	28

	Balls	R	W	Ave	Econ
Bowling	200	98	0	–	2.94

ONE-DAY INTERNATIONALS

	M	I	NO	Runs	HS	Ave	SR	50	Ct
Batting & Fielding	19	19	1	383	74	21.27	50.72	2	5

	Balls	R	W	Ave	BBI	SR	Econ
Bowling	38	26	2	13.00	2/20	19.00	4.10

FIRST-CLASS
(Career: 1959/60-1984/85)

	M	I	NO	Runs	HS	Ave	100	50	Ct
Batting & Fielding	387	684	40	24,160	203	37.51	50	120	326

	R	W	Ave	BBI	5	10
Bowling	7,478	235	31.82	7/34	8	0

LIST A

	M	I	NO	Runs	HS	Ave	100	50	Ct
Batting & Fielding	208	203	9	5,893	131	30.37	7	30	51

	Balls	R	W	Ave	BBI	SR	Econ
Bowling	1,172	959	36	26.63	3/19	32.55	4.90

SALEEM MALIK

The three-Test home series in which Pakistan played Australia from September to November 1994 was the most intense and fascinating ever contested between the two countries. The stage had been intriguingly set. Australia had become, by sheer force of character as much as talent, a far better team than the one that had last toured Pakistan in 1988/89. Since then they had recovered the Ashes, retained them twice and beaten everyone at home except the all conquering West Indies, to whom they had lost by the narrowest of margins in 1992/93. Not least among the new ingredients was Shane Warne, a superlative purveyor of aggressive but controlled leg-spin, now on his first visit to the subcontinent. But the Australians had not won a Test match in Pakistan since 1959/60. And now, for the first time for many years, they were without Allan Border, one of the principal architects of the new team. He had been succeeded as captain by the unflappable and articulate left-handed opener Mark Taylor.

Pakistan also had a new, or newish, captain but as was so often the case this was hardly the apparently seamless transition managed by their opponents. Two and a half years earlier Pakistan had been led to victory in the one-day World Cup by the talismanic Imran Khan. He, however, almost immediately retired and the comings and goings to and from the captaincy that followed were reminiscent of pre-Berlusconi Italian governments. The veteran Javed Miandad – who did a pretty good job in the English summer of 1992 – fell out with the Pakistan Cricket Board (PCB). Then there was Wasim Akram, who seemed in many ways to be Imran's natural successor. He was selected to lead the side to tour New Zealand in early 1994. After the touring party was chosen, though, ten of the senior players protested to the PCB at Wasim's appointment because of his 'domineering and abusive' captaincy. They wanted the vice-captain, Waqar Younis, to replace him. Instead a compromise candidate was picked, the experienced right-handed middle-order batsman, Saleem Malik.

This represented something of a resurrection for Malik. He had had a very poor World Cup in early 1992 – he made 51 against Sri Lanka at Perth but in eight other innings his highest score was 17 – and although he did well in England in 1992 he did not play in the series against the West Indies and Zimbabwe that followed. Imran, still influential behind the scenes, had never been more than lukewarm in his support of Malik, apparently regarding him as a flat-track bully and unreliable. Moreover, his captaincy credentials at international level seemed negligible. In 1992, England played a five-match one-day international series against Pakistan, with two games played before the five-match Test series and three games played after it. England won the first two. Pakistan won a hard-fought Test series. Malik led Pakistan in Miandad's absence in the third one-day game at Trent Bridge. It was an extraordinary game. Malik put England in and they scythed their way to 363 for 7, then a record total in one-day internationals. An outstanding attack including Wasim, Waqar and Mushtaq Ahmed bowled to attacking fields: Waqar went for 7 an over. Pakistan in turn were bowled out for 165.

But when the captaincy came to him in his own right, however indirectly, Malik took it with gratitude and in his stride. He led his team to comprehensive series victories in New Zealand (Test and one-day), Sharjah (one-day) and Sri Lanka (Test and one-day). He batted consistently and with his customary elegance without making any really big scores. There was some comical confusion about the toss in New Zealand, caused largely by his habit of calling in Urdu – although Dave Crowe seemed to suggest in one of his typically imaginative reports in *The Cricketer* that Malik liked to delay his call, in whatever language, until the coin had landed safely flat. And there was some consternation at the Singer World Series that followed Pakistan's series in Sri Lanka. Those two teams were joined by India and Australia in a quadrangular tournament that the world champions, who had won four of their five one-day games against Sri Lanka with varying degrees of ease, were clear favourites to win. In fact, they failed to win a match.

The Australian and Pakistan players flew on to Pakistan together – or at least on the same plane – and before long, battle was being joined in the First Test at Karachi – Pakistan's citadel, where they had yet to lose a Test. Taylor won the toss and batted. He was out fourth ball to Wasim (he was to achieve the rare and unwanted distinction of bagging a pair in his first Test as captain). Australia recovered well through the debutant Michael Bevan (82) and Steve Waugh (73) to reach a comfortable if unspectacular 337. Pakistan replied with 256, the elegant left-handed opener Saeed Anwar top-scoring with 85. In the final session of the third day Australia, in their second innings, reached 171 for 2 with David Boon and Mark Waugh seemingly in command. But once Waugh fell for 61, Wasim and Waqar demolished the innings, only Boon standing firm to make a defiant five-and-a-half-hour century.

Pakistan needed 314 to win. Again Anwar was in marvellous touch and put on 84 for the third wicket with Malik (43). The captain was out just before close of play on the fourth day with the hosts on 155 for 3; it really was too close to call. There was a flurry of wickets at the start of the final day with Warne removing Basit Ali and Wasim Akram, and Joe Angel dismissing Anwar for 77. When the seventh wicket fell on 174 the relatively inexperienced Inzamam-ul-Haq was left with the tail. Rashid Latif helped him put on 52 and Waqar Younis 22. By this time injuries were affecting Australia: Glenn McGrath was off the field and Tim May had a ricked neck. Even so, when Mushtaq Ahmed walked out to join Inzamam with 56 still needed, most people must have fancied Australia to win.

The last-wicket pair reached their target in 8.1 overs. As for Warne, how did he toil and spin! With 3 runs and 1 wicket separating the sides he bowled to Inzamam. The batsman moved down the wicket to hit over the top but failed to connect. He was well out of his ground but the ball kept horribly low and contrived to evade everything, going through wicketkeeper Ian Healy's legs. Was it byes or leg-byes? Nobody seems certain. Whatever it was, there were four of them and Pakistan had won a famous victory. Bob Simpson, the Australian coach, who has played in and watched some amazing cricket, said he had never seen a game of such fluctuating fortunes. Malik, whose team had made Pakistan's highest successful fourth innings run chase, was understandably elated: 'Until the last ball, we weren't expecting to win. I still can't believe it.' Warne had 3 wickets in the first innings and 5 in the second and was Man of the Match.

The Australians must have felt that they had won more sessions than they had lost at Karachi, only to lose the match by a whisker. They began the Second Test at Rawalpindi in equally dominant form. Asked to bat by Malik, they made 521 for 9 with Michael Slater making a typically buccaneering 110, and substantial contributions coming from most of the middle order. Pakistan responded with 260 – the opener Aamir Sohail made 80 – and were asked to follow on for only the second time at home. Surely, this time Australia would not let the prize slip away.

If ever a situation called for a captain's innings, this was it. Malik provided one, scoring a masterly 237 in over nine hours to deny Australia victory. He gave one chance, being dropped by Taylor at slip off Angel on 20 (dropped catches dogged the Australians on this tour). Malik hit 37 fours and played all the bowlers, Warne included, with utter composure. When he eventually fell – oddly enough as the third victim in a hat-trick for Test debutant Damien Fleming – Australia were out of the game, which was drawn.

A triangular one-day series involving South Africa followed, which Australia won, and then the two teams reconvened for the Third Test at Lahore. The sudden withdrawal from the Pakistan team of both Wasim and Waqar due to injury raised eyebrows, both having played in the one-day final two days before the Test. Ijaz Ahmed, Malik's brother-in-law, – who had had a successful time in the one-day series – returned to the Test side after a four-year absence. Malik won the toss and batted. He scored 75 but the main contribution came from Moin Khan, replacing the injured Rashid Latif, who scored his first Test century. Pakistan reached 373 but Australia easily overhauled this, making 455. Then McGrath, in the first truly incisive spell of his remarkable career, reduced Pakistan to 74 for 4 on the fourth evening. Once again, Australia had a real opportunity to win.

Once again, it was Malik who stood in their way. He batted for 314 minutes in all, making 143 and hitting 19 fours. Sohail also made a hundred and the game and the series were safe. Malik's achievement was genuinely outstanding. In the three Tests, he scored 557 runs at an average of 92.83. He was cunning, aggressive and indefatigable. But it was not just the figures, it was his impact on the series that was remarkable, Warne said that Australia had outplayed Pakistan and could have won all three Tests; not an outrageous assessment. Malik himself said that Australia batted and bowled better. Warne had a very successful series – 18 wickets in 181.4 overs. But he never dismissed Malik. Malik's performance against Australia, coupled with his and his team's achievements earlier in the year, appeared to indicate that, in a cricketing realm where palace revolutions were more frequent and regular than official birthdays, his position was secured. Indeed, Z.H. Syed, in *The Cricketer*, said that any attempt to remove him could only be 'viewed with disgust'.

How quickly and completely it all fell apart. The next assignment was a lengthy tour to southern Africa between November 1994 and February 1995, involving an inaugural Test and a quadrangular one-day series in South Africa and Tests and one-day games against Zimbabwe. The tourists started well in the Mandela Trophy, which also involved New Zealand and Sri Lanka, and reached the two-game final against the hosts, having lost only once in the round-robin stage. But Malik's tactics in both the final games caused bewilderment among teammates and pundits alike. In both games he won the toss and inserted the opposition. Both were day-night games, where the toss is highly significant. South Africa won both games with ease. They then won the Test by a massive margin of 324 runs. Malik scored 99 in the first innings but after the game he felt compelled to issue a statement denying rumours of a rift in the dressing room.

And that was just the beginning. The disconsolate party moved on to Zimbabwe where they lost the First Test, at Harare, by an innings and 64 runs; the hosts made 544 for 4. Zimbabwe then were nothing like the pushover they are now. Even so, it was their first ever Test victory and by any objective yardstick an extraordinary result: bookmakers in Delhi were said to be laying odds of 40-1 on a Zimbabwe victory.

The tourists appeared to pull themselves together and won the two remaining Tests, so that Malik became the first captain to lead his side to victory in a three-Test series after losing the first match. He gained a more unusual distinction, in the Third Test, also at Harare, by being fined for accusing the Zimbabwean umpire, Ian Robinson, of ball-tampering. The one-day series was drawn. Before the last match, vice-captain Rashid Latif and Basit Ali made an extraordinary announcement to the effect that they had retired from international cricket; Latif made it clear that the reason was his dissatisfaction with Malik's captaincy, and in particular his tactics during the Mandela Trophy finals.

On 12 February – between the Second and Third Tests, it was revealed that the Australian Cricket Board (ACB) had asked the International Cricket Council (ICC) to investigate allegations that Warne and May had been offered substantial sums to 'throw' the Karachi Test. The incident was said to have taken place on the evening of the fourth day. The bribe had been emphatically rejected. Pakistan won the match, it will be recalled, by 1 wicket. Three days later, on the eve of the third Zimbabwe Test, it was disclosed that Mark Waugh claimed to have been offered money to lose his wicket cheaply in a one-day game at Rawalpindi. Phil Wilkins, of the *Sydney Morning Herald*, claimed that, in both cases, the man who made the offer was Saleem Malik.

Malik at once denied the allegations. But he and the manager, Intikhab Alam, were both sacked on their return to Pakistan and an investigative process of sorts was initiated by the PCB. It has to be said that this was not especially well handled. Malik, the national captain, was suspended before he had had a chance to defend himself. For a while, not much happened. Malik went to court demanding reinstatement as a player but his claim was rejected. The Australian players meanwhile, hardly surprisingly, declined an invitation to go to Pakistan to give evidence. Their statements to the ACB had been provided in an affidavit form. Eventually a report was produced by former Supreme Court Justice Fekhruddin Ebrahim. Malik was cleared of the allegations made against him, the report suggesting that they had been 'concocted'.

Javed Burki, former national captain and chairman of the ad hoc committee running cricket in Pakistan, had spoken of the 'cultural gap' between Australia and Pakistan and questioned the delay in the making of the allegations. Asif Iqbal mischievously suggested that the players were upset at not having been paid. The timing was certainly odd. The first incident involving Warne and May apparently took place on the fourth evening of the First Test – on 1 October 1994. Australia played another Test, then a one-day tournament (the game at Rawalpindi where Malik reportedly made his second offer to Mark Waugh, was played on 22 October) and a third Test, which finished on 5 November. Warne has always made it clear that he reported the incident to Taylor and to Simpson, who presumably brought it up to the ACB. But clearly no complaint was made to the PCB during the tour. Taylor wrote a book about his first year as captain of Australia, starting off with the Pakistan tour. He writes about his thoughts as he left the country. 'Flying home, a kaleidoscope of memories played in my mind.' That is understandable. What were they? 'My First Test pair, our one-day triumph, the dropped catches, the pressure from the press.' And the fact that the captain of Pakistan tried to buy the First Test? It does not get a mention.

One senses the presence of our learned friends the lawyers here. If Malik were not proved to be guilty a report of the allegations might have been regarded as defamatory. Malik did indeed threaten to sue the Australian newspaper. But there was more to it than that. By the time he wrote his book, Taylor must have known that, in March 1995, Warne and Mark Waugh had been fined by the ACB for accepting money from an Indian bookmaker in exchange for pitch information during the Singer Cup in Sri Lanka. The ACB took the view that it was in everyone's best interests – and most of all, their own – to hush the matter up. In the circumstances, one can hardly blame Taylor for avoiding the issue. The information about Warne and Mark Waugh only came to light in December 1998. By that time, Waugh and Taylor – on behalf of Warne, who was injured – had testified before the inquiry under Justice Mohammad Malik Qayyum investigating allegations of corruption in Pakistan cricket. This occurred during the Australians' tour of Pakistan in 1998/99; again, nothing was said about the Australian dealings with the bookmaker and such was the outrage in Pakistan when the news broke that a special hearing of the Pakistani inquiry was convened in Melbourne so that Warne and Waugh could be cross examined. Peter Roebuck observed that the fact that the Australians were astonishingly dim-witted at best did not mean that Malik was innocent.

As it transpires, it seems to be more likely than not that he was guilty as charged (yes, it's those lawyers again: well, nothing's been proved). This emerged once Justice Malik Qayyum reported in late 1999. He concluded that the Australians were telling the truth. He also concluded, among other things, that suspicions about the Singer Cup and the Mandela Trophy finals were well founded. He recommended a life ban for Malik. The Qayyum inquiry, although the most comprehensive of the various inquiries to be held into match-fixing in Pakistan, was far from perfect. Kamran Abbasi called it Pakistan's *Oprah Winfrey Show*. Perhaps the most telling comment on it is that Justice Qayyum (now retired) is reportedly advising Malik on how to proceed with challenging his ban.

Malik had returned to the international scene after his exoneration by Justice Fekruddhin but the rest of his career had a slightly unreal quality about it: 'living and partly living' like a figure in a T.S. Eliot chorus. Perhaps inevitably his first return to the Test match scene was in Australia in 1995/96. He was a strange selection because his temporary suspension meant that he had not even played domestic cricket since returning from Zimbabwe. He had no sort of form and he was a pariah as far as the Australian public were concerned. Not surprisingly, he had a bit of an attitude problem too: 'I hate Australia: it's hell.' Warne got him for a duck in the First Test. 'It shows there's some justice,' said the leg-spinner, justifiably if somewhat self-righteously. They had a fascinating duel in the Third Test at Sydney, Malik making what *Wisden* called a 'skilful and bloody-minded' 36. Pakistan gained a consolation victory, losing the series 2-1. He toured England the following summer, playing in all three Tests and, to begin with, achieving little, pottering about ineffectively at Lord's in the second innings of the First Test when Wasim Akram was anxious to get a move on and declare. But at The Oval he made a stylish century in an apparently effortless manner. He lost his place after a more than usually meaningless one-day series against India in Toronto in the autumn of 1997 after he and Ijaz Ahmed were reported to have fallen out with skipper Rameez Raja. The series was memorable for a succession of hectic middle-order collapses by Pakistan against the previously innocuous bowling of Sourav Ganguly.

But he was back in the side in 1998/99, when Australia toured. This time it was Malik's turn to bag a pair at Karachi – in his ninety-ninth Test. Taylor made 334 not out at Peshawar. Malik returned to England once more, rather surprisingly as a belated selection to the World Cup squad in 1999. He played in four games and failed to reach double figures in any of them. The third of these was the notorious match in which Pakistan lost to Bangladesh, leading inexorably, it is sometimes said, to Bangladesh's inclusion among the Test playing elite. A recently established accountability committee launched an investigation into Pakistan's alleged under-performance in the World Cup campaign and attention was said to be focussed on Malik, Ijaz and Wasim. All were exonerated. But the Qayyum inquiry report was just around the corner.

No less a judge than Scyld Berry, writing of Malik as one of *Wisden's* Five Cricketers of the Year in 1988, said he was the natural successor to Zaheer Abbas and Javed Miandad as Pakistan's leading batsman. He showed immense promise at the start of his career, scoring a century against Sri Lanka on his Test debut in 1981/82 aged only eighteen. He was a keen and agile fielder too. When he made a hundred against England at Faisalabad in 1983/84 he became only the third player – after two giants of the game, George Headley and Graeme Pollock – to score three Test centuries before his twenty-first birthday. Loss of form limited his appearances in the short term. But by 1987, when he made his second tour of England, he seemed a seasoned campaigner. His 99 at Headingley in the decisive Third Test – Pakistan won the series 1-0, their first series win in England – was perhaps the most significant innings played by a Pakistan batsman all summer. He batted for most of the second day in challenging conditions and faced 238 balls. Coming in at a time of relative crisis at 86 for 4 he departed with his team comfortably placed at 280 for 7. England, who had batted feebly on the first day after winning the toss, collapsed to Imran on the fourth and lost by an innings. Malik scored a century – his first outside Pakistan – at The Oval, adding 234 for the fourth wicket with Miandad.

Malik's return to Headingley five years later was, if anything, even more impressive. This was the period when the Yorkshire ground's pitch was at its most treacherous and demanding for batsmen. The tour was almost the last of the old-fashioned tours, with a full set of county games. Four of Pakistan's batsmen made over a thousand first-class runs, none more than Malik's 1,184 at 78.93, which put him at the top of the national averages. Pakistan won a tense Test series 2-1. Malik made 488 runs at 81.33 in the five Tests. He and Miandad started where they had left off in 1987, putting on 322 for the fourth wicket in the first game at Edgbaston (Malik 165), still a record for any Pakistan wicket against England, but it was at Headingley in the Fourth Test – which England won by 6 wickets – that Malik really showed his mettle. Pakistan made 167 and 221. Intelligent seam bowling by Test debutant Neil Mallender troubled all the batsmen but Malik played wonderfully well. Patient, crafty and immensely skilful, he made 82 and 84 – both not out. Graham Gooch's epic first innings century was the key to England's success.

Gooch and Malik had been county colleagues the year before, when Essex won the Championship for the fifth time in thirteen years. Malik was in brilliant form, scoring almost 2,000 first-class runs at an average of over 73, with six hundreds, five of them over 150. Curiously he was relatively unsuccessful on his return in 1993, making 861 runs in fourteen Championship matches.

That Malik had it in him to be a genuinely great player is beyond dispute. Imran's dismissal of him as a flat-track bully seems snide and ill-considered. The two of them fell out during the 1992 World Cup, when Malik had a poor run of form and there was an unsavoury dispute about prize money. It is true that Malik had a better record at home than away – ten centuries in Pakistan compared to five elsewhere. But his record at Headingley, on a notoriously awkward surface where, in 1992, only one of his team-mates scored more than 30 – is testimony to his versatility, judgment and technique in conditions markedly different from those found at home. Nor did he lack courage. At Faisalabad, in the First Test against the mighty West Indies in 1986/87, he and Imran led a recovery on the first day from 37 for 5, the pair adding 53 before Malik's left arm was broken just above the wrist by a ball from Courtney Walsh. In the second innings he came out to bat at number eleven with his arm in plaster and helped Wasim Akram add 32 for the last wicket. He faced his first ball left-handed and then turned back to right. Acting-captain Malcolm Marshall objected to his having a runner, pointing out with irrefutable logic that it was his arm that was broken. Pakistan won the match by 166 runs. The unreliability tag with which Imran also adorned Malik seems equally harsh. In the late 1980s and early 1990s he was unquestionably one of the most consistent batsmen in world cricket, making runs against all the leading Test countries. He had a very good series against the West Indies in 1990/91, scoring a century in the victory at Karachi, and 74 and 71 in the defeat at Faisalabad; no other Pakistani made more than 32 in the match, and for the West Indies, only Richie Richardson with 70 not out in the second innings scored more than 44.

Strong wrists, exquisite timing, decisive footwork and a sound technique were the key to Malik's success. At his best he was a sumptuous stroke maker with all the shots. He could be patient but he was rarely purely defensive. Even in a crisis such as Headingley in 1992 he showed rare judgment as to when to attack. And when the moment was right he could be blisteringly aggressive. The best example of this was his astonishing onslaught against India in the second-one day international at Calcutta in February 1987. Chasing 239, Pakistan were struggling at 161 for 5 when Malik came in, with 78 still needed at more than 10 an over. More than 90,000 spectators watched incredulously as Malik conjured up a six and 11 fours to lead Pakistan to a remarkable 2-wicket victory. Another example was in the Nehru Cup semi-final against England at Nagpur in 1989/90. England made 194 for 7 in their 30 overs. Rameez Raja and Malik put on 122 from 77 balls for the fourth wicket, Malik hitting 3 sixes and 6 fours in his 66 off 41 balls. Gooch, England's captain, called it an 'innings of genius'. Pakistan won by 6 wickets with 9 balls to spare.

As Berry has observed, Malik's greatest achievement was his mastery of Warne. The batsman had no false modesty about this. After his epic innings at Rawalpindi

Above left: Saleem Malik celebrates his century in the Fifth Test against England at The Oval, 1987.

Above right: Saleem Malik batting against Bangladesh in the World Cup match at Northampton, 1999.

he said that, although Warne was a great bowler, he, having learned his cricket as a teammate of Abdul Qadir, had no difficulty reading him. Warne respected Malik as a batsman ('a difficult customer'), who read the flight and spin better than most and had plenty to say at the crease. He also admired his placement, recalling how Malik had found the fielders with unerring accuracy during a strange passage of play in a one-day game in Sri Lanka. Later, Malik was to say that Warne was a negative bowler, the equal neither of Qadir nor Muttiah Muralitharan. By then, however, his statements were often acquiring a bitter and twisted air. He has continued to maintain his innocence of the match-fixing and bribery allegations, and has filed various appeals against his life ban. His public exculpatory statements, however, have tended to be along the lines of 'What about the others?' rather than 'It wasn't me.'

What a waste. Malik's decline and fall seemed gradual but in hindsight they were precipitate. The 1994/95 season was *mirabilis* and *horribilis* all in one. Rarely in any field of human endeavour, let alone sport, can zenith and nadir have accompanied one another with such startling intensity.

SALEEM MALIK
Right-hand bat, right-arm medium-pace/off-break
Born: 16 April 1963, Lahore
Major Teams: Pakistan, Lahore, Habib Bank, Sargodha, Essex

TESTS
(1981/82–1998/99)

	M	I	NO	Runs	HS	Ave	100	50	Ct
Batting & Fielding	103	154	22	5,768	237	43.69	15	29	65

	Balls	R	W	Ave	BBI	SR	Econ
Bowling	734	414	5	82.79	1/3	146.80	3.38

ONE-DAY INTERNATIONALS

	M	I	NO	Runs	HS	Ave	SR	100	50	Ct
Batting & Fielding	283	256	38	7,170	102	32.88	76.41	5	47	81

	Balls	R	W	Ave	BBI	5	SR	Econ
Bowling	3,505	2,959	89	33.24	5/35	1	39.38	5.06

FIRST-CLASS
(Career: 1978/79–1999/2000)

	M	I	NO	Runs	HS	Ave	100	50	Ct
Batting & Fielding	269	417	56	16,586	237	45.94	43	81	167

	Balls	R	W	Ave	BBI	5	10	SR	Econ
Bowling	5,784	3,283	93	35.30	5/19	4	0	62.19	3.40

LIST A

	M	I	NO	Runs	HS	Ave	100	50	Ct
Batting & Fielding	426	385	61	11,856	138	36.59	12	78	141

	Balls	R	W	Ave	BBI	5	SR	Econ
Bowling	5,745	4,656	160	29.35	5/35	1	35.90	4.90

SAQLAIN MUSHTAQ

In 1998/99 Pakistan made their first Test tour to India since 1986/87. Indeed, the two sides had not played each other in Test cricket since India's tour of Pakistan in 1989/90. A new generation of players had grown up in the meantime and interest in both countries was intense. Political sensitivities were also running high and there was a very real threat of direct action from Hindu extremists.

In fact, the visit went smoothly and the cricket played was of the highest order. On slow, turning wickets both Tests (the scheduled third, at Calcutta, became part of the Asian Test Championship involving Sri Lanka too) were dominated by spinners. The series is always remembered because Anil Kumble, the Indian leg-spinner, took 10 wickets in Pakistan's second innings in the Second Test at Delhi to win the match and square the rubber. But Kumble was not the Man of the Series. That honour went to Pakistan's Saqlain Mushtaq.

The first game, at Chennai, was a classic Test match. Pakistan batted first and made 238, Kumble taking 6 wickets. India started solidly and were 71 for 2 when Sachin Tendulkar came to the crease. Seeking to dominate from the start, Tendulkar advanced down the pitch to the third ball he received, from Saqlain, but misjudged the length and succeeded only in slicing the ball to Saleem Malik in the gully. Tendulkar was gone for a duck. India were restricted to a 16-run lead and Saqlain took 5 for 94. A responsible maiden Test century from Shahid Afridi set the game up beautifully: India's target was 271. Their highest-ever successful run chase had been 256 against Australia back in 1964/65, so the odds were against them. The situation looked hopeless when Waqar Younis reduced them to 6 for 2, and no better at 82 for 5. But Tendulkar was still there, and he was prepared to graft. Nayan Mongia stayed with him while 136 was added and the Pakistanis began to get worried. Conditions were not easy. The heat and humidity were energy-sapping and the home crowd were passionate in their longing for a big innings by Tendulkar. It was difficult for him too because, halfway through his innings, he began to experience back spasms. At 218, Wasim Akram removed Mongia. Sunil Joshi hung around while Tendulkar upped the tempo, anxious to ease his increasing back pain as much as anything else. He hit 3 fours in an over from Saqlain. Then at 254 – 17 runs away from victory – Tendulkar slogged at Saqlain and was caught at mid-off. Saqlain polished off the tail to take 5 for 93 and Pakistan won by 12 runs. They got a standing ovation from the Chennai crowd. Kumble was the undisputed hero of Delhi but it was impossible to ignore Saqlain. He took 5 for 94 and 5 for 122, to give him 20 wickets in the series. His only other 10-wicket haul has been against Zimbabwe at Bulawayo in 2002/03.

Saqlain's potent form continued into the English 1999 season. First there was the World Cup, in which Pakistan were highly fancied. They got to the final but were there eclipsed by Australia. Saqlain had a good tournament, taking 18 wickets including 5 in the controversial loss to Bangladesh at Northampton and a hat-trick – his second in one-day internationals – against Zimbabwe at The Oval.

It was to The Oval that he returned at the end of the World Cup, to rejoin Surrey as one of their overseas players. Saqlain had signed for Surrey in 1997 when, in eight games, he took 32 wickets and headed their averages. He was an even more dominant figure in 1998 when Surrey were pressing for the championship title and were only thwarted in the final game. Saqlain's early departure to join the Pakistan side was a factor in their failure to win. Three times at The Oval he had 11 wickets in a match. First, Worcestershire were bowled out for 186, with Saqlain taking 7 for 46, a then career-best. He bettered that a month later, precipitating a startling collapse by Sussex on the first day. They went from 93 for no wicket to 125 all out. Saqlain, whose final figures were 7 for 30, had a spell of 7 for 17 in 65 balls, and 4 for 0 in 7 balls. In the next home match, against Derbyshire, he took 8 for 65 in the second innings.

In 1999, Surrey finally reached the pinnacle they had been striving for. Adam Hollioake's immensely strong combination established themselves as the outstanding county team of modern times. Saqlain's contribution to the 1999 title was critical, even though he only played seven games. He took 58 wickets at 11.37. He started with 5 for 72 and 7 for 38 against Durham. There were 5-wicket hauls in the next three games, against Hampshire, Warwickshire and Glamorgan (5 for 18) and then Sussex were annihilated at Hove (7 for 19 including a hat-trick in the first innings, 10 in the match). At one point, in their first innings, Sussex were 103 for 2: they were all out for 115. Eight in the match against Derbyshire and 7 against Nottinghamshire saw Saqlain to the end of his season. All the games mentioned were won. He missed the final two matches because of a knee injury.

Surrey retained the title in 2000, the first year of the two-division Championship. Saqlain was fifth – as opposed to first the previous year – in the first-class averages, taking 66 wickets at 15.39. A bizarre match against Derbyshire was over by tea on the second day. Derbyshire were bowled out for 118, with Gary Butcher, brother of the England batsman Mark, taking 4 wickets in 4 balls. Surrey made 260. Derbyshire's openers put on 68 before Ian Salisbury, often Saqlain's partner in these successful years for Surrey, took 2 wickets in an over. Then Saqlain took over, taking 7 wickets for 5 runs. His final analysis was 7 for 11 – Derbyshire were all out for 97. He remained a force to be reckoned with when Surrey won the title again in 2002.

In between these triumphs in England, Saqlain had had mixed experiences in Test cricket. In Australia in 1999/2000, Pakistan lost all three Tests, but they should probably have won the second at Hobart. Pakistan, put into bat by Steve Waugh, made 222.

Saqlain Mushtaq in action for Surrey,

Australia, largely through a typically dazzling display from Michael Slater, were at one point 191 for 1 but were all out for 246. Saqlain took 6 for 17 in 8 overs and his overall figures were 6 for 46. A century from Inzamam-ul-Haq enabled Wasim Akram to set Australia what appeared to be an academic target of 369. But they got them, despite slipping to 126 for 5. Saqlain's figures were 2 for 130 off 44.5 overs. Six months later, a schoolboy fielding error by Saqlain, fluffing a run-out chance in a moment of panic, enabled the West Indies to win the match by 1 wicket and thus secure the series.

It can perhaps be seen from the achievements recorded here that Saqlain was an unusual sort of spinner. The county games show that he could run through sides and cause precipitate collapses. At Hobart in 1999/2000, he caused genuine mayhem in Australia's first innings. The fact is that, although always described as an off-spinner, Saqlain was never an off-spinner pure and simple. Like Cleopatra, he had infinite variety. In particular, he had a 'mystery ball'. It was Saqlain, rather than Muttiah Muralitharan, who invented the 'doosra' – Urdu for the 'other one'. As early as 1995/96, when he toured Australia, it was acknowledged that he could bowl what was in effect, a leg-break with an off-spinner's action. Australians were reminded of their own 'mystery spinner' John Gleeson.

He took a little while to get established in the side. Against Zimbabwe at Sheikhupura in October 1996 he made 79, helping Wasim Akram add 313 for the eighth wicket; but he was unable to bowl Pakistan to victory. He was to make a – very dull – Test hundred against New Zealand at Christchurch in 2000/01. He helped secure victory in the First Test at Auckland, taking 4 for 48 and – in 25.4 overs – 4 for 24. He was the leading wicket-taker, with 14, in the two Test series in Sri Lanka in 1996/97. He was involved in a bizarre incident on the tour of South Africa in 1997/98. The Pakistani management requested the postponement of the First Test because two of their players – Saqlain and Mohammad Akram – had been mugged outside the team hotel. Eyewitnesses reported the players as having been seen at various exotic nightspots. The players' story changed various times and before long the team management were virtually hiding from the press.

Be that as it may, Saqlain was a high-class performer, who was equally effective in one-day cricket. Indeed he came to be regarded as something of a one-day specialist. Only Muralitharan, Kumble and Shane Warne have taken more wickets in one-day internationals than Saqlain, and they have all played more matches. And his strike rate is better than any of them, the fifth best in one-day internationals. He was the youngest bowler to reach 100, 150 and 200 one-day wickets.

He has a lovely side-on action after a curious stuttering run-up. He is also an expert at varying his pace and his line of attack. He has never been a big spin-ner of his orthodox off-break and his real strength is the doosra. Even as careful a player of spin bowling as Michael Artherton said he found it difficult to pick the doosra out of the hand: it was delivered with a slightly higher arm action. The doosra wreaked havoc with tail enders. Atherton felt that if a batsman could deal with the doosra, Saqlain was much less of a handful then Muralitharan. Interestingly, Abdul Qadir, the guru of modern Pakistani spinners, felt that Mushtaq Ahmed was a more effective spinner than Saqlain. Certainly Mushtaq, although he ended up with fewer wickets, won more matches. Murali and the other great unorthodox finger spinner, Harbhajan Singh, have won far more games at home than Saqlain.

England's batsmen certainly proved equal to the task in 2000/01. Saqlain took 8 wickets in the first innings of the First Test, but they cost 164 runs. And although Saqlain took 3 for 64 in England's second innings in the Third Test at Karachi, he could not prevent them from securing an historic 6-wicket victory, Pakistan's first defeat at the National Stadium. Revenge, of a sort, was gained six months later at Old Trafford when, in the second and final Test, Saqlain's unusual – for a slow bowler – tendency to bowl no-balls was overlooked by the distracted umpires as he helped skittle England's lower order to gain a series-equalling victory in a frantic final session. Saqlain took 4 for 74 in a marathon spell of 47.4 overs.

In recent years a series of injuries have blighted Saqlain's progress. First a wrist injury, suffered in an accident at home in 2003, made it difficult to bowl the doosra; then a knee injury ended his 2004 county season before it had started. In what was, to date, his last Test appearance, against India at Multan in 2003/04, he seemed distinctly out of sorts, having Virender Sehwag dropped off his bowling in a promising opening spell and then dropping him himself. Sehwaq made 309, India got 675 for 5 and Saqlain took 1 for 204. He unveiled yet another variation – the teesra – but whatever he bowled Sehwag seemed to like it. Danish Kaneria is doing the slow bowling in the Tests and Shoaib Malik – a good enough batsman to open for Pakistan in Test cricket – is doing it in the one-day internationals. Saqlain, meanwhile, started the 2006 English season playing for Ireland. It remains to be seen where he goes from there.

SAQLAIN MUSHTAQ
Right-hand bat, off-break
Born: 29 December 1976, Lahore
Major Teams: Pakistan, Islamabad, Pakistan International Airlines, Surrey, Ireland

TESTS
(1995/96-2006)

	M	I	NO	Runs	HS	Ave	100	50	Ct
Batting & Fielding	49	78	14	927	101*	14.48	1	2	15

	Balls	R	W	Ave	BBI	5	10	SR	Econ
Bowling	14,070	6,206	208	29.83	8/164	13	3	67.64	2.64

ONE-DAY INTERNATIONALS

	M	I	NO	Runs	HS	Ave	SR	Ct
Batting & Fielding	169	98	38	711	37*	11.84	49.58	40

	Balls	R	W	Ave	BBI	5	SR	Econ
Bowling	8,770	6,275	288	21.78	5/20	6	30.45	4.29

FIRST-CLASS
(Career: 1994/95-2006)

	M	I	NO	Runs	HS	Ave	100	50	Ct
Batting & Fielding	176	242	54	3,109	101*	16.53	1	12	64

	Balls	R	W	Ave	BBI	5	10	SR	Econ
Bowling	41,544	18,026	775	23.25	8/85	96	15	53.60	2.6

LIST A

	M	I	NO	Runs	HS	Ave	Ct
Batting & Fielding	315	177	66	1,307	38*	11.77	79

	Balls	R	W	Ave	BBI	5	SR	Econ
Bowling	15,780	10,975	473	23.20	5/20	7	33.36	4.17

SARFRAZ NAWAZ

A brief survey of the career of the mercurial fast-medium bowler Sarfraz Nawaz could do worse than concentrate on his performances on Pakistan's tour of Australia in 1978/79. The circumstances under which the tour was conducted were not without controversy. This was the heyday of World Series Cricket and most of Australia's leading players had signed for Kerry Packer and hence were banned from Test cricket. Pakistan's Packer players, however, were allowed by their home board, after initially being banned, to resume their official Test careers. Asif Iqbal made some very ill-judged comments before the series started about the Australians being a bunch of schoolboys. Imran Khan said that the series was played in as ugly an atmosphere as he ever experienced. Both teams had been busy. Australia's inexperienced side had had a harrowing time of it in a six-Test Ashes series, losing 5-1. Pakistan had beaten India in Pakistan – this hugely anticipated series had been the catalyst for the return of their Packer players – and New Zealand away. Sarfraz headed the bowling averages against India with 17 wickets in the three Tests, at an average of 25. He was a major force in Pakistan's two victories at Lahore and Karachi. At Lahore, there was more grass on the pitch than usual and some help for the seamers. Mushtaq Mohammad won the toss and put India in. Sarfraz came on first change, after Saleem Altaf had dismissed Sunil Gavaskar, and took 4 for 46. India struggled to 199. They were always on the back foot after that and Pakistan won by 8 wickets. At Karachi, a pitch of varying pace and bounce produced a game with many notable features. Pakistan's margin of victory was the same; they reached their target of 164 in 100 minutes with 7 balls to spare. Gavaskar scored twin hundreds for India, while for Pakistan it was again magnificent pace bowling from Imran and Sarfraz that made the difference. Sarfraz took 9 wickets for 159 runs off 55.2 overs in the match. In New Zealand he saved his best for the final drawn Test at Auckland, where he took 3 for 56 and 4 for 61.

The first game in the short two-Test series in Australia was played at Melbourne, unusually late, in March. Graham Yallop won the toss and put Pakistan in. An aggressive opening spell from Rodney Hogg had the visitors in trouble early on and they were always struggling; Sarfraz, often a useful performer with the bat, top-scored with 35 out of 196. Australia fared even worse against Imran (4 for 26) and Sarfraz, totalling 168 (debutant Dav Whatmore 43). Pakistan declared their second innings at 353 for 9. By the close of the fourth day, Australia were 117 for 2 with Andrew Hilditch and Whatmore both out to Sarfraz. Australia needed 265 to win on the final day.

Yallop was out early but Allan Border and Kim Hughes combined for the biggest partnership of the match, putting on 177 for the fourth wicket. The twenty-three-year-old Border made what would later come to be seen as a typically dogged six-and-a-quarter-hour century, his first in Tests. The new ball had been taken shortly before tea but Pakistan appeared to be handicapped by Imran suffering from the after-effects of food poisoning. The fourth-wicket pair took the score to 305: 77 needed for victory. Then Sarfraz, cutting his run-up by half and holding the seam upright, struck, bowling Border with a beauty that cut sharply back.

What followed was scarcely believable. Australia were all out for 310. Sarfraz took all the remaining wickets – 7 including Border's – at a personal cost of 1 run in 33 balls. His final figures, 9 for 86 in 35 eight-ball overs, were then the best by a visiting bowler in Australia; indeed they were at the time the best figures ever achieved by a pace bowler in Test cricket. Hughes was caught at mid off trying to revive the run-getting; Yallop had been run out: everyone else was either bowled, leg before or caught behind. Mushtaq Mohammad described Pakistan's 77-run victory as a miracle.

Australia won the Second Test at Perth with relative ease, by 7 wickets. Pakistan, put in by Hughes, in his first Test as captain, never recovered from losing 5 wickets before lunch. Sarfraz made useful runs at the end of that first innings but his most memorable contribution came as Australia approached their victory target of 236. The opening pair had put on 87 when the non-striker, vice-captain Hilditch, bent down and picked up the ball, which had been lobbed in by a fielder, and handed it, as if it were a cup of tea or a letter, to the bowler Sarfraz. Sarfraz promptly appealed. Hilditch was given out 'handled the ball'. Gerald Brodribb, the expert on all matters of cricket law, called the incident 'shameful'. It was a direct retaliation to Sikander Bakht having been run out while backing up in Pakistan's second innings.

To say that this was typical of 'Saf' would be misleading because it would suggest that he was mean and calculating. Which he was not. Well, not often; usually he was charming and companionable. But he was a bit unpredictable, not to say contrary: a controversialist. In the middle of the 1977/78 series against England he simply vanished, flying to England in a fit of pique about terms and conditions. Peter Roebuck put it well: deadly serious but incredibly funny. And he was always well aware of his 'rights': hence the appeal. Brodribb conceded that Hilditch was silly to pick the ball up; there are, after all, eleven fielders who can do that.

At the time of Pakistan's next big series – in India in 1979/80 – Sarfraz was not even in the touring party. Dicky Rutnagur put his omission down to a 'clash of personalities'. Imran was more explicit. He said that the new captain, Asif Iqbal, did not want Sarfraz in the side because he could not handle him. When Imran became

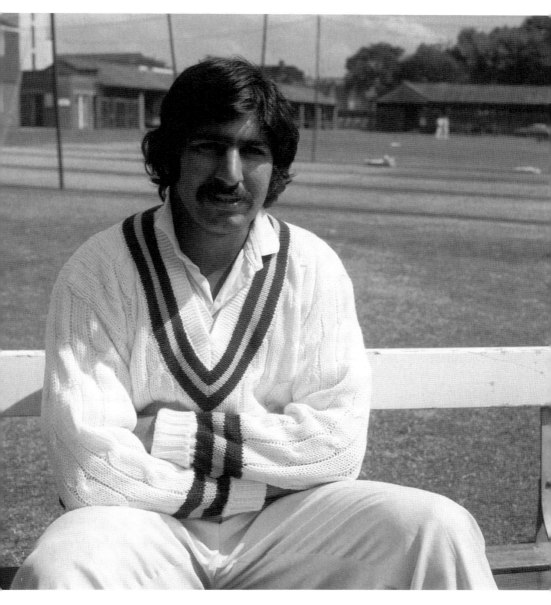

Sarfraz Nawaz.

captain, he sometimes had to fight to get Sarfraz into the team, as in the series against India in 1982/83 when Imran took 40 wickets. Sarfraz rendered splendid support, taking 19 wickets including 11 in the innings victory at Hyderabad but Imran had had to appeal to the president of the cricket board to get him into the side. Imran was not around to get Sarfraz into the squad for the tour of India in 1983/84 and he duly missed it. But he was recalled during the tour of Australia later that season and bowled splendidly in the Third Test at Adelaide, prompting thoughts of a Pakistan victory. Even in his bowling he could be quite mad, loving to bowl bouncers at fellow fast bowlers – mild-mannered men like, er, Jeff Thomson. Riled by Tony Greig at The Oval in 1974, he bowled a beamer at him.

Sarfraz and Imran were a very considerable pair, both immensely hard-working although Imran was naturally fitter. Sarfraz was Robert Mitchum to Imran's Cary Grant, bulkier, moodier more threatening in some ways. Sarfraz was older and took Imran under his wing in the early days, teaching him Punjabi, a necessary language in the Pakistan team. In Imran's first great Test performance, at Sydney in 1976/77, when Pakistan gained their first victory in Australia, Sarfraz took three important wickets in each innings. They combined formidably in the Caribbean a few months later in a fascinating series won 2-1 by the home side. Sarfraz's swing bowling, in support of Mushtaq's leg-spin, helped Pakistan to victory in the Fourth Test at Port-of-Spain. The best game of the series was the fascinating draw in the First Test at Bridgetown. Imran has written of how he and Sarfraz had the West Indies in trouble in the first innings and in particular how they swung the old ball. Mushtaq Mohammad wanted to take the new ball, Sarfraz urged Imran to dissuade him – he knew Mushtaq would listen to Imran, not him – but even Imran could not change the captain's mind. The new ball was taken and the West Indies recovered.

Sarfraz was among the earliest exponents of reverse swing and he was never shy of explaining how he helped to teach Imran the proper way to shine a cricket ball. *Wisden*, in its report of Pakistan's tour of Australia in 1972/73, remarked on the late swing obtained by the opening bowler Saleem Altaf. In the Third Test at Sydney, Pakistan gained a first innings lead of 26 and then bowled Australia out for 184. Saleem and Sarfraz took 4 wickets each, Sarfraz took 8 for 109 in the match. Ray Robinson called the third day, which closed with Australia on 94 for 7, Pakistan's best day against Australia since they beat Australia in Karachi in 1956/57. But the batsmen collapsed to Max Walker (6 for 16).

Reversing needs one side of the ball to be distinctly shinier than the other rougher, heavier one and there were dark mutterings as succeeding generations of Pakistan's fast bowlers demonstrated exceptional prowess at reverse swing. The mutterings culminated in a tabloid article by Allan Lamb at the end of Pakistan's tour of England in 1992 in which he said that Sarfraz, while they were county colleagues at Northamptonshire, explained how best to rough up a cricket ball. Sarfraz sued, but withdrew the case before it got to court. Somehow the lawsuit against Lamb was a very Sarfrazian epilogue to his relationship with Northamptonshire. That relationship had been mutually beneficial. It had started many years before. Sarfraz made his Test debut in the riot-shortened Karachi Test against England in 1968/69. The Northamptonshire captain Roger Prideaux was on that MCC tour, although he was not playing in the match (his place had been taken by another Northants player, Colin Milburn, who scored a century in what tragically turned out to be his last Test). Mushtaq Mohammad– yet another Northants player – recommended Sarfraz to Prideaux, who liked what he saw. Sarfraz signed for the county and had two spells with them, a brief and not entirely convincing one in 1970 and 1971 and a longer and much more distinguished one from 1974 to 1982.

In the mid 1970s, the county were as strong as they have ever been. Their greatest strength was the variety of their bowling – Sarfraz and Bob Cottam, the left-armer John Dye and two genuinely exotic spinners, Bishan Bedi and Mushtaq. In 1975, Sarfraz took 101 first-class wickets at 20.30. Peter Lee of Lancashire was the only other bowler to take a hundred wickets. The following year, although his figures did not look as good, he was more influential. He took 82 wickets at 22.76 – being the fifth-highest wicket taker in the country – and was a genuine match-winner. Northants came second in the Championship and won the Gillette Cup, their first honour. He also scored over 600 championship runs. In 1977, he was fourth in the national averages with 73 wickets at 17.06. He headed the county's bowling averages again in 1979 and in 1980 he was a leading figure in the county's triumph in the Benson & Hedges Cup, taking three for 22 in the quarter-final against Nottinghamshire, 5 for 21 in the semi-final against Middlesex and 3 for 23 in the final against Essex, which Northants won by 6 runs.

Sarfraz finished with over 500 wickets for the county. He took 1,005 wickets in all. As suggested above, he was a more than useful batsman too. His forceful 53 at Headingley in 1974 in difficult conditions was the second highest score of an intriguing draw. He took 7 wickets as well. He made invaluable runs – 29 and 51 – in both innings of Mushtaq's victory at Port-of-Spain in 1976/77. In his fifty-fifth and final Test, at his home ground of Lahore, against England in 1983/84, he went in at number ten in the first innings and scored 90, putting on 161 for the ninth wicket with Zaheer Abbas and becoming the third Pakistani, after Imran and Intikhab Alam, to achieve the Test match double of a thousand runs and a hundred wickets. In that last series, at the age of thirty-five, he bowled 150 overs in the three Tests.

Sarfraz has rarely been out of the news for long since giving up playing cricket. He had a spell in politics and for a while was a special adviser on sport to the Pakistani government. It seems almost like Tony Blair making Wayne Rooney a special adviser on football: don't laugh – it could still happen. He was always a stirrer. As England began preparations for what was always going to be a difficult tour of Pakistan in 1987/88, he put a little fuel on the fire by suggesting that the English umpires Dickie Bird and David Shepherd – sainted figures both – had been a little less than even-handed in their handling of the World Cup semi-final between Australia and Pakistan. Sarfraz's first explanation for Pakistan's defeat was that they had thrown the match, but he changed his mind about this after the captain, Javed Miandad, sued for defamation.

Even his relations with Imran became difficult. Ivo Tennant, in his biography of Imran, said that he and Sarfraz were no longer speaking to one another. That was 1994. When the match-fixing scandal broke in 1995, however, they began exchanging pleasantries. It emerged that Imran had been involved in the decision to sack manager Intikhab Alam and the captain Saleem Malik after the crisis-ridden tour of southern Africa. Sarfraz – ever the moderator – alleged that Imran should be stoned to death as a cheat and an adulterer. Imran responded, alleging that Sarfraz was an inveterate gambler who, when in England, could always be found in Ladbrokes.

All good clean fun. On one point, though, the two appeared to be in agreement. There was only one punishment appropriate for someone found guilty of match-fixing: the death penalty.

SARFRAZ NAWAZ
Right-hand bat, right-arm fast medium-pace
Born: 1 December 1948, Lahore
Major Teams: Pakistan, Lahore, Punjab University, Punjab, Railways, United Bank, Lahore City, Northamptonshire

TESTS
(1968/69–1983/84)

	M	I	NO	Runs	HS	Ave	50	Ct
Batting & Fielding	55	72	13	1,045	90	17.71	4	26

	Balls	R	W	Ave	BBI	5	10	SR	Econ
Bowling	13,951	5,798	177	32.75	9/86	4	1	78.81	2.49

ONE-DAY INTERNATIONALS

	M	I	NO	Runs	HS	Ave	SR	Ct
Batting & Fielding	45	31	8	221	34★	9.60	64.05	8

	Balls	R	W	Ave	BBI	SR	Econ
Bowling	2,412	1,463	63	23.22	4/27	38.28	3.83

FIRST-CLASS
(Career: 1967/68–1984/85)

	M	I	NO	Runs	HS	Ave	50	Ct
Batting & Fielding	299	367	72	5,709	90	19.35	17	163

	Balls	R	W	Ave	BBI	5	10	SR	Econ
Bowling	55,692	24,750	1,005	24.62	9/86	46	4	55.41	2.66

LIST A

	M	I	NO	Runs	HS	Ave	50	Ct
Batting & Fielding	228	161	49	1,721	92	15.36	3	43

	Balls	R	W	Ave	BBI	5	SR	Econ
Bowling	11,937	6,662	319	20.88	5/15	3	36.16	3.46

SHAHID AFRIDI

Who is the most exciting cricketer in the world in 2006? Not the best, or the most skilful, or the most successful, but the most exciting? There are a lot of candidates. It is an exciting time in Test cricket even if the one-day game has became tediously mundane and formulaic.

In England, they will say Andrew Flintoff or Kevin Pietersen. Maybe Flintoff is too good to be described merely as exciting: a genuinely great player. Pietersen really is a one-off: unorthodox, aggressive and a magnificent hitter, the holder, with Wasim Raja, of the record for the number of sixes hit in a Test series. In Australia, there is Adam Gilchrist, who has revolutionised batting in both Test and one-day cricket and Andrew Symonds, renowned for his batting exploits for Gloucestershire in the County Championship in the mid-1990s. He has become one of the most dangerous one-day players in the world and is beginning to take that confidence into the Test arena. Australia also have Brett Lee who, like Shoaib Akhtar, is able to generate that special frisson that comes with bowling of extreme pace. The new Indian wicketkeeper Mahendra Singh Dhoni is another who generates real enthusiasm; he has come to Test cricket by way of the one-day game and become an instant success.

But if you are seeking someone who can bring a crowd to its feet just by walking to the wicket then you need look no further than the charismatic Pathan Shahid Afridi. Afridi must now be the most feared batsman in the world because of his ability to demolish and demoralise an attack. In the year or so up to January 2006, he has added an unprecedented degree of consistency to the astonishing power of his hitting.

The starting point was the tour of the Caribbean in 2004/05. Some commentators have attributed the new, more consistent approach to Bob Woolmer, Pakistan's coach since the middle of 2004. Woolmer is thought to be more inclined to let Afridi play the way he wants to. Whatever the reason, Afridi made 122 in the First Test at Bridgetown, which Pakistan lost, and 33 and 43 in the second at Kingston, which they won. At Bridgetown he opened in the first innings, scoring 16 (1 six, 1 four). In the second, he went in at number six. His 122 was made in 93 balls and included

6 sixes and 9 fours. In the course of the first game, he apparently had a furious row with stand-in captain Younis Khan. But Younis and Afridi, guided by returning skipper Inzamam-ul-Haq, were able to put their differences behind them and all contributed significantly to the victory in Jamaica.

Then came the series against England at the end of 2005. He was not picked for the First Test at Multan but made an authoritative, indeed dismissive 92 in the second, at Faisalabad. Again he was batting at six and the stand of 138 between Inzamam and Mohammad Yousuf provided the ideal platform for him. On 57 not out overnight, he launched into Matthew Hoggard on the second morning, when 45 runs came off the first 5 overs. Hoggard got him in the end though. Afridi picked up 3 wickets in England's first innings but his most telling contribution came in the field. He was seen to be scuffing up the pitch, on a length, during a drinks interval – taken after the momentary panic after a gas canister exploded at the ground – and this earned him a one-Test ban.

The culmination of his batting transformation came in Pakistan's next home series against India in January 2006. The first two Tests were high-scoring draws on placid pitches at Lahore and Faisalabad. The bowlers did not have much of a chance and all the batsmen on both sides, except, amazingly, Sachin Tendulkar, filled their boots at some stage or other, but even so Afridi stood out. At Lahore, he came in with the score at 456 for 4 and made 103, holing out to Ajit Agarkar as soon as he had reached three figures. He hit the hapless Harbhajan Singh for 27 in an over with four successive sixes, all in an arc between square-leg and long on. Apparently, it was a premeditated attempt to hit six sixes in an over, something no one has managed in Test cricket. In all he hit 7 sixes and 7 fours, in 80 balls – Kamran Akmal, incidentally, took 81 balls to score 102.

When he came in to bat at Faisalabad, Pakistan were almost in a crisis – 217 for 4 – and he received a tumultuous reception from the crowd. The corollary of this had been seen in the Faisalabad game against England: in the second innings Afridi was out first ball to Flintoff. The crowd just got up and walked out. He and Inzamam took the score to 467. Afridi made his highest Test score of 156 off 128 balls with 20 fours and 6 sixes. He made 60 in the second innings at Karachi – when seven Pakistan batsmen made at least fifty – and finished the series with an average of 66.

It had not always been thus. His Test record has been a curiously patchy affair. He got off to an impressive enough start. He was brought in for his First Test against Australia at Karachi in 1998/99 as a last-minute replacement for opening batsman Saeed Anwar. On the first day, he took 5 for 32 with his leg-breaks: 'slightly flattering' figures, *Wisden* reports. Opening the innings with Aamir Sohail, he made 10 and 6. But in his second match, against India at Chennai three months later, again opening the innings, he made a highly responsible 141 in Pakistan's second innings of 286, batting for over five hours and hitting 21 fours and 3 sixes: he was seventh out with the score at 279. Pakistan won a thrilling match by 12 runs. He made 32 and 41 in the Second Test – Kumble's match – at Delhi, being the highest scorer in the first innings and the second highest scorer in the second.

Shahid Afridi takes the aerial route. Faisalabad, 2006, Second Test against India.

In the second game of the Asian Test Championship that followed the Indian series against Sri Lanka at Lahore, he scored 84 in the second innings, having been dropped four times, and put on 156 for the first wicket with Wajahatullah Wasti. But after that, his Test appearances were sporadic. By the time he toured the Caribbean in 2004/05, he had only played seventeen Tests – as opposed to over 200 one-day internationals altogether and had made just one more century, against the West Indies at Sharjah in 2001/02.

It was as a one-day player that Afridi initially established himself and in a singularly spectacular manner. The context was what would otherwise have been a forgettable series in Kenya, involving the hosts, Sri Lanka, South Africa and Pakistan. Afridi was playing in his second one-day international – he had not batted in the first – at the (alleged) age of 16 years and 217 days. Pakistan's opponents at the Nairobi Gymkhana were Sri Lanka, whose attack included Chaminda Vaas and Muttiah Muralitharan. Pakistan, batting first, made 371 for 9. Anwar, opening with Saleem Elahi, made 115 but the real sensation was Afridi, who batted at number three. Afridi made the fastest ever one-day international hundred, off 37 balls with 11 sixes and 6 fours. 'Crikey O'Riley!' as Mark Nicholas – but, one feels, very few others – might say.

The previous fastest centurion, Sanath Jayasuriya, was there to see his record broken: his 10 overs went for 94 runs. What everyone who saw the innings agreed on was that Afridi was not a slogger: they were good cricket hits and the sixes would have been six anywhere. That was a point Greg Chappell, the Indian coach, made after Afridi's pyrotechnics in 2006 – that his sixes were real sixes. Chappell's opposite number, Woolmer, agreed that Afridi was something special – even he, he said, would be prepared to pay to watch Afridi bat. He is twentieth on the list of Test match six-hitters but everyone above him on the list has scored at least twice as many runs. Chris Cairns of New Zealand, who is second on the list after Adam Gilchrist, is perhaps the closest comparison to Afridi. In one-day internationals he is already number one. He averages only 23 but he has a staggering strike rate of 108. Gilchrist's, by way of example, is 96.

Against India, Afridi tended to start with a frantic flourish and then steady down and, if not exactly graft, then at least exercise a little discretion and careful shot selection. That was what was missing in earlier years. A good example was the time he spent with Leicestershire in 2001. There were some genuinely spectacular displays. Opening the innings in a Championship match against Northamptonshire, he made a hundred off 74 balls – by the ninth over there were five men on the boundary. In all, he made 164 with 22 fours and 6 sixes. By that stage of the season, Leicestershire's principal interest was in the 50-over knock-out cup, the Cheltenham & Gloucester Trophy. Afridi powered them through the quarter-final against Worcestershire – 67 in 44 balls including 25 in an over from Stuart Lampitt – and the semi-final against Lancashire – 95 off 57 balls with 8 fours and 6 sixes. Leicestershire faced Somerset in the final at Lord's. Somerset made 271 for 9 – Afridi took 3 wickets. Then he opened the innings with Trevor Ward. It was almost embarrassing. Afridi was clearly out to impress the capacity crowd, but Somerset's new-ball attack of Andrew Caddick and Richard Johnson was more than equal to the task. Afridi was out for 20 off 10 balls and Somerset secured a comfortable win.

Afridi's fastish, skiddy leg-breaks give his cricket an extra dimension in both the shorter and longer versions of the game. He has a faster ball that is genuinely quick – it has been timed at over 80 miles an hour. He played a key role with Danish Kaneria in bowling Pakistan to their historic victory at Bangalore in 2004/05. He picked up a couple of wickets in the first innings, including Sachin Tendulkar for 45. In the second, he struck three decisive blows, removing Tendulkar, V.V.S Laxman and Sourav Ganguly: his figures were 3 for 13 in 17 overs.

In April 2006, with Test matches and one-day games going on in various parts of the world, there were two cricket-related stories of particular interest. One was the hurried departure of England's vice-captain, Marcus Trescothick, from the tour of India shortly before the First Test. Weeks after the event, Trascothick said he had been suffering from a 'virus'. Initially, his departure was explained by reference to 'personal' or 'family' reasons. The second story was Shahid Afridi's sudden, if temporary 'retirement' from Test cricket to concentrate on one-day internationals in preparation for the World Cup in 2007. It is curious that he has never really 'fired' in a World Cup: his main achievement so far has been to be banned by his own board for sledging in the match against India in 2003. There was a view that his announcement had been made in a fit of pique after being dropped during the recent Test series in Sri Lanka: this seemed to be borne out when his retirement was rescinded almost as suddenly as it had been announced. Be that as it may, Afridi's statement raised directly an issue that Trescothick's raised indirectly, namely the threat of 'burn-out' facing the world's top players. I can assure you, dear reader, simply from the experience of preparing this slim volume, that there is simply far too much international cricket being played.

Shahizaha Mohammad SHAHID Khan AFRIDI
Right-hand bat, leg-break & googly
Born: 1 March 1980, Kohat
Major Teams: Pakistan, Karachi Whites, Karachi Blues, Leicestershire, Derbyshire, Griqualand West, Kent

TESTS
(1998/99-2006)

	M	I	NO	Runs	HS	Ave	100	50	Ct
Batting & Fielding	24	43	1	1,634	156	38.90	5	8	10

	Balls	R	W	Ave	BBI	5	10	SR	Econ
Bowling	2,735	1436	44	32.63	5/52	1	0	62.15	3.15

ONE-DAY INTERNATIONALS

	M	I	NO	Runs	HS	Ave	100	50	Ct
Batting & Fielding	219	209	9	4,787	109	23.93	4	26	81

	W	Ave	BBI	5	SR	Econ
Bowling	184	26.19	5/11	2	46.90	4.62

FIRST-CLASS
(Career: 1995/96-2006)

	M	I	NO	Runs	HS	Ave	100	50	Ct
Batting & Fielding	86	147	4	4,624	164	32.33	11	22	55

	Balls	R	W	Ave	BBI	5	10	SR	Econ
Bowling	10,360	5,345	184	29.04	6/101	6	0	56.30	3.09

LIST A

	M	I	NO	Runs	HS	Ave	100	50	Ct
Batting & Fielding	297	284	11	6,883	112	25.21	5	42	97

	Balls	R	W	Ave	BBI	5	SR	Econ
Bowling	11,993	9,160	267	34.3	5/11	3	44.91	4.58

SHOAIB AKHTAR

There are few more valuable commodities in world cricket than Shoaib Akhtar. He is a fast bowler of quite exceptional pace. From the very beginning of his career as a teenage tearaway for Rawalpindi it has been clear that he has wonderful natural ability and the sheer speed to disconcert the opposition. He has always caused problems for the best players in the world and provoked mayhem in many batting orders if he is in the mood; even now, perhaps especially now, as a middle-aged tearaway – well, the Rawalpindi Express is over thirty – he is that rarest of treasures, a genuine match-winning bowler.

Shoaib can do serious damage in more ways than one. A good example came during Pakistan's first Test against South Africa at Lahore in October 2003. It looked like being a difficult game for the home side. They had recently been thrashed by South Africa in a series there. They had lost the one-day series 4-1 after winning the first game. They were without their new captain and best player, Inzamam-ul-Haq, who was injured. And South Africa won the toss and batted and halfway through the first afternoon were taking control of the match at 159 for 3.

Pakistan won the match on the morning of the fifth day. It was a valiant team effort in which a number of the side played notable parts. The opener Taufeeq Umar made 111 and Asim Kamal 99 on debut as Pakistan gained a first innings lead of 81. Danish Kaneria took 5 wickets in South Africa's second innings. Taufeeq also got runs in the second innings as Pakistan won by 8 wickets.

But arguably the match-winner was Shoaib. In South Africa's second innings, as they were building a lead, it was he who made the vital breakthrough that allowed Kaneria in. South Africa started the fourth day on 99 for 1, Shoaib having dismissed Graeme Smith the previous evening. In that morning session, he took 3 vital wickets – Herschelle Gibbs, Jacques Kallis and Boeta Dippenaar – to return figures of 4 for 36 in 19.3 overs. But his most important contribution had come on that first afternoon. South Africa's most experienced batsman, the combative left-handed accumulator Gary Kirsten, was constructing what had the potential to be a formidable total when Shoaib felled him with a bouncer. Kirsten is a tough customer, like all the South Africans. Not only did he retire hurt, he did not bat again in the innings. Although he came in again at number six second time around he had a broken nose and left eye socket. Next ball, Shoaib bowled Neil McKenzie with an inswinging yorker. Later, he had Andre Nel leg before, but the damage had already been done. The psychological balance of the game had shifted and although South Africa were not yet beaten, Pakistan were in the ascendancy from the moment Kirsten was hit.

With Shoaib, of course, you get a package – the good is marvellous but you have to take the bad and the ugly as well. He bowled 19.3 overs, rather than 20, in that second innings not because he polished off the tail but because he had to leave the field in the middle of an over with a strained hamstring. Fitness has been a persistent and sometimes tiresome issue. Fast bowling is a strenuous and stressful pastime but some of Shoaib's fitness issues have been rather dubious – not that this was one of them. Anyway, he missed the Second Test at Faisalabad not because of the strained hamstring but because he had been banned for a game. The ban was imposed by the match referee Clive Lloyd after an incident on the first afternoon of the First Test when Shoaib directed what Lloyd deemed to be 'obscene' language at the South African tail-ender Paul Adams. It was doubtless just a bit of banter but behaviour had become an issue after a disagreeable incident involving Andrew Hall and Yousuf Youhana (as he then was) in a one-day game at Peshawar, and Lloyd came down hard. Shoaib was a bit unlucky really but, unfortunately, this is the sort of thing that tends to happen to him.

Shoaib is also the sort of bowler who can make a dramatic impact on the dullest of days when there is no hope of a result. The series between Pakistan and India in early 2006 was a very curious affair. There were two immensely high-scoring draws, at Lahore and Faisalabad. Then at Karachi, there was a hat-trick by Irfan Pathan in the first over of the match and Pakistan went on to win by 341 runs. Shoaib made a crucial breakthrough in the second innings at Karachi, getting Rahul Dravid early, but the decisive bowling came from Mohammad Asif. Shoaib's most memorable spell of the series had come in the previous game at Faisalabad. The match was following a similar pattern to that at Lahore. Pakistan had made 588 and early on the third afternoon India were 230 for 1 with Dravid and V.V.S. Laxman looking ominously well set. Then, suddenly, both were out – Dravid run out – within a few minutes of each other and India had two new batsmen at the crease. Inzamam brought Shoaib back on and, just for a few moments, a burst of 6 overs, it was a different game. Asif removed Yuvraj Singh and Shoaib launched a terrific assault on Sachin Tendulkar and Mahendra Singh Dhoni. It really did look like a contest between bat and ball. Tendulkar was hit on the helmet and before long fenced at one outside the off stump and was caught behind for 14. Dhoni, a naturally aggressive player, was made to struggle as he had never had to before in his brief Test career. But he survived, and Shoaib tired. Dhoni, batting at number six, made 148. India got 603. Shoaib took 1 for 100 in 25 overs.

Shoaib had 'previous' when it came to Tendulkar. Their paths first crossed in the first game of the Asian Test Championship at Calcutta in February 1999. The game, reportedly watched by more than 450,000 people over the five days, resulted in a Pakistan victory by 46 runs. Shoaib took 4 wickets in each innings. The match started sensationally. Wasim Akram won the toss and chose to bat but before long his side were reeling at 26 for 6. Javagal Srinath, who took 13 wickets in the match, did most of the damage.

The Rawalpindi Express. The First Test against India, Lahore, 2006.

Pakistan eventually made 185. India were well in control at 147 for 2 when Shoaib, bowling with venomous pace and just beginning to reverse the old ball, yorked Dravid and Tendulkar with successive balls. It was Tendulkar's first golden duck in Tests. Shoaib was – quite accidentally – involved in Tendulkar's second innings dismissal too. Tendulkar was run out going for what should have been a straightforward third run. With his eye on the ball he failed to observe Shoaib backing away as the ball was thrown at the stumps. They collided and Tendulkar failed to make his ground. The incident resulted in two riots, the second of which, on the final day, resulted in almost all the spectators being forcibly ejected from the ground before Wasim and Shoaib performed the last rites.

India and Pakistan only met sporadically for the next few years in one-day games, including two World Cups. Shoaib was unquestionably one of the stars of the 1999 tournament in England. His pace was electrifyingly generated by a dramatic sprint of a run-up; his heels virtually touched the seat of his pants as he ran in, such was the energy generated. His first ball of the competition, in the game against the West Indies at Bristol, was edged over the slips by Sherwin Campbell and went for six. Campbell's stumps were reorganised in Shoaib's next over. In the following game he and Wasim reduced Scotland to 19 for 5. He had a thrilling spell against the South Africans at Trent Bridge, his bowling touching 95mph, but even he could not stop Lance Klusener, another of the tournament's stars, taking South Africa to victory in that Super Six game. Tendulkar had the better of what turned out to be India's day at Old Trafford, opening aggressively and making 45. Shoaib took 1 for 54 and India won by 47 runs.

He shattered the stumps three times in the semi-final against New Zealand at Old Trafford; Stephen Fleming was well set on 41 when he was bowled by a 91mph yorker. But even Shoaib was powerless in the final when Australia cruised to an easy win.

Pakistan seemed to be in a sorry state during the next World Cup in southern Africa in 2003 where, despite being outshone by Ricky Ponting in the final, Tendulkar was the batting giant. They lost their first game to the holders, Australia, at Johannesburg and never really recovered. Shoaib beat his arch-rival, the Australian Brett Lee, in the race to be the first to the 100mph mark, while bowling to England's Nick Knight at Cape Town. He took 1 for 63 in 9 overs and England won. Shoaib made 43 off 16 balls. One of the great matches of the tournament came just over a week later, at Centurion: India *v.* Pakistan – Tendulkar *v.* Shoaib. Pakistan batted first and made 273 for 7. India reached 100 in the twelfth over. Shoaib's first over went for 18, all to Tendulkar including a cut for six and 2 fours. He made 98 from 75 balls. Shoaib got him in the end but India won by 6 wickets.

Shoaib was dropped for a while after the World Cup and then got banned for a game or two for ball-tampering in a one-day tournament in Sri Lanka. But things got better as 2003 moved into 2004. This was good because India were due to make their first Test tour of Pakistan since 1989/90. It seemed the ideal stage for Shoaib to re-establish his status as one of the world's great fast bowlers.

Just four months before the Indians arrived, he had made a sensational impact in New Zealand. He had only played one Test against them before: that was the only Test in the 2001/02 series that was cut short because of a dreadful bomb blast in Karachi. In that game, at Lahore, Pakistan made 643 (Inzamam 329; Shoaib helped him add 78 for the ninth wicket) and bowled New Zealand out for 73 and 246. In the first innings, which lasted 30.2 overs, Shoaib bowled 8.2 of them and took 6 for 11. Five of his victims were bowled and one leg before, four of those wickets coming in 25 balls to reduce New Zealand from 12 for 0 to 21 for 4. Then he injured his ankle in his follow through but came back to polish off the tail the next morning. He did not bowl in the second innings. In that Test it was a controlled, focussed Shoaib. In the first one-day game, at Karachi, ten days earlier, he had gone for all-out pace: the result had been equally spectacular: 6 for 16 in a 9-over spell.

So the New Zealanders knew what to expect in December 2003. They still seemed to find it a bit of a shock though. Shoaib missed the First Test at Hamilton with a muscle strain. New Zealand were lucky to escape with a draw despite making 563 in the first innings. Mohammad Sami reduced them to 96 for 8 in the second. At Wellington, in the second and final Test, it was Shoaib's turn. He worked very hard to get himself fit. He started the match well, dismissing Lou Vincent and Fleming for ducks in his first two overs – spread over a long period because of a break for bad light. He took 5 for 48 but even so New Zealand seemed to be in a good position as the match progressed. They made 366 and Pakistan fell well behind that with 196. In the middle of the fourth morning, New Zealand were 273 ahead with 3 wickets down and Mark Richardson doing his adhesive damnedest. And then Shoaib struck. It was a genuine strike, like a hurricane, blowing away everything in its path. From 95 for 3, New Zealand were all out for 103.

Shoaib Akhtar in action against Derbyshire on
the tour of 2001.

Shoaib took 6 for 30. Fleming was matter of fact about it after the game, saying, 'We don't
get exposed to 150kph in-swingers that often.'

So there was a lot of expectation when India arrived in March 2004. And a lot of
people were very disappointed. India won the series, something very rare for India
away from home. Pakistan had been inpregnable at home for so long – they lost one
series at home between 1969/70 and 1995/96, to the West Indies in 1980/81. It was,
in one way, just another home defeat. But to India… One head rolled – that of the
coach, Javed Miandad. Of the players, the one who bore the brunt of the criticism,
along with skipper Inzamam – who certainly batted well enough – was Shoaib.

Things started all right, or at least not too badly, in the ding-dong one-day series
that India ended up winning 3-2. Shoaib dismissed Tendulkar twice, once for 28
and once for 7. The Little Master made 141 at Shoaib's home ground, Rawalpindi,
but Pakistan won by 12 runs. Shoaib had his best game, taking 3 wickets, including
Virender Sehwag and Mohammad Kaif, the latter deceived by what was becoming a
speciality, a superlative slower ball. The Test series, though, started badly and finished
worse. Sehwag and Tendulkar murdered the Pakistani bowling at Multan. India lost
5 wickets in the match – none to Shoaib – and won by an innings. Pakistan fought
back well at Lahore, where Shoaib took 3 wickets in India's second innings. So they
went to Rawalpindi for the final game all square.

Sourav Ganguly won the toss and put Pakistan in. India were 23 for 1 by the close,
Pakistan having been bowled out for 224, with Lakshmi Balaji taking 4 for 63. When
India batted Sehwag was out first ball to Shoaib. The second day was mostly Dravid: he
was in the process of compiling a massive 270. To begin with he was partnered by the
stand-in opener, wicketkeeper Partiv Patel. Patel was out just after lunch for 69 and

was replaced by Tendulkar. Inzamam called up Shoaib at once, and Tendulkar fell to his first ball, caught behind. Shoaib also yorked a startled Laxman, who said later that he had never faced bowling so fast. By then, though, India were 261 for 4. Laxman had made a sublime 71. Dravid just went on and on; at close of play India were 342 for 4.

By then, Shoaib had departed. Shortly after bowling Laxman he slipped and fell in his follow-through. He finished that over, but in the middle of the next left the field. He not only failed to reappear, except for a brief period when he was told by the umpires that he could not bowl for a while, but he did not appear on the third day either. Dravid and the rest of them made the most of it. India were finally dismissed for 600, Dravid last man out. It was not entirely clear what the problem was with Shoaib. Various explanations circulated: thumb, wrist, back. But many people were flummoxed when, on the fourth day, with Pakistan in distress at 179 for 7, Shoaib went out to bat and played as if he was in a beer match on a village green, slogging 28 off 14 balls. At the disagreeable post-match press conference, Inzamam made his views very clear. A medical commission was appointed by the Pakistan board to inquire into Shoaib's injury: Imran Khan helpfully advised Shoaib to sue the board for defamation. The commission was inconclusive, although it emerged later that there was a chronic rib problem. More serious really were the concerns routinely being expressed by senior cricket people in Pakistan about Shoaib's commitment or lack of it, and the dire state of his relations with Inzamam in particular and the management generally.

The tour of Australia in 2004/05 did not really help Shoaib's cause either. He had had mixed fortunes against them before. His darkest hours in international cricket had come in Australia, on the tour in 1999/2000. The tour in general was a disappointing one for Shoaib: in the three Tests he took 8 wickets at an average of 67.66. But worse than that was the fact that he was banned from bowling in international cricket because of doubts about the legality of his action when bowling the bouncer. The ban was lifted immediately in relation to one-day cricket and his action was officially cleared in time for Pakistan's next series against Sri Lanka, but the experience was a chastening, indeed devastating one.

The Australians ran into Shoaib twice in 2002, each time getting a taste of the real thing. In the First Test at the neutral venue of Colombo in October, Shoaib almost brought about what would have been a miraculous Pakistan win. Australia made 467 in their first innings and Pakistan replied with 279. Midway through the third day Justin Langer and Matthew Hayden had taken Australia to 61 for no wicket. Then Saqlain Mushtaq dismissed Langer and Shoaib returned for a second spell. He dismissed Ponting and the Waugh twins in 4 balls – two bowled, one leg before – and yorked Adam Gilchrist in the next over. Australia went from 74 for 1 to 74 for 5 to 89 for 7. Shoaib took 5 for 21 in 8 overs. Australia made 127. Pakistan fought hard in their second innings but lost by 41 runs. That, at least, was better than the second game at Sharjah, where the scores were Pakistan 59 and 53, Australia 310. (Hayden 119). Four months earlier, in Brisbane, Shoaib had effectively obliterated Australia's middle order in a one-day game, dismissing Ponting, Damien Martyn, Darren Lehmann, Michael Bevan and Jason Gillespie in his 8 overs at a cost of 25 runs.

In 2004/05, Shoaib headed the bowling averages and obtained 5-wicket hauls at both Perth and Melbourne (he broke down in Sydney during Australia's first innings). But Australia won the first of those games by 491 runs and the second by 9 wickets.

So, at home anyway, the jury was still out. He did not play much in the first part of 2005 but there was talk of a rapprochement with Inzamam. When the series against England started late in the year, we saw a committed and enthusiastic Shoaib bowling his lethal combination of yorkers, out-swingers and in-swingers at alarming pace and mixing them up with his equally devastating slower ball. He took 17 wickets in the series, leading the attack with rapacious vigour in the thrilling victories at Multan and Lahore. By the end of the series he was fourth in the ICC rankings. If not yet in the Gillespie league, he even batted responsibly as a nightwatchman. Still running in at breakneck speed, luxuriant hair still flopping extravagantly, still one of the biggest and most exuberant personalities in the game, Shoaib Akhtar may just be embarking on the next and most productive phase of his career.

SHOAIB AKHTAR
Right-hand bat, right-arm fast
Born: 13 August 1975, Rawalpindi
Major Teams: Pakistan, Rawalpindi, Pakistan International Airlines, Agriculture Development Bank of Singapore, Khan Research Labs, Durham, Somerset, Worcestershire

TESTS
(1997/98-2006)

	M	I	NO	Runs	HS	Ave	Ct				
Batting & Fielding	42	62	12	537	47	10.74	11				

	Balls	R	W	Ave	BBI	5	10	SR	Econ
Bowling	7,490	4,240	165	25.69	6/11	12	2	45.39	3.39

ONE-DAY INTERNATIONALS

	M	Runs	HS	Ave	Ct
Batting & Fielding	124	299	43	9.96	16

	W	Ave	BBI	5	SR	Econ
Bowling	193	23.16	6/16	4	30.00	4.62

FIRST-CLASS
(Career: 1995/96-2006)

	M	I	NO	Runs	HS	Ave	50	Ct
Batting & Fielding	120	168	47	1,503	59*	12.42	1	37

	Balls	R	W	Ave	BBI	5	10	SR	Econ
Bowling	18,696	11,294	428	23.81	6/11	28	2	43.68	3.62

LIST A

	M	I	NO	Runs	HS	Ave	50	Ct
Batting & Fielding	173	93	34	720	56	12.20	1	27

	Balls	R	W	Ave	BBI	5	SR	Econ
Bowling	8,190	6,383	268	23.81	6/16	6	30.55	4.67

WAQAR YOUNIS

Waqar Younis's reported age was a bit like a New Labour economic survey; you knew it couldn't be right but there was no way of proving it. When he joined Surrey in 1990 and produced a series of devastating spells in a summer memorable for gargantuan run-scoring, it seemed impossible that he was a mere eighteen years old. Not that it mattered. A little matter of fourteen years later he turned up, almost by accident, playing for Warwickshire and took 39 Championship wickets in eight matches, expending as much energy and competitive spirit – Waqar could sledge with the best of them – as ever. In between, Waqar was arguably the most feared, and destructive – and certainly the most accurate – fast bowler in the world.

The statistics certainly go some way towards proving that. In 83 Test matches he took 373 wickets at an average of 23.56, which is commendable by any standard. But it is the strike rate that is the thing. At 43.49 Waqar's is the third best of any Test bowler with 75 wickets or more, just ahead of his compatriot and successor Shoaib Akhtar. Of the others in the top ten, all apart from Frank Tyson and Malcolm Marshall played a hundred years or so ago.

Waqar, born in a cotton-growing area in Multan but growing up in Sharjah, was brought to Surrey's attention by his mentor Imran Khan. In that first season, he took 57 Championship wickets at 23.80. Remarkably, 29 of his victims were bowled and 8 were leg before. *Wisden* in 1991 carries a graphic illustration of his potency, showing Leicestershire's Tim Boon, Peter Willey and James Whitaker having their stumps rearranged. Waqar took 4 wickets in 26 balls on the first day after Leicestershire had won the toss. He had 6 in all in the match: 5 bowled.

Waqar's greatness lies in what he achieved in international cricket for Pakistan, but this thrilling and decisive performance in a Championship match at The Oval tells much about his method and approach. There were three essential ingredients. First, there was the in-swinging yorker. Right from the start, this was Waqar's trademark, what Mike Atherton called his signature ball. Reinforced toecaps became a required accessory for batsmen confronted by this alarming projectile, delivered apparently at will and, in the beginning, at extreme speed. Even after the serious back injury – of the type that ended the career of his great West Indian contemporary Ian Bishop – when his pace had declined somewhat, Waqar could wreak havoc with that yorker. In a one-day game at East London during the Mandela Trophy in 1994/95, he finished the New Zealand innings with a hat-trick – all in-swinging yorkers, all bowled. Rarely was his ability to bowl this startling ball on demand seen to greater effect than at the Lord's Test in the English summer of 1996, when Pakistan played a three-Test series in the second half of the season.

Graeme Hick had been talked up by the English media: this was going to be his second – or was it third? – coming. The Worcestershire batsman had emerged from the three-match series against India that preceded Pakistan's visit with an average of 8.75, so his confidence, never high at this level, may well have been particularly low. And he and Waqar had, of course, met before: Hick had been yorked on a belter at New Road in 1991 for 145. In each innings at Lord's Hick was bowled by Waqar for 4. In the first innings, after a promising start to their reply to Pakistan's 340, England had lost Nick Knight and Alec Stewart on 107. Hick lasted 20 balls. In the second innings, Atherton and Stewart added 154 for the second wicket in a determined effort to save the match. The turning point was Mushtaq Ahmed's change of ends. England lost their next 7 wickets for 18 runs. Waqar made a special return for Hick, who lasted 6 balls (in the course of which he was also out to Mushtaq, but reprieved by umpire Steve Bucknor). Each time Hick walked to the wicket, everyone knew a leg-stump yorker was on its way. As David Gower – himself a victim on more than one high-profile occasion – said at the time, knowing it was coming was one thing; playing it was quite another. Hick's generous back-lift and initially ponderous footwork must have seemed like a welcome mat at the home of an old and trusted friend to one of Waqar's missiles.

But perhaps the single most striking example of the in-swinging yorker came relatively late in Waqar's career. The West Indies toured Pakistan from October to December 1997. They were well on their way down the steep incline from world domination to profound mediocrity but they still had some great players. Both Waqar and Wasim had had injury problems and Waqar had been mysteriously omitted from the First Test of this three-match series, which Pakistan won by an innings and 19 runs. They were together for the second, at Rawalpindi. Wasim won the toss and the visitors batted. They lost 2 early wickets and Brian Lara came in. Lara had scored 3 and 37 in the defeat at Peshawar: the tour was dominated by rumours of a power struggle between him and the captain, Courtney Walsh. At Rawalpindi he immediately sought to attack Waqar, hitting him for 10 runs in 3 balls. Then it came – a rapid in-swinging yorker that knocked out the leg stump and left the batsman literally on all fours, West Indies lost that game by an innings and the third by 10 wickets.

Along with the trademark in-swinging yorker, there was the fact that Waqar's later spells always seemed the most devastating. Imran, writing before the 1996 tour of England, went so far as to say that it really was time Waqar learned how to use the new ball properly. The commentary in *Wisden* on Surrey's 1990 season referred to Waqar's 'two-way swing'. In the following English summer, Waqar was even more effective, taking 113 wickets at the extremely healthy average of 14.95. Peter Roebuck, memorialising his achievements as one of *Wisden's* Five Cricketers of the Year, observed that Waqar found the old ball easier to control and swung it even more than the new ball. Roebuck referred to 'rumours' that bowlers in Pakistan – where the wickets had little to offer them – roughed up one side of the ball and were able to generate prodigious swing, perplexingly against the shine: hence 'reverse' swing. Roebuck further observed that umpires had shown special interest in balls used by Waqar and his compatriot at Lancashire, Wasim, during the 1991 season in England but had identified no cases of interfering with the ball.

Roebuck's mention of rumours must have been at least in part a reference to events in Pakistan's two home series, against New Zealand and West Indies in 1990/91. In the New Zealand series Waqar and Wasim shared 39 wickets; in the three Tests against the West Indies they shared 37. Both visiting teams made complaints about interference with the condition of the ball by the Pakistanis.

The New Zealand case was the more intriguing. The tourists sent an inexperienced side and many of their batsmen had no clue against Waqar in particular. Their captain, Martin Crowe, was a notable exception. He had a superb series, averaging 61 and making a masterly century in the Second Test at Lahore. He was quoted at the time as saying that Waqar was the best fast bowler he had ever faced. In his autobiography, however, Crowe said that the tour would be remembered for the alleged ball-tampering that went on throughout the series. Crowe claimed that he first realised something was wrong during his Lahore century: he picked the ball up at one point and allegedly saw that, on one side, it was totally mutilated with slashes apparently gouged out by some sort of sharp instrument. The other side was very red and shiny. Crowe said that though he accepted that Waqar and Wasim were brilliant bowlers, he lost some respect for them at that point because of the assistance they were allegedly getting. The Third Test was won by Pakistan by a slightly narrower margin than the other two. In Pakistan's first innings, the New Zealand opening bowler Chris Pringle, playing in his third Test match, took 7 for 52. Reports of the match suggested that he showed admirable control of line and length and summoned up an extra yard of pace. It transpired, however, that the New Zealanders allegedly used bottle tops to tamper with the ball.

It is worth noting that when the two sides next met in a Test match – a one-off Test in 1992/93 – they had a thrilling encounter that New Zealand, without the injured Crowe, appeared to have in the bag when they bowled Pakistan out for 174 in their second innings, leaving themselves 127 to win. Wasim and Waqar swept the visitors to victory, bowling New Zealand out for 93. Waqar took 5 for 22 in the second innings, and 9 for 81 in the match (four bowled, three leg before). In a three-Test series in New Zealand in 1993/94, Wasim and Waqar once again cut a swathe through the home side's batting, taking 43 wickets between them. Pakistan won the series 2–1: Crowe was again absent, with a knee injury. Waqar was equally effective in the one-day series. In the fourth game, at Auckland, he bowled Brian Young with an in-swinging yorker in his opening spell – not much scope for tampering there – and the last 6 wickets fell for 19, with the match being tied with 2 balls to spare, Waqar took 6 for 30 (three bowled, two leg before).

All the muttering about interfering with the ball's condition was very much to the fore when Pakistan embarked on a full tour of England in the following year, 1992. The series came soon after the conclusion of the World Cup held in Australasia, in which Pakistan had beaten England in the final, Wasim sealing the Englishmen's fate with a phenomenal display of swing bowling. The tabloid press was in a fever of near-xenophobic speculation about ball-tampering. Pakistan won a close-fought series 2-1. Tension was often high, each side nursing a variety of historical if not hysterical grievances. Waqar, who had missed the World Cup with his back problem, was not fully fit until the end of the tour. But he played a leading role in the Second Test at Lord's where both England innings followed a similar pattern. Graham Gooch won the toss and he and Stewart put on 123 for the first wicket with apparent ease. They slumped, however from 197 for 3 to 255 all out, Waqar destroying the tail with 4 wickets in 40 balls at a cost of 17 runs. In the second innings, England went from 108 for 2 to 172 all out. Waqar came on first change and took 2 middle-order wickets, although Mushtaq Ahmed and Wasim were the chief destroyers. Waqar and Wasim took 13 wickets in the match and they were the principal protagonists in the game's thrilling climax, putting on 46 unbeaten and hard-earned runs as Pakistan edged home by 2 wickets.

In the Fourth Test at Headingley, which saw England draw level, their first innings followed a similar pattern to that at Lord's. Gooch made a superb – in effect, a match-winning – century and received sterling support from Atherton and Robin Smith. But 270 for 1 became 320 all out. This time Waqar took 5 wickets for 13 runs in 38 balls (three bowled, two leg before). When the innings closed, the ball was a remarkable 118 overs old. By now, Waqar had recovered most of his former pace and this carried over to the Oval Test, the decider, won by Pakistan. Unusually for Waqar, it was his opening spell in England's second innings that was his most lethal. The hosts, trailing by 173, were reduced to 59 for 3 at tea on the third day, Waqar having dismissed Gooch, Stewart and Atherton. Wasim engendered startling collapses in both England innings.

At the press conference at the end of the Oval Test, the England manager Micky Stewart was asked for his views on suspicions that the Pakistan bowlers were 'interfering' with the ball. The normally forthright and straightforward Stewart gave a non-committal and somewhat mangled response. The floodgates burst after the fourth one-day international at Lord's. Pakistan won the match, which stretched over two days, by 3 runs in the last over. The game was exciting enough but not nearly as dramatic as the aftermath. It was disclosed soon after the game ended that, during the second-day lunch interval, umpires John Hampshire and Ken Palmer had changed the ball being used by Pakistan. The umpires and match referee Deryck Murray remained tight-lipped about why it was changed. Intikhab Alam, the Pakistan manager, said it had gone out of shape. The ball itself was never seen again: for a certain type of English pundit – Chris Cowdrey was perhaps the leading example – it became a sort of cricketing Holy Grail. The official silence was seized upon by both sides but essentially served only to heighten speculation that ball-tampering had been detected. The storm reached its height when Allan Lamb – who had been dropped after the Lord's Test but was retained for the one-day series – published a newspaper article in which he accused Pakistan of cheating. It was Lamb who had drawn the umpires' attention to the state of the ball at Lord's. The controversy rumbled on inconclusively. Lamb was fined for his unauthorised publication. Soon afterwards another lamb, of the sacrificial variety, appeared: Assadullah Butt,

Waqar Younis.

of Habib Bank, became the first bowler to be suspended for ball-tampering in Pakistan. The ICC issued a typically non-committal statement. Surrey were fined for infringements of Law 42.5 ('Unfair Play') in separate incidents over three years, some of them occurring in games in which Waqar played and some of them not.

So the jury was still out. But the slur remained. Jack Bannister, nobody's fool and technically well versed in the mysteries of seam and swing, had the temerity to suggest that the reason Waqar and Wasim achieved such extraordinary results might just have something to do with the fact that they had exceptional talent. Aqib Javed, the third seamer, used the same ball but with markedly less success. Maybe Devon Malcolm, Chris Lewis and the rest had more in common with him than with his illustrious teammates?

Nonetheless, when the countries next met in England in 1996 the pundits' pencils – and knives – were being sharpened. The beginning of the Test series coincided with the end of a slightly absurd court case, involving Lamb, Ian Botham and Imran Khan. The former England players were suing Imran for defamation because of comments attributed to him in an article in the magazine *India Today*. The thirteen-day trial ranged far and wide but ball-tampering was never far away. The cricketing great and good – from Atherton to Brian Close, by way of umpire Don Oslear – another obsessive in the Cowdrey mould – were put through their paces. It was all a lot of nonsense really, and made some wealthy barristers even wealthier at the expense of some rather silly people. And there was a fear that it would set the tone for another summer of ball-tampering allegations.

Pakistan won the First Test at Lord's by 164 runs. Waqar was Man of the Match, taking 4 for 69 in the first innings and 4 for 85 in the second, with a combination of searing pace and what *Wisden* called 'wicked swing'. His first two overs in the first innings went for 19. Seven of his wickets in the match were bowled or leg before, the eighth was caught behind. Roebuck heaved a weary if metaphorical sigh as the whispering started. He commended the superior quality of the Pakistan bowlers and in particular their brilliance with old cricket balls subject to regular inspection by the umpires. By the end of the tour, it is fair to say that that was the majority view.

Wasim and Waqar were lucky in their timing. When they first came to prominence as a pair, cricket's opinion-formers in the West, who tended to come from England and Australia, were becoming increasingly frustrated by the dominance of the West Indies. That dominance owed much to the presence for a long time – the individual components changed over the years – of a quartet of fast bowlers who could be rotated throughout the day. The preponderance of short-pitched bowling grew wearisome. Pakistan had something different to offer: a left-arm right-arm combination operating at a full length for a start. And when it came to pace, they conceded nothing to the West Indians.

That was the other ingredient of Waqar's success: along with the in-swinging yorker and the use of the old ball, he had electrifying pace, especially in his early years. Waqar's extreme pace marked him out as special when he first appeared on the international scene, against India in 1989/90. The sixteen-year old Sachin Tendulkar and a slightly less youthful Waqar each made his debut in the First Test. There was another notable first: neutral umpires – the Englishmen Hampshire and John Holder – stood in all the Tests. The series was played in a good spirit. Nobody said anything about ball-tampering, Wasim bowled beautifully, mesmerisingly, especially with the new ball. Kapil Dev's swing was more effective with the old ball. With Waqar, who reportedly passed his eighteenth birthday during the match, it was sheer pace that caught the eye.

Roebuck said it was Waqar whose pace persuaded Crowe to fix a visor to his helmet during the series in Pakistan in 1990/91, although Crowe in his autobiography says it was Wasim. It would hardly have been surprising if it had been Waqar. His pace was phenomenal and several of the New Zealanders found it impossible to cope with. In the three Tests he took 29 wickets at 10.86, including 7 for 86 in the Second Test at Lahore (four bowled, two leg before) and 7 for 76 in the Third Test at Faisalabad (three bowled, one leg before). His single most incisive spell came in the visitors' first innings at Faisalabad. Early on he was pitching too short. In his third over a bouncer reared up and hit opener Matt Horne in the nose: he was stretchered off bleeding. Mark Greatbatch was his next victim. After surviving a barrage of short balls, he edged a fuller delivery to Salim Yousuf behind the stumps. Trevor Franklin was an unwilling, even unwitting participant in what Shoaib Albi called the homing-device ritual, his stumps shattered by a vicious in-swinging yorker. The next ball was even faster. Ken Rutherford simply had no answer and was bowled. The hat-trick delivery hit a motionless Dipak Patel on the toe. He seemed to have been classically 'Wackered' but umpire Badal said no. Eighteen of Waqar's victims in the series were bowled or leg before. He was just as much of a force in the one-day series that followed, taking 5 for 11 (two bowled, three leg before) at Peshawar, and 5 for 16 (four bowled, one leg before) at Sailkot.

When he toured England two years later, his pace at first seemed to have diminished as a result of his back injury. But Atherton who, in a long career, faced all Waqar's great contemporaries from Malcolm Marshall to Shoaib Akhtar, said that the spell Waqar bowled to him in England's second innings in The Oval Test was the fastest through the air he ever faced.

Waqar in full flight was certainly a magnificent spectacle. He was not as tall as Wasim, about six feet, compact and sturdy. The effort he put into his bowling was immense. It is hardly surprising that he suffered stress fractures of the back. The initial impression on Atherton, when the pair first encountered one another in a county match, was the run up. There was its length – literally back to the sightscreen at Old Trafford. Then there was its speed, a genuine sprint, like Malcolm Marshall's. Then a bounding leap, a classically high side-on action powering through to a long follow-through. Even at the end of his career when his pace had slackened Waqar was an impressive sight. By then, he no longer had the classically high arm action. Indeed, by 1992, after the back operation, the action had become more round-arm, and the trend intensified as he got older. Robin Smith thought Waqar had lost his out-swinger after the operation. A change of arm action signalled the one that held its own, but there was not a lot of time to adjust.

When he had his marvellous year for Surrey in 1991 Waqar had taken 5 wickets in an innings on thirteen occasions. The last home game of the season, against Hampshire, gave a clear indication of his powers. Batting was never easy. Only Surrey's Darren Bicknell (119 and 54) and Monte Lynch (51) scored more than 42 in the match. Hampshire managed 119 and 155. In their second innings, the captain, Mark Nicholas, had the knuckle of his left hand broken by Waqar, thus ensuring that he would miss the final of the NatWest Bank Trophy between the two sides, won by Hampshire. Waqar's figures were 6 for 45 and 6 for 47 (six bowled, two leg before). But in that season the county managed fifth place in the Championship. Their inability to capitalise on their possession of the most potent weapon in world cricket was a telling comment on what a miserable outfit Surrey were in their pre-Hollioake days.

Waqar was back in England in 1997 but he had changed counties: he was now with Glamorgan. Glamorgan were imaginatively led by Matthew Maynard. Their coach was the Zimbabwean Duncan Fletcher, since generally acknowledged as one of cricket's greatest man-managers, or man-readers – Mike Brearley in a tracksuit. They were never going to repeat Surrey's mistake. Waqar was lured to the Principality at considerable expense and let nobody down. In mid-June Glamorgan played Lancashire at Old Trafford, in a match greatly affected by rain and shaped by forfeited innings. The upshot was that Lancashire required 273 to win. They were annihilated: all out for 51. Waqar took 7 for 25 in 7 overs (three bowled, two leg before). Five days later, they met Sussex at Swansea. Glamorgan struggled to 172 after being put in and then dismissed Sussex for 54. Waqar took 8 for 17 in 11.5 overs (two bowled, two leg before). Glamorgan went on to win the Championship for the first time since 1969 and the gregrarious and fun-loving Waqar was a hero in the valleys.

The exertions of the English season seemed to affect him on his return to international duty and he was not consistently at his best in the home series against South Africa. But he returned to form on the return visit to South Africa, taking 6 for 78 (three bowled) and 4 for 55 (three bowled) in a losing cause in the Third Test at Port Elizabeth. By this time Waqar was very much a senior figure in the Pakistan side. On the whole, he 'weathered' less well than Wasim although in occasional bursts, as in Sri Lanka in 2000/01, he could still trouble the best; that tour and the one to the West Indies that followed it were perhaps the last hurrah of Waqar and Wasim as a pair.

Waqar was never a natural captain, but in Pakistan it is best to be prepared as your turn is likely to come sooner or later. He had captained the team in the First Test of the home series against Zimbabwe in 1993/94 (Wasim was injured). Still only twenty-two, he became Pakistan's youngest ever captain. Pakistan won the two-Test series 2-0, Waqar taking 27 wickets at 13.81. In his first match as captain he was absolutely outstanding, taking 13 for 135 (7 for 91 and 6 for 44: five bowled and seven leg before). In the first innings Zimbabwe collapsed from 280 for 5 to 289 all out. In the second innings it was a similar story, as they slid from 61 for 2 to 92 for 8.

Eventually, for the 2001 tour of England, Waqar became captain in his own right after some typically convoluted manoeuvres behind the scenes. Pakistan lost the First Test by an innings. Waqar showed he was still a force to be reckoned with by taking 5 for 23, including a hat-trick, in a comprehensive victory over Leicestershire (three bowled, two leg before). Then Pakistan squared the series in a controversial manner at Old Trafford. Close-up television pictures of Waqar 'working on' the ball revived memories of the good old days of ball-tampering. But, as so often in these clashes, it was the umpiring that made the headlines. Pakistan's victory was gained with the help of at least three wickets that, so the television cameras suggested, should have been classified as no-balls. Pakistan were too good for England in the triangular one-day series (Australia were involved too). In the game at Headingley, marred by terrible and disturbing crowd behaviour, Waqar again revived memories of the previous decade by taking 7 for 36 as England stumbled to 156 all out.

He remained in charge for the tour of Bangladesh, which resulted in a predictably comfortable victory for Pakistan. The West Indies were scheduled to tour in January 2002 but the world was now a different place because of the events of 11 September 2001. It seemed that the West Indies would cancel the tour but it was agreed that the series would take place on neutral territory, in Sharjah. Pakistan won both Tests, and Waqar, still captain, played a critical role in both games. In the First Test Pakistan made 493 with centuries by Yousuf Youhana (as he then was) and Rashid Latif. At 325 for 5 at the close of the third day, the West Indies seemed to have made the game safe but Waqar demolished the tail, finishing with 4 for 93 (two bowled). Pakistan made quick runs in their second innings and gained a comfortable victory. The second victory was even more comprehensive. Waqar took 3 quick wickets in a superlative spell of reverse swing in the second innings, taking 4 for 44 (two bowled, two leg before). There followed unhappy series against Australia (played in Colombo and Sharjah) and in southern Africa where Pakistan beat Zimbabwe but lost to South Africa. By this time, the Pakistan team was becoming fractious again. Waqar's relations with Wasim had reached a new low; wary regard for one another had long ago replaced mutual affection. The situation had deteriorated during the tour of Australia in 1999/2000 when Waqar felt Wasim had treated him poorly: he was quoted as saying that he could respect Wasim as a cricketer but not as a leader. But Waqar had far from universal respect as a leader either. The 2003 World Cup, also in southern Africa, was a disaster and Waqar was sacked as captain.

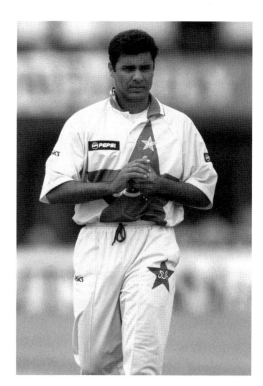

Waqar Younis during the World Cup match against Bangladesh, 1999.

There remained the swansong at Edgbaston in 2003. It really was almost an accident. Waqar happened to go to Edgbaston to watch Mushtaq Ahmed in a county game while he was visiting friends in Birmingham. It became apparent that the New Zealander Shane Bond, Warwickshire's new overseas signing, would not be coming and Waqar was signed as a replacement. He took more Championship wickets (39) than anyone else at the club, at a lower average (23.51). He was still capable of remarkably incisive performances. The county, who were draw specialists even when they won the Championship the following year, only managed four victories and Waqar was usually instrumental. Perhaps the most impressive display was against Middlesex at Edgbaston. It was a close-fought match with the teams being more or less level on first innings. On the fourth day, Middlesex needed 88 to win with 8 wickets in hand. Seven wickets fell for 30 runs as Waqar produced devastating swing and took 5 for 40 and 9 for 109 in the match (four bowled, two leg before).

WAQAR YOUNIS
Right-hand bat, right-arm fast
Born: 6 November 1969, Vehail
Major Teams: Pakistan, Multan, United Bank, Lahore, Rawalpindi, Redco, National Bank, Surrey, Glamorgan, Warwickshire

TESTS
(1989/90-2002/03)

	M	I	NO	Runs	HS	Ave	Ct
Batting & Fielding	87	120	21	1,010	45	10.20	18

	Balls	R	W	Ave	BBI	5	10	SR	Econ
Bowling	16,224	8,788	373	23.56	7/76	22	5	43.49	3.25

ONE-DAY INTERNATIONALS

	M	I	NO	Runs	HS	Ave	SR	Ct
Batting & Fielding	262	139	45	969	37	10.30	67.05	35

	Balls	R	W	Ave	BBI	5	SR	Econ
Bowling	12,698	9,919	416	23.84	7/36	13	30.52	4.68

FIRST-CLASS
(Career: 1987/88-2003/04)

	M	I	NO	Runs	HS	Ave	50	Ct
Batting & Fielding	228	283	61	2,972	64	13.38	6	58

	Balls	R	W	Ave	BBI	5	10	SR	Econ
Bowling	39,182	21,350	956	22.33	8/17	63	14	40.98	3.26

LIST A

	M	I	NO	Runs	HS	Ave	Ct
Batting & Fielding	411	215	66	1,553	45	10.42	56

	Balls	R	W	Ave	BBI	5	SR	Econ
Bowling	19,611	15,083	674	22.37	7/36	17	29.39	4.56

WASIM AKRAM

Wasim Akram's cricket was an intriguing blend of the dazzlingly straightforward and the profoundly mysterious. Whether batting or bowling, he was one of the most compelling and charismatic players of his generation. The scorer of 257 not out (with 12 sixes) from number eight in a Test match and the only man to have taken two hat-tricks in both Tests and one-day internationals, there were not many cricketing challenges he did not seem capable of meeting successfully. One of the most brilliant of new-ball bowlers, his ability to swing the old ball was a source of constant bewilderment.

Wasim's various periods at the tiller of that wayward vessel the Pakistan national cricket team tell their own story. There was never any doubt that he would, one day, become captain. A tall, impressive-looking man, he was the son of affluent middle-class parents. He was educated at Cathedral School, Lahore and it was clear almost from the start that he was going to be a leader. Even so, the appointment came at a very early age.

Javed Miandad had often deputised for Imran Khan when the all-rounder was, for whatever reason, unavailable and when Imran withdrew from the tour of England that followed Pakistan's triumph in the World Cup in 1992 and subsequently announced his retirement, Miandad's appointment seemed secure for some time to come. But a poor tour of Australia and New Zealand, in which a succession of one-day defeats was only partly redeemed by victory in a one-off Test at Hamilton, orchestrated by Wasim and his friend and fellow pace bowler Waqar Younis, led to Miandad's removal. Wasim was the new captain, and Waqar his deputy. It seemed a risky strategy to place such responsibility on the shoulders of two young and brilliant opening bowlers. The first significant assignment, a tour to the Caribbean in 1992/93, was not a success. Pakistan had more than held their own in recent series against the West Indies but this time they lost the three-match series 2-0. To compound their misery, Wasim, Waqar, Mushtaq Ahmed and Aqib Javed were hauled off to a police station in Grenada on the eve of the last warm-up match and charged with 'constructive possession' of marijuana. The charges were dropped but it was an unwanted distraction. Both Wasim and Waqar seemed reluctant to bowl in the West Indies' second innings in the First Test at Port-of-Spain when Desmond Haynes and Brian Lara were in full flow. The home side won that Test, and the second at Bridgetown.

Wasim remained in charge for a trip to Sharjah and Test and one-day series at home against Zimbabwe, comfortably won by the hosts. Wasim took 5 for 15 in the one-day game of Karachi. But shortly after his reappointment for the forthcoming tour of New Zealand, a group of ten senior players rebelled against Wasim's captaincy, claiming that it was too domineering. It was also alleged that he had tried to keep Miandad and Saleem Malik out of the side. His great friend, Waqar, said that the players had more confidence in him.

The three-man 'ad hoc' committee appointed to run cricket in place of the Pakistan Cricket Board (PCB) accepted the broad thrust of the players' complaints and replaced Wasim, not with Waqar but with Malik. Writing some two years later (by which time Wasim was back in charge) Imran lambasted the decision to remove him. He said it was the wrong move in principle because Wasim should have been given time to develop and learn. But it was also wrong to give in to a players' revolt because it meant that the captain was always looking over his shoulder, and that this was the position during Malik's period in charge. That period ended when Malik was sacked after the controversial tour of southern Africa in 1994/95 when allegations of bribery and match-fixing were swirling around. Rameez Raja – who had been out of the side since 1992/93 and was seen as free of any sort of taint – took over for the three-match series in Sri Lanka, which the visitors won 2-1. Wasim was a key figure with bat and ball in Pakistan's victory in the First Test at Colombo. That was it for Rameez and Wasim was back for what turned out to be his most successful stint in the captaincy. This included two challenging tours, to Australia in 1995/96 and England in 1996. The Australian tour was challenging because three of the Australian players had accused Malik of offering them bribes to play badly during Australia's tour of Pakistan in 1994/95. A judicial inquiry in Pakistan had cleared Malik and effectively accused the Australians of lying. That was a sensitive enough situation for Wasim – and his Australian counterpart Mark Taylor – to deal with. Moreover, Malik was back in the Pakistan side, as were Rashid Latif and Basit Ali – who had announced their retirements from international cricket at the end of the trip to southern Africa. This potentially explosive situation was handled with considerable skill by the captains and the series passed off without incident. On the field, Pakistan were no match for Australia.

The tour to England had its own share of combustible elements, engendered by concerns about umpiring and ball-tampering hanging over from previous tours. In this case there was great good fortune in that the two captains, Wasim and Mike Atherton, were old friends, having played for Lancashire together for years. The series was played in an unprecedently good spirit. Pakistan, particularly their bowlers, Wasim, Waqar and Mushtaq, were far too good for England.

In between these two tours was the World Cup, held in India, Pakistan and Sri Lanka in early 1996. Pakistan were the holders. For a variety of reasons this was probably the least successful World Cup, although Sri Lanka played some consistently brilliant cricket to win it. It took a very long time to conclude which of the (then) nine Test-playing countries and three associate members would contest the quarter finals, and not many people were surprised when the qualifiers turned out to be the Test nations minus Zimbabwe.

India and Pakistan were drawn to meet each other in one of those quarter-finals and India won a well-contested game. Great was the rage and grief in Pakistan. One man apparently shot his television and then himself. Effigies of Wasim were burned in the streets of Karachi and Lahore, always a bad sign. Wasim had not even played in the critical clash: he pulled out with an injury. That, though, was part of the problem. Speculation about match-fixing had reached new heights during the competition and rumours spread that his withdrawal had sinister implications, strenuously denied by Wasim.

After the successful tour of England, Pakistan played a two-Test series against Zimbabwe in October 1996. The series, which Pakistan won 1-0, was a triumph for Wasim. The First Test, at Sheikhupura – it was the first first-class match played there – was the occasion of his amazing 257 not out. When he came to the crease Pakistan were 183 for 6. They were all out for 553. It was not the strongest attack in the world – Heath Streak was not play-ing, for a start – but even so it was an extraordinary, almost outrageous display. To show that he was not a wholly one-dimensional player, Wasim proceeded to win the Second Test at Faisalabad almost on his own; taking 6 for 48 and 4 for 58 in a 10-wicket victory.

An injured left shoulder restricted Wasim's appearances over the next few months. 1997/98 was a turbulent season, in terms of the national captaincy, even by Pakistan's standards. Wasim's injury kept him out of the Pepsi Asia Cup in Sri Lanka, where Rameez Raja was recalled to lead the side. He was replaced by Saeed Anwar for the home Test series against South Africa. Wasim returned to the side for the Third Test. He bowled beautifully in South Africa's first innings, taking 4 for 47, but South Africa won the match and thus the series, 1-0. Wasim was then restored to the captaincy for the home series against the West Indies. This turned out to be one of those pivotal series that mark a turning point in international cricket, like Bodyline or Australia v. West Indies in 1960/61. It was not that Pakistan played exceptionally well: they were certainly competent. The remarkable thing was how bad the West Indies were. Pakistan won the first two Tests by an innings and the third by 10 wickets. Soon we were to get used to West Indies losing all the Tests in an away series but at this stage, it was still a shock, if not entirely a surprise. Wasim certainly played his part, with inspiring leadership and some incisive spells of hostile swing bowling with old and new ball in each of the Tests. He finished with 17 wickets at 17.49.

That series was followed almost immediately by the Akai Singer Cup in Sharjah, contested by Pakistan, the West Indies, India and England. To almost universal conster-nation, a new-look England side led by one-day specialist Adam Hollioake, won. Mike Selvey noted in *Wisden* that hindsight would show that Sharjah was the starting point for England's build up to the 1999 World Cup. Not many people, even in England, cared very much about England's victory. Pakistan's failure to qualify – although they did defeat India – was a different matter altogether. The burning of effigies was child's play compared to what confronted Wasim on his return home. There were death threats to him and his family and there were reports that his brother had been kidnapped. He resigned from the captaincy saying he would not lead the side again. The obligatory match-fixing inquiry was instituted by Majid Khan, the chief executive of the PCB. Wasim was then omitted from the side that toured South Africa under Rashid Latif, although he was flown out to join the team for the final Test, which Pakistan lost. It was Latif's first match as captain – he had been unfit earlier in the series and Aamir Sohail led the side in the first two Tests, the second of which Pakistan had won. There was a feeling that Wasim's return did not do an enormous amount for team spirit.

Nonetheless, it was not long before he was yet again recalled as captain for the highly sensitive tour of India in 1998/99. Pakistan had not toured there since 1986/87; Wasim and Saleem Malik were the only survivors from that side. The tour was politically controversial – Hindu extremists in India were violently opposed to it. This resulted in the venue of the first Test being switched from Delhi to Chennai, and there was constant tight security. In fact, there was almost no trouble during the series and some high-class cricket. Pakistan won an enthralling encounter at Chennai, and were given a standing ovation as they did a lap of honour. India squared the series at Delhi through Anil Kumble's historic 10-wicket haul. Wasim took 1 for 23 and 3 for 43 on a spinner's paradise, and overtook Imran as Pakistan's leading wicket-taker.

The series was followed by the inaugural Asian Test Championship for which India and Pakistan were joined by Sri Lanka. Pakistan won, and it was a triumph – again – for their captain. The first game, at Calcutta, was originally scheduled to be the Third Test of the India-Pakistan series. Here there was crowd disturbance, although it was not politically motivated; the game concluded in an empty stadium. Pakistan won by 46 runs having been 26 for 6 on the first morning. Wasim, with 38, top-scored in their first innings of 185 and took 5 wickets in the match. They then drew with Sri Lanka at Lahore in a match where seven hours were lost to rain. The game's most memorable passage of play was the conclusion of Sri Lanka's first innings, which subsided from 320 for 6 to 328 all out. Wasim took all 4 wickets, including Pakistan's first Test hat-trick: Romesh Kaluwitharana caught behind and two tail-enders yorked. The final, at Dhaka, was also between Pakistan and Sri Lanka and Pakistan secured a massive victory, by an innings and 175 runs. Ijaz Ahmed and Inzamam-ul-Haq scored double centuries for Pakistan but yet again the most enduring contribution came from Wasim who, in Sri Lanka's second innings, took his second hat-trick in successive Tests. Then, after victories in one-day tournaments in India and Sharjah, it was off to England for the 1999 World Cup.

Given their recent form, Pakistan were clearly among the favourites and they had a good blend of youth and experience. There was a troubled prelude, with the coach, Miandad, resigning shortly before the competition started. But on the field, everything seemed to go according to plan. Their group included Australia, the front runners, and dark horses New Zealand, but Pakistan won their first four matches. Then there was a glitch. They lost, quite sensationally, to Bangladesh. They then lost two games in the Super Six stage but there was never any doubt that they would qualify for a semi-final spot. There they clinically disposed of New Zealand. They then prepared to meet Australia in the final. Rarely has such a big match been such a damp squib, Wasim won the toss and batted on an overcast day. That was not an unreasonable decision. This was a Lord's final but it was June, not September. Yet the game was effectively over by lunch. Pakistan were bowled out for 132 in 39 overs and Australia won by 8 wickets.

Bewilderment in St John's Wood was rapidly followed by alarm and despondency in Pakistan. A recently established 'accountability' commission instituted a match-fixing inquiry, focussing on alleged under-achievement at vital times by various players who were suspended from playing before being cleared. Wasim could justly claim that his team had, in fact, had a very good tournament, and he himself had played well, taking 4 for 40 in the crucial first round game against Australia.

Wasim was reinstated to lead the side in Australia in 1999/2000 but the tour was not a success for Pakistan. They lost the series 3-0 – they should probably have won at Hobart – and Wasim asked to be relieved of the captaincy before the home series against Sri Lanka. Then came Justice Mohammad Malik Qayyum's report into match-fixing, which contained criticisms of Wasim. He did not captain the side again. Ironically, Qayyum's report enabled Wasim to tour Sri Lanka for the return series in the (English) summer of 2000. He was scheduled to be a Channel 4 commentator but that august organisation, in its self-appointed role as guardian of public morals, which also led it to boycott the eponymous Geoffrey, cancelled the contract.

A review of Wasim's captaincy encompasses as many highs and lows as a trip down the Karakoram Highway. Victory in England, match-fixing allegations, demolition of the West Indies, humiliation in Sharjah, it was all there. That seemed in keeping with Wasim's personality. Peter Roebuck expressed it best: a cricketing genius and 'a rascal… whose practical face and gleaming eyes hinted at a darkness within.' A charmer too, with plenty of friends in English cricket, he had to captain his nation because, in a country of limitless talent, he was, quite simply, the best.

Wasim, to a greater extent than Waqar, did literally come into big cricket from nowhere. He was in a training camp in Lahore in 1984/85 when Javed Miandad spotted him in the nets. Drafted into a strong BCCP Patron's XI against the touring New Zealanders at Rawalpindi, he took 7 for 90 and was selected for the return tour in early 1985. In the Third Test at Dunedin he took 5 for 56 and 5 for 72. The game was a tight one, which New Zealand won by 2 wickets largely thanks to a coura-geous unbeaten hundred by their captain, Jeremy Coney. Wasim impressed with his pace and line and his movement off the seam. He also showed a keen appreciation of the value of the short-pitched ball, hitting the helmetless Coney on the head and being warned for intimidation. He did well in the Benson & Hedges World Championship of Cricket that took place in Australia after the New Zealand tour, taking 5 for 21 against Australia at Melbourne.

A new prodigy had arrived. Steady progress followed over the next couple of years under the tutelage of Imran Khan, including good performances at home against the West Indies in 1986/87. In the victory at Faisalabad he took 6 for 91 in the West Indies' first innings; going in at number nine in Pakistan's second innings with the score on 224 for 7 he scored 66, taking the total to 328. In England in 1987 he took 3 for 36 and 2 for 55 and scored 43 off 41 balls, with 4 sixes and 2 fours, in Pakistan's innings victory at Headingley.

During the English tour he signed for Lancashire and this turned out to be a highly significant event. He was to remain a Lancashire player until 1998. He had

Wasim Akram bowls to Mike Atherton during the second Test at Old Trafford, 2001.

started his Test career batting at number eleven. He batted at seven in that first season for Lancashire and scored his first first-class century in his second game, against
Somerset at Old Trafford. Against Surrey at Southport he took 5 for 58 and 3 for 58
and scored 58 and 98. Injury restricted his appearances, though, as it did in 1989,
when he headed the county's bowling averages with 50 Championship wickets at
19.86. Lancashire won the Sunday League. They came second in 1990 but their one-
day form generally was reviving memories of the early 1970s as they won both the
NatWest Bank Trophy and the Benson & Hedges Cup. In the final of the premier
competition, the NatWest, Wasim played a vital supporting role to Phillip DeFreitas
but he was the outstanding performer in the Benson & Hedges final against
Worcestershire. When DeFreitas joined him at the fall of the fifth wicket Lancashire
had scored 146 in 42 overs. They added 55 in 5 overs, Wasim's 28 including 2 sixes
– one an immense straight drive into the Lord's Pavilion – in an over from Neal
Radford. Lancashire finished on 241. Coming on after 13 overs, Wasim's pace was
too much for Worcestershire's most reliable batsmen, Tim Curtis and Graeme Hick.
Lancashire won by 69 runs. He again headed the Championship bowling averages in
1991, despite further injury problems.

All in all, Wasim had eight seasons with Lancashire: he missed 1992 and 1996 because Pakistan were touring and he hardly played at all in 1997 because of injury. There were a couple of seasons in the late 1980s and early 1990s when injury restricted him. As for Pakistan, when he was fit and fully committed, he was a formidable performer. His best year as a bowler was 1995 when he took 81 Championship wickets at 19.72, including 7 for 52 against Hampshire at Portsmouth (on Andrew Flintoff's first-class debut). In his final year, 1998, he headed the county's bowling averages for the fifth time with 48 wickets at 21.35 and scored 531 runs at 31.23. That was his first – and only – year as official captain of the county. It was not exactly a failure: second in the Championship, first in the AXA League and winning the Benson & Hedges Cup. Yet at the end of it, he was replaced as overseas player for 1999 by Muttiah Muralitharan. During Wasim's period as their overseas player, Lancashire won six one-day trophies.

Injury was a serious problem in the late 1980s but, as the decade turned, Wasim came into his own as an international cricketer of the highest class. This was clearly demonstrated in his all-round performances against India at home and away against Australia in 1989/90. Against India he was by some distance the best bowler on either side, taking 18 wickets at 30.61 in a high-scoring series and troubling all the batsmen (all the matches were drawn). In Australia, Pakistan, weakened by illness and injury to key players, lost a three-match Test series 1-0. Wasim was again the outstanding performer. He was Man of the Match in the First Test at Melbourne, which Australia won by 92 runs. In the first innings he took 6 for 62, finishing the innings with 3 wickets in 8 balls. In the second innings he took 5 for 98. In the Second Test at Adelaide, he was equal top scorer, with 52 from 89 balls in Pakistan's first innings of 257. He then took 5 for 100 in 43 overs – including 3 wickets in the last over – as Australia replied with 341. Pakistan appeared to be facing defeat at 90 for 5 when Wasim joined Imran. Master and pupil, in their contrasting but equally commanding and eye-catching styles, put on 191, both men scoring hundreds. Wasim's flamboyant 123 occupied 244 minutes and included 18 fours and a six. The match was drawn.

He was magnificent too at home against the West Indies in 1990/91, when the three-Test series was drawn 1-1, Wasim took 21 wickets at 14.19. In the third, drawn Test at Lahore, where Brian Lara made his Test debut, Wasim took 5 for 28 in the West Indies' second innings, polishing off the tail with 4 wickets in 5 balls. Imran dropped a catch off the hat-trick ball. Wasim was in his prime. Pakistan, for a couple of years, had the astonishing luxury of being able to field him, Waqar Younis and Imran Khan together. Waqar missed the 1992 World Cup in Australasia, where Pakistan triumphed under Imran, and Wasim was the leading wicket-taker, with 18. Imran retired almost immediately after the World Cup and was obviously in decline as a fast bowler towards the end of his career.

Of these three immensely skilful bowlers, Wasim was arguably the greatest. Even if he had not been supremely gifted Wasim would have added variety to Pakistan's attack simply by virtue of being a left-armer. But what variety, and at what a pace! No left-arm fast bowler can expect to succeed at the highest level unless he is able to bring the ball back into the right-handed batsman. Prior to Wasim's emergence, the supreme master of this craft, certainly since the Second World War, had been the Australian Alan Davidson. Imran recognised the standards set by him. Writing in 1988, he said he thought Wasim had it in him to be the greatest left-armer since Davidson. They were certainly bowlers of a similar type. Both were big, tall men. Both had relatively short but busy and eager run-ups. Both, at their peak and when firing on all cyclinders, were genuinely fast, albeit in Davidson's case short of the very highest pace. Each generated the pace through an exceptionally speedy arm action. Imran said Wasim's first spell in the Second Test at Port-of Spain in 1987/88 was possibly the fastest bowled by anyone in the series; the West Indies' bowlers included Malcolm Marshall, in his prime, and Patrick Patterson.

Simon Wilde, in *Letting Rip*, his brilliant study of fast bowling, said that one of the things that made Wasim – and Waqar – different was their ability to swing the ball late in its flight. John Woodcock said that Davidson had exactly that ability, adding that Davidson himself was uncertain as to how the ability arose. For Wasim wrist position was critical. Richie Benaud, who knew Davidson's bowling better than anyone, said he had never seen a bowler swing the ball as late as Davidson. Davidson, like most opening bowlers – by definition – was at his most potent with the new ball. Wasim was a master with the new ball too but, as Wilde eloquently illustrated, he was no less effective with the old one. This was well demonstrated in Pakistan's tour of England in 1992. Wasim had a marvellous tour, taking 82 wickets – more than he ever took in a season for Lancashire – at 16.21. In four Tests, he took 21 wickets at 22.00.

He missed the First Test with a stress fracture of the shin. On his return to the side for the match against Nottinghamshire, bowling off a seven-pace run-up (a dozen sufficed even when fully fit) he took 4 for 7 in 13 overs; all the wickets came in a 9-over spell that did not cost a run. In the next game, against Northamptonshire, he took 5 for 43 and 5 for 74. So he was nicely warmed up for the Second Test at Lord's. There, in England's first innings, he played a supporting role to Waqar but, in the second innings, where again England got off to a bright start against the new ball, it was he who limited the target Pakistan would be set by taking the last 3 wickets in 4 balls. The finish was tighter than had seemed likely: Wasim, who made 45 not out, hit the winning runs.

He bowled beautifully in the drawn Third Test at Old Trafford, taking 5 for 108 (and conceding 32 no-balls). But he saved his best for The Oval, where Pakistan won to clinch the series 2-1. As so often, England started well and, forty minutes after tea on the first day were 182 for 3 with Atherton and David Gower well set. Gower played on to Aqib Javed and then Atherton looked on as the tail capitulated to a succession of in-swinging yorkers from Wasim. He took 5 for 18 in 7.1 overs – all bowled or leg-before – to finish with 6 for 67. He eliminated the tail in a similarly brusque manner in the second innings, taking 3 for 36 and being named Man of the Match.

Allegations of ball-tampering followed these brilliant performances by Wasim (and Waqar), particularly after a one-day international at Lord's dealt with elsewhere in

Wasim Akram in action for Lancashire in a Benson & Hedges Cup match against
Nottinghamshire, 1998.

the book. The fact remains that, as Imran had previously observed, English umpires regularly inspected the ball. There was a strange incident involving Wasim in a county game at Derby the following year, 1993. Lancashire scored 477 (Wasim 117) and 327 for 8 (Wasim 42). Derbyshire made 426 in their first innings (Wasim 0 for 83 in 17 overs). Derbyshire were coasting at 242 for 2 in their second innings when Wasim came on and took 6 for 11 in 49 balls. Lancashire won by 111 runs. Derbyshire were sufficiently disgruntled to send the ball to Lord's, presumably for some sort of forensic analysis. It all added spice to the Benson & Hedges final between the same sides a fortnight later, a game that the unfancied Derbyshire narrowly won and which was memorable for Wasim hitting the Derbyshire batsman, Chris Adams, on the shoulder with what looked suspiciously like a beamer.

Atherton, writing much later, recalled standing at the non-striker's end during The Oval Test in 1992 and watching as Wasim bowled Derek Pringle. The ball, said Atherton – and Pringle, perhaps not surprisingly, confirmed the same, again long after the event – was simply unplayable. It appeared to swing both ways on its rapid progress towards and into Pringle's stumps. Roebuck described this effect perfectly: how Wasim's deliveries 'embarked upon journeys more complicated than any previously undertaken between popping creases. They seemed to have second thoughts halfway down the pitch, whereupon they would change direction, thereby confounding carefully constructed defences.' It made him a handful at the best of times but a real problem for the tail or, indeed, for any new batsman. It accounted for his ability to generate startling collapses and his clinical expertise in dismantling the tail. In his two one-day international hat-tricks, all six victims were bowled. A classic example in county cricket was his performance for Lancashire against Somerset at Southport in 1994. Somerset, who lost by an innings, were out for 160 in their second innings. Wasim took 8 for 30 in 16.4 overs. Three times he was on a hat-trick, and he took the last 5 wickets in 28 balls.

Davidson took a while to reach his peak and remained there for perhaps four or five years –in those days Australian players departed relatively young to get real jobs. Wasim arrived as, if not the finished article, then as a highly effective operator, and he just seemed to go on and on. His longevity is all the more remarkable given that he has suffered from diabetes since 1997. Of course, it would be absurd to claim that he was always unplayable. He played so much cricket, a lot of it for Lancashire and a lot of inconsequential one-day stuff. But right to the end, he was capable of turning it on. In June 2002 at the Colonial Stadium in Melbourne he dismissed Adam Gilchrist and Ricky Ponting in the first three balls of a one-day international. And he had the universal respect of opposing batsmen. Justin Langer attributed Australia's historic series win in Pakistan in 1998/99 to the fact that their batsmen were able to blunt the threat posed by Wasim.

Despite the cloud of the Qayyum report hanging over him he enjoyed highly successful tours of the West Indies and Sri Lanka in 1999/2000. In Antigua, in the Third Test against the West Indies, which resulted in a thrilling 1-wicket victory for the home side, he took 6 for 61 and 5 for 49. The West Indian captain Jimmy Adams guided his side to victory: television replays suggested that Wasim had him caught behind by Moin Khan in the course of a devastating burst on the fourth afternoon.

Before that in Sri Lanka, where Pakistan won both Tests, he was again at his glorious best. In the First Test at Colombo, he came in at 160 for 6 and made a watchful 78, shepherding the tail to a competitive 266 in response to Sri Lanka's 273. When Sri Lanka batted again he swiftly removed Russel Arnold to claim his 400th Test wicket in his ninety-fifth Test. He disposed of the tail in the classic Wasim manner, with a succession of fast swinging deliveries: 5 for 45, and another match award. He picked up yet another one at Galle, where he was an admirable foil to Waqar as Sri Lanka's batsmen twice succumbed meekly. And he was Pakistan's fourth centurion in a total of 600 for 8, making 100 – his third Test century – from 86 balls with 6 sixes and 8 fours.

At the time of his great series in Australia in 1989/90 people started saying that Wasim was going to be one of the world's greatest all-rounders. That never quite happened: his Test batting average was 22.64. Davidson, also a destructive batsman on his day, averaged 24.59 with the bat and 20.53 with the ball. Garfield Sobers, the other great left-handed all-rounder, was on another plane – although his bowling average was 34.03.

But perhaps it is unreasonable to expect someone who has taken 916 international wickets – Wasim took his 500th one-day international wicket during the 2003 World Cup – to be worth his place in a side purely as a batsman. At his best, he was a glorious striker of the ball with a wonderful free swing of the bat. Even if, arguably, he did not fulfil his potential as an all-rounder, he was capable of remarkable all-round performances in individual games. Against Hampshire in 1991 at Basingstoke – ah, exotic Basingstoke, actually a delightful ground, greatly missed – he came in on the first afternoon when Lancashire were 106 for 4, on a damp pitch and, dropped at 16, made 122 off 165 balls with 2 sixes and 15 fours. Lancashire made 312. Rain then prompted two declarations and Hampshire were set 350 in 74 overs. At one stage they were 171 for 3 but Mike Watkinson broke though the middle order and Wasim, who finished with 5 for 48, took the last 4 wickets – including that of intrepid skipper Mark Nicholas who had mysteriously dropped down the order – in 9 balls without conceding a run. Against Nottinghamshire in 1998, Lancashire had a first innings lead of over a hundred, but they were struggling at 137 for 6 when Wasim came in. He made a brilliant 155, with 5 sixes and 14 fours to get Lancashire to 357. He then took Nottinghamshire apart with 5 for 56.

He was always vulnerable early on but, once set, no bowler was safe. And he was never predictable. Against Sussex at Horsham in 1994, Lancashire were set 451 to win on the final day. When Wasim came in they were 207 for 6 and there were 25 overs left. He launched a dramatic assault on the Sussex attack, making 98 with 8 sixes and 10 fours, before being last man out.

So much talent, such genuinely remarkable achievements over so many years. Could one be identified as outstanding? Yes: a brief passage of play on a floodlit night at Melbourne in March 1992. It was the final of the World Cup, between Pakistan and England. Pakistan had won the toss and batted, making 249 for 6 in their 50 overs. Ian Botham fell for a duck to a controversial catch behind off Wasim and England made a shaky start. A determined effort by Graham Gooch ended in the twenty-first over with the score on 69 for 4. Then a typically inventive display from one-day specialist Neil Fairbrother, aided by Allan Lamb, took the score to 141: 109 to win in 15 overs. Imran needed a breakthrough. He brought Wasim back on. Bowling round the wicket, he dismissed Lamb with a genuinely unplayable ball, one of his two-way specials that started outside leg-stump and hit the top of off. Next ball he clean bowled Chris Lewis with one that started wide of off-stump. Pakistan were into the tail: it was all over.

Wasim was Man of the Match. The crowd of 87,000 at the MCG had witnessed something special, something out of the ordinary. There are a lot of words that are excessively and inappropriately used in sports writing but there really is only one way to describe Wasim Akram's bowling that night.

It was magic.

WASIM AKRAM
Left-hand bat, left-arm fast
Born: 3 June 1966, Lahore
Major Teams: Pakistan, PACO, Lahore, Pakistan International Airlines, Lancashire, Hampshire

TESTS
(1984/85-2001/02)

	M	I	NO	Runs	HS	Ave	100	50	Ct
Batting & Fielding	104	147	19	2,898	257★	22.64	3	7	44

	Balls	R	W	Ave	BBI	5	10	SR	Econ
Bowling	22,627	9,779	414	23.62	7/119	25	5	54.65	2.59

ONE-DAY INTERNATIONALS

	M	I	NO	Runs	HS	Ave	SR	50	Ct
Batting & Fielding	356	280	55	3,717	86	16.52	88.28	6	88

	Balls	R	W	Ave	BBI	5	SR	Econ
Bowling	18,186	11,812	502	23.52	5/15	6	36.22	3.89

FIRST-CLASS
(Career: 1984/85-2003)

	M	I	NO	Runs	HS	Ave	100	50	Ct
Batting & Fielding	257	355	40	7,161	257★	22.73	7	24	147

	Balls	R	W	Ave	BBI	5	10	SR	Econ
Bowling	50,277	22,549	1,042	21.64	8/30	70	16	48.25	2.69

LIST A

	M	I	NO	Runs	HS	Ave	50	Ct
Batting & Fielding	594	467	97	6,993	89★	18.90	17	147

	Balls	R	W	Ave	BBI	5	SR	Econ
Bowling	29,719	19,303	881	21.91	5/10	12	33.73	3.89

WASIM BARI

Wasim Bari is a significant figure in the history of Pakistani cricket. He is by some distance the best wicketkeeper the country has produced, although there are signs that his supremacy may be challenged by the talented Kamran Akmal. To a greater extent than anybody else he provided a link between the bad old days of the 1960s, when Pakistan's Test cricketers lurched from defeat to humiliation, and the years of plenty under Imran Khan. By the time he retired, at the end of Pakistan's tour of Australia in 1983/84, not only had he appeared in more Test matches than any of his countrymen (81) but he was third on the all-time list for dismissals, behind his great contemporaries Alan Knott of England and the Australian Rodney Marsh. Not surprisingly perhaps, he had more stumpings than either.

Bari was not a showman in the way that to some degree both Knott and Marsh were. He was more the quiet, dependable type. Well, not necessarily quiet. In later years, he transformed from being principal boy – he made his debut as a teenager in England in 1967 – to being chorus leader, a valiant aide to Abdul Qadir in particular, in his global campaign to persuade umpires purely by force of decibel levels that batsmen ought to be given out if they are struck on the pads. Bari was not in the Salim Yousuf class as an opportunistic appealer, but he was enthusiastic enough. David Gower was one opponent who found it hard to take Imran's assumption of the moral high ground seriously when it came to umpiring and Bari was an invaluable if unwitting ally: Gower has written about an incident in the 1982 series when he stayed put after nicking one to Bari off Qadir and being given not out. He was given the full treatment from behind the stumps – he said Bari's vocabulary made Bernard Manning sound like Mary Whitehouse – but Gower was not unduly bothered. He said it was ironic coming from someone who thought nothing of appealing when the ball had missed your bat by a yard. But even if he was verbally aggressive and noticeable, Bari was calm and methodical behind the stumps rather than effusively acrobatic. He could dive acrobatically when he had to and he was genuinely athletic, but he relied to a great extent on keen anticipation, decisive footwork and a very dependable pair of hands.

Bari did not drop much. Right from the start he was recognized as solid and secure. His wicketkeeping in England in 1967 was described by *Wisden* as almost infallible and that set the standard. He had an outstanding game at The Oval in 1971, outshining Knott, then at his peak, and taking eight catches in the match, equalling the record. He played in all Pakistan's Tests after that until the Third Test against New Zealand in 1976/77 when he was mysteriously omitted in favour of Shahid Israr. The game was an immensely high-scoring draw – its 1,585 runs was the highest aggregate for a Test on the subcontinent until the Test against India at Faisalabad in 2005/06 – and New Zealand's avoidance of a third successive defeat owed something to the new keeper's spillage of four chances.

Bari was swiftly restored for the tours of Australia and West Indies and then found himself in the invidious position of captaining an inexperienced side, deprived of its Packer players, in back-to-back series against England in 1977/78 and 1978. The captaincy did not sit easily on Bari's shoulders. Let us turn, for an assessment, to that exceptionally objective bystander, the reasonable man's reasonable man, Bari's team-mate, Javed Miandad. 'Bari was a total failure; he knew next to nothing about captaincy and his bland management only added to the tedium.' Well, there we are. Certainly Bari was not a success. The Tests in Pakistan were drawn, neither side being good enough to rise above the somnolent pitch conditions. The Pakistanis sank without trace in England, but if Mike Brearley had been captaining them instead of the home side it would probably not have made a difference. Geoffrey Moorhouse though did note the contrast, in terms of enthusiasm and organisation, in the two sides' warm-ups before the Lord's Test in 1978.

Back in the ranks when Mushtaq Mohammad and the other Packer players returned, Bari enjoyed a remarkable statistical peak against New Zealand at Auckland in 1978/79, catching 7 of the first 8 wickets to fall in New Zealand's first innings. Almost more extraordinary than that was the fact that he secured no more victims during the remainder of the match. It remains the record for the number of dismissals in a Test innings, although it has been equalled.

He lost his place for a while in the early 1980s, to Taslim Arif, who was a better batsman, and he had another spell out of the side following the senior players' revolt against Miandad's captaincy after the tour of Australia in 1981/82. But once Imran was in charge Bari was a fixture again until he retired; indeed more than once Imran had to dissuade him from retiring. Imran had a very high regard for Bari's keeping, although he felt he was sometimes a little slow on the leg-side. Miandad, whatever his views on Bari's captaincy, was unstinting in his praise of the wicket-keeper. He said Bari was the best he ever saw. He was competent as a batsman too, coming in anywhere between eight and eleven and always liable to hang around. He put up some courageous displays, especially in the Caribbean in 1976/77. A Colin Croft bouncer forced him to retire hurt in the final Test at Kingston. Majid Khan had to keep wicket, and dropped an important chance off Gordon Greenidge. At Adelaide, in the opening Test of the 1972/73 series, Pakistan's vaunted batting line-up had been exposed by excellent pace and swing bowling from Dennis Lillee

Wasim Bari.

and Bob Massie. Bari, along with the captain Intikhab Alam (64), responded positively, driving fearlessly and exhibiting nimble footwork against the spinners Ashley
Mallett and Kerry O'Keefe to hit 10 fours in his 72. The Adelaide crowd gave him
a standing ovation. Australia won by an innings. His highest Test score came as
nightwatchman in the Second Test against India at Lahore in 1978/79. Pakistan's
first innings of 539 for 6 was the platform for their historic 6-wicket victory. Bari,
going in first wicket down, made 85 and was the dominant partner in a second-
wicket stand of 125 with Majid. Curiously, Bari had made more ducks – 19 – than
any other Pakistan batsman until he was overtaken by Waqar Younis.

When Bari finally retired he left the scene with barely a smidgeon of interest
from the national press. He has since been honoured with a Lifetime Achievement
Award given during celebrations of fifty years of nationhood. Wasim Bari is currently
Pakistan's chairman of selectors.

WASIM BARI
Right-hand bat, wicketkeeper
Born: 23 March 1948, Karachi
Major Teams: Pakistan, Karachi, Pakistan International Airlines, Sind

TESTS
(1967–1983/84)

	M	I	NO	Runs	HS	Ave	100	50	Ct	St
Batting & Fielding	81	112	26	1,366	65	15.88	0	6	201	27

	Balls	R	W	Ave	Econ
Bowling	8	2	0	–	1.50

ONE-DAY INTERNATIONALS

	M	I	NO	Runs	HS	Ave	SR	Ct	St
Batting & Fielding	51	26	13	221	34	17.00	51.27	52	10

FIRST-CLASS
(Career: 1964/65–1983/84)

	M	I	NO	Runs	HS	Ave	100	Ct	St
Batting & Fielding	286	357	92	5,751	177	21.70	2	681	144

	R	W	Ave	BBI
Bowling	30	1	30	1/11

LIST A

	M	I	NO	Runs	HS	Ave	50	Ct	St
Batting & Fielding	85	47	20	451	54	16.70	1	95	20

WASIM RAJA

Wasim Raja was a buccaneering left-handed batsman of style and panache and a purveyor of more than passable slow-medium top-spinners. There is little doubt that he had the talent to be one of his country's highest run-scorers. Yet, for whatever reason – perhaps a lack of ambition or of the special instinct that propels sportsmen to the very top – he did not quite manage that. He had a long career in Test cricket. He started in 1972/73 in New Zealand and he finished there in 1984/85. But his 57 Test matches were spread over twenty-three different series, an indication that the national selectors – not themselves the most reliable of arbiters – were never entirely convinced. He also had his supporters as a potential captain, particularly in the early 1980s. He is an educated and articulate man, if a little outspoken. But although he had captained an Under-25 side he never got the top job.

He had his first chance with the national side on the tour of New Zealand in 1972/73 when Saeed Ahmed and Mohammad Ilyas had been sent home after the Australian leg of the trip. Wasim had had an impressive domestic season, taking 5 for 77 and 5 for 23 and scoring 117 for Pakistan Universities against PWD at Lahore. He played in all three Tests and did enough with bat and ball to show that he had real potential. The tour of England in 1974 gave an indication of what was to come. He could hardly get a game at the beginning of the tour and was not picked for the First Test. Then he got a hundred against Glamorgan and the runs started to flow. He topped the tour batting averages, with 486 runs at an average of 54. He played in the two remaining Tests and, although he did not make big scores, he showed tremendous character at Lord's in exceptionally difficult circumstances, sharing a long partnership in the second innings with Mushtaq Mohammad, defending rigorously against devilish bowling by Derek Underwood but hitting straight and hard when the opportunity presented itself: he had made 24 in the first innings when conditions were even worse. John Woodcock called him a rare find. He built on the confidence gained in England in Pakistan's next series, against the West Indies at home in 1974/75. He made his maiden century in the Second Test at Karachi, adding 128 for the seventh wicket with Wasim Bari. There was a two-and-a-half hour interruption

when he reached his century. Dozens of spectators rushed onto the field to congrat-
ulate him and when the police were sent out to restore order a full-scale riot ensued.
Wasim strained an ankle ligament when bowling and was due to take no further part
in the match. But he came out at the end of Pakistan's second innings with his leg in
plaster, hoping to see Sadiq Mohammad to his century. But Wasim was bowled with
Sadiq stranded on 98.

He played in the World Cup in England in 1975 with some success but, in the following year, competition for places in the middle order hotted up with Javed Miandad
and Haroon Rashid making their Test debuts. Miandad has said that Majid Khan
moved up the order to open because there was no room in the middle order. Whether
or not that is true, Wasim seemed to have a problem finding a slot in 1976/77. He

Wasim Raja.

was dropped after one Test against New Zealand. He also played in none of the Tests in Australia that followed, despite a thrilling two-hour century against Queensland, which included 5 sixes and 11 fours. But he came into his own in the series in the Caribbean, of which more shortly.

The Packer imbroglio, which saw Pakistan lose, among others, Mushtaq Mohammad, Zaheer Abbas and Asif Iqbal, should have given Wasim his big chance. But he did not seize it, having moderate series against England in 1977/78 and 1978. When the Packer players returned for the hugely important visit of India in 1978/79 Wasim had to make way. He toured New Zealand and Australia after that but was in and out of the side. But he played in all six Tests against India on the ill-fated tour of 1979/80, making two 90s and two other scores of over fifty, heading Pakistan's averages with 450 runs at 56.25. In Pakistan's best game of the series, the Second Test at Delhi, he top scored in both innings, a swashbuckling and extravagant 97 being followed by a circumspect and sedate 61. He also played magnificently for 94 not out in the rain-affected draw at Kanpur. Kapil Dev made everybody else struggle, taking 6 for 65. Sadiq Mohammad, with 47, and Iqbal Qasim (32) stayed for two hours: nobody else made 20.

After that it was very much an 'in and out' sort of career. He was always likely to make a useful contribution, usually from number six; but the big scores came less frequently. When his favourite bowlers, from the Caribbean, toured Pakistan in 1980/81 it almost goes without saying that he headed the home side's batting averages with 246 runs in the four Tests at 61.50. In the Second Test at Faisalabad he top scored with 38 not out as Malcolm Marshall and Colin Croft harried Pakistan to their first home defeat since losing to New Zealand in 1969/70. Man of the Match in a low-scoring draw at Karachi, he made the game's highest score, 77 not out in the second innings.

When he was dropped after one Test in England in 1982 – with Majid in the squad too Imran Khan seemed to have had at least one senior batsman too many – it seemed all over, but Wasim had not quite finished yet. In 1983/84, he scored two more hundreds. Against India at Jullundur in the Second Test of a series in which all three games were drawn, he made 125 going in at number seven. He put on 95 for the eighth wicket with Tahir Naqqash and, when Tahir was dismissed, hit with familiar vigour until he was last out. A series against England came next. In the First Test at Karachi his brother Rameez made his debut. Rameez was a right-handed, clean-shaven obdurate opener, now Pakistan's answer to Mark Nicholas (they go to the same hairdresser). He made an interesting contrast with his left-handed bearded and flamboyant sibling. In the Second Test, at Faisalabad, Wasim made a splendid hundred with 2 sixes and 14 fours, reaching his century with boundaries to long off, cover and square leg off Neil Foster.

That was Wasim at his glorious best. That was how it had been in his greatest series, against the West Indies in 1976/77. He had not got into the side against Australia. But Zaheer Abbas was injured before the First Test at Bridgetown and Wasim seized his chance. Pakistan began the opening day of the series well, with

Majid in marvellous touch, but by the end of it they were in relatively poor shape at 269 for 6, Colin Croft and Joel Garner having removed the upper middle order. Wasim, batting at number seven, galvanized the tail expertly. Imran, Sarfraz Nawaz and Salim Altaf all made handy runs and the total reached 415. Wasim made 117 not out. He batted for four hours and twenty minutes and hit a six and 12 fours, most of them struck sweetly through the off-side, The West Indies made 421 in reply and a draw seemed the most likely result. But Croft and Andy Roberts ripped through the Pakistan batting to leave them reeling at 126 for 7, then 158 for 9. Wasim was still there though, and riding his luck as the West Indies' out-cricket mysteriously fell apart. He was dropped four times and just kept hitting. He put on 133 for the last wicket with Wasim Bari: Raja made 71. The West Indies had ample time to make the 308 they needed but struggled after a good start. There was great tension in the last hour when Pakistan needed 2 wickets to win but the batsmen held out.

The West Indies won the Second Test at Port-of-Spain by 6 wickets. The decisive blow was struck on the first day when Croft took 8 for 29. Wasim, remarkably, again top-scored in both innings, making 65 (out of 180) and 84. The high-scoring draw at Georgetown seemed to lack appeal – he made 5 and 0. But he shared big partnerships with Mushtaq in the victory at Port-of-Spain in the Fourth Test and with Asif in the valiant fourth innings of the decider at Kingston, which the West Indies won.

Wasim made 517 runs at 57.44 in the series, a truly remarkable statistic. But not the most remarkable of his series. That honour goes to his achievement in hitting the West Indian bowlers for 14 sixes in the series. Kevin Pietersen equalled his record in the Ashes series in 2005. Other batsmen had success against the West Indian pace battery but surely none did it with the flair, the enterprise or the extravagance of Wasim Raja. The faster Croft, Garner and Roberts bowled, the harder he hit, usually free-swinging drives and cuts. Bare-headed and manifestly enjoying himself, he was indeed a sight to behold.

Wasim really couldn't do a thing wrong on that tour. In the Fourth Test at Port-of-Spain, Pakistan were closing in for a win. Only 3 wickets to get, victory out of the question for the home side. Then Deryck Murray and Roberts dug in and put on a bit of a stand. Minutes turned to hours, 154 for 7 became 196 for 7. The fielding side began to panic. Unpleasant memories of the World Cup in 1975 were rekindled: Murray and Roberts had foiled them then. Mushtaq wondered who he should turn to. He himself had 8 wickets in the match but he knew he could not do it. Saf? Knackered. Imran? Sulking. Majid? The umpire's looking worried. Inti? Oh yes, we dropped him. Just a minute, who's that down at fine leg? 'Hey, Waz, can you give me a couple of overs?'

That was nearly all it took. It was his first bowl of the match. There it is, in the book: Wasim Raja 3.5-1-22-3.

WASIM Hasan RAJA
Left-hand bat, leg-break & googly
Born: 3 July 1952, Multan
Major Teams: Pakistan, Lahore, Sargudha, Punjab University, Universities, Pakistan
International Airlines, Punjab, National Bank

TESTS
(1972/73-1983/84)

	M	I	NO	Runs	HS	Ave	100	50	Ct
Batting & Fielding	57	92	14	2,821	125	36.16	4	18	20

	Balls	R	W	Ave	BBI	SR	Econ
Bowling	4,082	1,826	51	35.80	4/50	80.03	2.7

ONE-DAY INTERNATIONALS

	M	I	NO	Runs	HS	Ave	SR	50	Ct
Batting & Fielding	54	45	10	782	60	22.34	66.95	2	24

	Balls	R	W	Ave	BBI	SR	Econ
Bowling	1,036	687	21	32.71	4/25	49.33	3.97

FIRST-CLASS
(Career: 1967/68-1987/88)

	M	I	NO	Runs	HS	Ave	100	Ct
Batting & Fielding	250	379	54	11,434	165	35.18	17	156

	R	W	Ave	BBI	5	10
Bowling	16,211	558	29.05	8/65	31	7

LIST A

	M	I	NO	Runs	HS	Ave	50	Ct
Batting & Fielding	89	75	15	1,412	60	23.53	4	37

	Balls	R	W	Ave	BBI	5	SR	Econ
Bowling	22,061	1,529	60	25.48	6/39	1	39.39	4.04

ZAHEER ABBAS

When, in a cricket video 'magazine' programme, Mike Atherton was asked to nominate an innings that was memorable for its style and aesthetic quality he chose the 274 made by Zaheer Abbas against England at Edgbaston in 1971. The choice was surprising only in that Atherton, who muttered in his then somewhat dour and dispiriting tones what an impact the innings had made on him, could not have been more than three and a half-years old at the time it was played.

The choice was spot on, though, for more than purely aesthetic reasons. In that respect, Zaheer certainly stood out as a stylist. When he joined Gloucestershire the following year, the older locals, depending on precisely how old they were, would have been reminiscing about Tom Graveney and Walter Hammond when they saw him. He had watched Graveney and Colin Cowdrey bat for England in Karachi and their style had influenced him. He played his off-side strokes with particular relish, skillfully finding gaps to the left and right of cover point with wristy last-minute adjustments. But he was far from being an exclusively off-side player; indeed a slightly open stance made him, if anything, more naturally inclined to the leg-side. But he had strokes all round the wicket, including a magnificent square cut and an enthusiastic if not always effective hook. A tall, slim, bespectacled figure, one of the distinctive features of his play was an unusually high, oddly loopy backlift that must have helped what, on a good day, was purringly satisfactory timing. As Frank Keating wrote, at his best 'Zed' was incapable of an ugly shot.

So, from the aesthetic viewpoint, Athers was right. The innings was important for other reasons too. It marked a watershed in Pakistan's Test cricket. After an encouraging and relatively successful start in the 1950s the country's Test cricket had been in the mire for much of the 1960s, locked in a negative mindset. The decade had ended with an humiliating home defeat at the hands of New Zealand. The 1971 tour seemed to herald a new beginning. Zaheer was playing in only his second Test match when he scored his marvellous 274. Imran Khan made his debut in the same game. England, under their immensely experienced captain Ray Illingworth and with players of the calibre of Cowdrey, Geoff Boycott and John Edrich at their disposal, eventually won the series, but they were forced to follow on at Edgbaston. Zaheer's innings symbolised a new Pakistan and as they moved through the 1970s into the 1980s, confidence grew and they began to learn how to win.

There was, of course, more to the innings than just looking nice. It showed various things about Zaheer apart from the fact that he had a graceful style. It showed that he had considerable powers of concentration. His innings started in the first over, Aftab Gul having retired hurt after being hit on the head by a bouncer from Alan Ward. Zaheer had one piece of good fortune: the great John Snow was not playing. At the end of the first day, Zaheer was 159 not out. In all he batted for nine hours ten minutes and hit 38 fours. In the course of the innings, he became the first man in the country to reach a thousand runs for the season.

That was the other thing that the innings, by definition, demonstrated: Zaheer just loved batting. Of course, you might say, all batsmen love batting, otherwise what is the point? But there is a difference in degree with all of these things. 'Why have you got so many children?' Groucho Marx famously asked a – presumably distant – female acquaintance. 'Because my husband loves me,' came the reply. 'Well, I love my pipe', said Marx, 'but sometimes I take it out of my mouth.' All batsmen love success. Some are fascinated by the technique of batting or just love the feel of creaming a ball to the boundary. Philip Mead, the Hampshire left-hander who played from 1906 to 1936 and made more runs for the county than anybody else has ever done for any side in first-class cricket, was a case apart. It was said of him that he did not love batting. What he loved was making runs. Zaheer was not really like that. The shrewd and mellifluous David Foot said it was patently wrong to call him a run-machine. But there was something about his avarice for runs that was reminiscent of the gluttony of the 1930s. His second Test century was also a double, also on a perfect batting track against what became a labouring England attack, 240 at The Oval in 1974. His third Test century, against Australia at Adelaide in 1976/77 (he made 85 in the first innings and 90 in the first innings of the next Test at Melbourne) was his fifty-first in first-class cricket. He finished with 108 first-class centuries. Among non-English batsmen only Don Bradman and Vivian Richards (all right then, and Graeme Hick) have scored more. On eight occasions, he scored two separate hundreds in a match, more than anyone else. For Gloucestershire in 1976 he twice scored a not out century and double century in the same match without being dismissed, and he repeated the feat in 1977, becoming the first person to score a double and a single century in the same match three times. He had previously shared the record not with Hammond or Bradman but with the Leicestershire opening batsman Maurice Hallam. Twice he was the leading run-scorer with the highest average in an English season, in 1976 (2,554 runs at 75.11 with eleven centuries) and 1981 (2,306 runs at 88.09, almost 20 ahead of the next man Javed Miandad, with ten centuries), a quite phenomenal achievement. In 1981 he yet again scored a double century and a century in the same match, both not out, against Somerset at Bath (5 sixes and 22 fours in the double century) and scored a thousand runs in June alone.

In Test cricket too he went in for big numbers. He made twelve Test centuries, of which four were doubles and another four were 168 or more. As his county form shows, when he had a purple patch he really enjoyed it. When India toured Pakistan in

Zaheer Abbas.

1978/79 Zaheer was in the curious position of being a world-class player with little to show for it in his native land, although he scored heavily in domestic cricket for PIA. He soon put the record straight. In the bore-draw at Faisalabad, which appeared to be continuing the long-standing tradition of inconclusive games between the neighbours, he made 176 and 76. He shared a big stand with Miandad in the first innings. Miandad said Zaheer 'pulled rank' and insisted on monopolising the ageing off-spinner Erapalli Prasanna. Pakistan won the remaining two Tests by 6 wickets. At Lahore Zaheer made 235 not out, out of 539 for 6, and 34 not out, hurrying Pakistan to victory with Asif Iqbal. Zaheer was in superlative form, outscoring all his partners – during the six and a half hours he was at the crease only Mushtaq Mohammad (67) made more than 35 – and hitting 2 sixes and 29 fours. At Karachi, he made 42. The series was the beginning of the end for the great Indian spin quartet. Zaheer was always a master of spin bowling. In this series Bhaghwat Chandrasekhar headed the Indian bowling figures with 8 wickets at 48 apiece. Prasanna took 2 wickets for 251 runs.

On India's next visit in 1982/83 there was further triumph for the home side, and for Zaheer. This was a series dominated by the phenomenal swing bowling of Imran and Sarfraz

Nawaz. It also saw monumental scoring feats by the Pakistani batsmen. Pakistan were on a roll, having beaten England in England and thrashed Australia 3-0 in Pakistan. Against Australia Zaheer scored 91 in the First Test at Karachi, 126 in the Second at Faisalabad and 52 in the Third at Lahore. He also scored a century in the one-day international at Lahore. Against India, he just carried on. He scored 215 in the First Test at Lahore. It was his hundredth first-class century. He followed that with 186 in the Second Test at Karachi, 105 in the one-dayer at Lahore and 168 in the Third Test at Faisalabad. After that he took a bit of a break as Miandad and Mudassar Nazar cashed in.

There was one difference, though, between Zaheer's performances against India in 1978/79 and in 1982/83. In the former series, he was batting in what had become his accustomed position at number three. That was where he always batted for Gloucestershire too, more or less until he retired in the middle of a stale, flat and unprofitable 1984 county season. But in 1982/83 he was in the middle order, usually at five. The drop down the order came about as a result of a rather traumatic series against the West Indies at home in 1980/81. The visitors won the four-Test series 1-0. Malcolm Marshall, Colin Croft and Sylvester Clarke were their principal bowlers. They shared 15 wickets in the victory at Faisalabad. Zaheer missed the First Test and his performance in the others was woefully below par: 57 runs at 14.25. A Croft bouncer put a two-inch dent in his helmet. Imran was unsparing in his autobiography. In the Second Test, Zaheer 'was in a terrible state against Marshall and Clarke, actually backing away from the fast bowling. I knew that this was the beginning of the end of Zaheer's reputation.' Imran's opinions on his seniors – especially those from Karachi – often seems unduly critical, but Zaheer's record against high pace was poor. He had struggled in the Caribbean in 1976/77, making one good score on a relatively comfortable wicket at Georgetown. Dennis Lillee rated Zaheer highly but said that he often had problems with the shorter ball. He was also very much a form player generally. When he was good he was very very good, but… Against New Zealand in 1972/73, he could not get going at all, making 35 runs in five innings. Between his two gorging series against India, Pakistan toured there in 1979/80. In five Tests, Zaheer made 157 runs at 19.62. Kapil Dev got him five times.

Zaheer was a paradoxical figure in some ways. Quiet and outwardly unassuming – though from a prosperous background – off the field, as a batsman he was ruthless and inclined to dominate bowlers when conditions allowed – which at Bristol, Cheltenham, Lahore and Faisalabad they often did. A career record of a hundred centuries and a first-class average of over 50 puts him in the top rank. Yet he made 'only' twelve centuries in Tests, two more than Mushtaq Mohammad and one more than Asif Iqbal. David Green, in a generous tribute in *Wisden*, justifies this by saying that Pakistan played relatively few Tests but really that will not do. Also he made no centuries against the West Indies and only two against Australia. One was in a losing cause at Adelaide, the other on a featherbed at Faisalabad. Lillee said he must have had Zaheer half a dozen times: the batsman realised that if he kept his head down and his pads in front he would be all right.

Unassuming and quiet he may have been, but he did not lack ambition. The captaincy of Pakistan was something he came to hanker after. He was bitterly disappointed as first Miandad and then Imran were preferred. He got his chance at last when Imran declined to go to India in 1983/84 (some cynics said Imran was concerned he might suffer the fate of Asif Iqbal after the 1979/80 tour). Like many things that people desperately want, once he had got the captaincy Zaheer did not seem to know quite what to do with it. The Indian series was a dull draw. Zaheer seemed to find it difficult to inspire the team on the difficult tour of Australia that followed. They were two-down after two Tests and, although things improved markedly when Sarfraz Nawaz joined the party, it remained 2-0 after five. It could not have helped that Imran was in the party: he played in the last two Tests as a batsman. It was almost with relief that he handed the job back for those games. Zaheer regained the job for the drawn series against England a couple of months later and in home series against India (drawn) and New Zealand (a 2-0 win) in 1984/85.

If this piece seems carping, it isn't meant to be. Like Atherton – but, perhaps a bit earlier – I watched that innings at Edgbaston in 1971 on television as this bare-headed, bespectacled, studious-looking man unreeled a succession of glorious drives. Zaheer Abbas will long be remembered as one of the most watchable batsmen of his time.

Syed ZAHEER ABBAS Kirmani
Right-hand bat, off-break
Born: 26 July 1947, Salkot, India
Major Teams: Karachi, Public Works Department, Dawood Industries, Sind, Pakistan International Airlines, Gloucestershire

TESTS
(1969/70-1985/86)

	M	I	NO	Runs	HS	Ave	100	50	Ct
Batting & Fielding	78	124	11	5,062	274	44.79	12	20	34

	Balls	R	W	Ave	BBI	SR	Econ
Bowling	370	132	3	44.00	2/21	123.33	2.14

ONE-DAY INTERNATIONALS

	M	I	NO	Runs	HS	Ave	SR	100	50	Ct
Batting & Fielding	62	60	6	2,572	123	47.62	84.80	7	13	16

	Balls	R	W	Ave	BBI	SR	Econ
Bowling	280	223	7	31.85	2/26	40.00	4.77

FIRST-CLASS
(Career: 1965/66-1986/87)

	M	I	NO	Runs	HS	Ave	100	Ct
Batting & Fielding	459	768	92	34,843	274	51.54	108	278

	R	W	Ave	BBI	5
Bowling	1,146	30	38.20	5/15	1

LIST A

	M	I	NO	Runs	HS	Ave	100	50	Ct
Batting & Fielding	323	309	33	11,240	158*	40.72	19	72	78

	Balls	R	W	Ave	BBI	SR	Econ
Bowling	828	689	16	43.06	3/48	51.75	4.99

BIBLIOGRAPHY

Cricinfo

Wisden Cricketers' Almanack
The Cricketer
The Cricketer International
Wisden Cricket Monthly
The Wisden Cricketer
Playfair Cricket Annual

Mike Atherton, *Opening Up*, Hodder & Stoughton, 2002
John Barclay, *The Appeal of the Championship*, Fairfield Books, 2002
Jack Bannister, *The Innings of My Life*, Headley, 1993
Rahul Bhattacharya, *Pundits from Pakistan*, Picador, 2005
Scyld Berry, *A Cricket Odyssey*, Pavilion Michael Joseph, 1988
Lt-Colonel (Ret'd) Shuja-ud-din Butt and Mohammad Salim Pervez, *The Chequered History of Pakistan Cricket*, Milestone Communications, 2003
Stephen Chalke, *At the Heart of English Cricket*, Fairfield Books, 2001
Phil Edmonds (with Scyld Berry), *100 Greatest Bowlers*, Macdonald Queen Ann Press, 1989
Graham Gooch, *Captaincy*, Stanley Paul, 1992
David Gower, *Gower: The Autobiography*, Collins Willow, 1992
Ramachandra Guha, *A Corner of a Foreign Field*, Picador, 2002
Imran Khan, *All Round View*, Chatton & Windus, 1988
Javed Miandad, *Cutting Edge*, Oxford University Press, 2003
Peter Roebuck, *It Takes All Sorts*, Allen & Unwin, 2005
Dicky Rutnagur, *Test Commentary*, Vikas Publishing House Pvt Ltd, 1978
Mark Taylor, *Taylor Made*, Macmillan, 1995
Ivo Tennant, *Imran Khan*, Witherby, 1994
Shane Warne, *My Own Story*, Swan Publishing, 1997
Shane Warne, *My Autobiography*, Hodder & Stoughton, 2001
Simon Wilde, *Letting Rip*, Gollancz/Witherby, 1994
Simon Wilde, *Number One*, Victor Gollancz, 1998
John Woodcock, *The Times One Hundred Greatest Cricketers*, Macmillan, 1998

Other titles published by Tempus

The Indian Masters
BILL RICQUIER

India has given the world some of the most exciting cricketers in the history of the game. This book looks at fifteen of the finest of them, including Ranjitsinhji, Duleepsinhji, Pataudis Senior and Junior, Sunil Gavaskar, Sachin Tendulkar and Anil Kumble, featuring personal and playing biographies, detailed statistics and many superb illustrations, plus a foreword by Farokh Engineer.

0 7524 3405 5

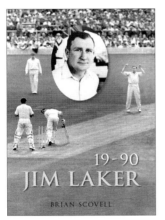

Jim Laker 19-90
BRIAN SCOVELL

This is the untold story of one of England's greatest cricketers, the Yorkshire-born off-spinner Jim Laker. Laker's greatest achievement, 19-90 against the Australians at Old Trafford, is a record that will probably never be beaten, yet four years later he was controversially stripped of his honorary life memberships of both Surrey CCC and the MCC. Brian Scovell presents a fascinating new insight into the life of a courageous and misunderstood man.

0 7524 3932 4

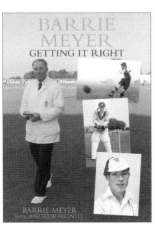

Barrie Meyer Getting it Right
BARRIE MEYER WITH ANDREW HIGNELL

Barrie Meyer has had a lifetime in professional sport, as a cricketer with Gloucestershire, a footballer with Bristol Rovers and Bristol City (amongst others), and twenty-five years as a first-class and Test match umpire. With a supporting cast including cricketing legends such as Ian Botham, Viv Richards, Dickie Bird and Curtly Ambrose – amongst countless other famous names – this autobiography offers a unique perspective on cricket in the 1970s, '80s and '90s.

0 7524 4007 1

If you are interested in purchasing other books published by Tempus, or in case you have difficulty finding any Tempus books in your local bookshop, you can also place orders directly through our website

www.tempus-publishing.com